Missionary Methods

Other Books in the EMS Series

About EMS

WWW.EMSWEB.ORG

The Evangelical Missiological Society is a professional organization with more than 350 members comprised of missiologists, mission administrators, teachers, pastors with strategic missiological interests, and students of missiology. EMS exists to advance the cause of world evangelization. We do this through study and evaluation of mission concepts and strategies from a biblical perspective with a view to commending sound mission theory and practice to churches, mission agencies, and schools of missionary training around the world. We hold an annual national conference and eight regional meetings held throughout the United States and Canada.

Evangelical
Missiological
Society
Series

no. **21**

Missionary Methods

RESEARCH, REFLECTIONS, AND REALITIES

Craig Ott and J. D. Payne, Editors

WILLIAM CAREY
LIBRARY

Published by William Carey Library
1605 E. Elizabeth Street
Pasadena, CA 91104 |www.missionbooks.org

Melissa Hicks, editor
Brad Koenig, copyeditor
Hugh Pindur, graphic designer
Rose Lee-Norman, indexer

William Carey Library is a ministry of the
U.S. Center for World Mission
Pasadena, CA | www.uscwm.org
Printed in the United States of America

17 16 15 14 13   5 4 3 2 1 BP 1200

Library of Congress Cataloging-in-Publication Data

Missionary methods : research, reflections, and realities / edited by Craig Ott and J. D. Payne.
    pages cm. -- (Evangelical Missiological Society series ; 21)
    ISBN 978-0-87808-043-4
    1. Missions. I. Ott, Craig, 1952- editor of compilation.
    BV2061.3.M65 2013
    266--dc23
                        2013015372

Contents

PART I – Biblical Understandings of Missionary Methods

PART II – Praxis and Case Studies of Missionary Methods

Acknowledgments

As editors we would like to express our appreciation to all those persons who contributed to bringing this volume together. We are grateful to the Evangelical Missiological Society for their trust in us as editors and for taking up this very important topic. We offer many thanks to the contributors who completed their work in a timely and efficient fashion, making our work as editors much easier. A special shout-out of appreciation goes to Craig's assistant, Dee Yaccino, for her attention to detail in formatting and editing. We are deeply grateful to the institutions that we serve, Trinity Evangelical Divinity School and The Church at Brook Hills, for allowing us to devote time and energy to this project. Finally, much appreciation goes to the wonderful people with William Carey Library for their partnership with the Evangelical Missiological Society to provide this monograph series. They are to be commended for their labors to make this book available to readers for kingdom advancement.

Craig Ott
Deerfield, Illinois

J. D. Payne
Birmingham, Alabama

Contributors

Robert H. Bennett (PhD, Concordia Theological Seminary) is an adjunct professor of mission at Concordia Theological Seminary in Fort Wayne, Indiana, and administrative pastor of Trinity Lutheran Church and School in Reese, Michigan. His publications include *I Am Not Afraid: Demon Possession and Spiritual Warfare* (Concordia Publishing House, 2013). He may be contacted at theoreader@gmail.com.

Anthony Casey (PhD candidate, Southern Baptist Theological Seminary) is an adjunct instructor of missions and evangelism at Boyce College and Southern Seminary in Louisville, Kentucky. His interests include orality in church planting and urban ethnographic research. He may be contacted at acasey@sbts.edu.

John Cheong (PhD, Trinity Evangelical Divinity School) currently collaborates with the Global Diaspora Network, serves as full-time senior lecturer in mission and intercultural studies in a Southeast Asian seminary, while equipping leaders for and ministering to Muslim background believers as well. He previously served in church planting ministries in Southeast Asia in the 1980s and 1990s and in evangelism of international students and Muslims in the Chicago area during the past decade. He can be contacted at eaglexian@hotmail.com.

Gary R. Corwin is staff missiologist with the international office of SIM and associate editor of *Evangelical Missions Quarterly*. He has served with SIM since 1981 in Ghana and in various research and education roles internationally. He holds three master's degrees (East Stroudsburg University, Trinity Evangelical Divinity School, and Northwestern University) and is coauthor of *Introducing World Missions: A Biblical, Historical, and Practical Survey* (Baker Academic, 2004). He may be contacted at garcorwin@aol.com.

Robert L. Gallagher (PhD, Fuller Theological Seminary) is department chair, director of the master of arts program in intercultural studies, and associate professor of intercultural studies at Wheaton College Graduate School in Chicago where he has served since 1998. He previously served as president of the American Society of Missiology (2010–11) and as an executive pastor in Australia (1979–90), as well as being involved in short-term theological education in Papua New Guinea and the South Pacific since 1984. His publications include coediting of *Footprints of God: A Narrative Theology of Mission* (MARC, 1999); *Mission in Acts: Ancient Narratives in Contemporary Contexts* (Orbis Books, 2004); and *Landmark Essays in Mission and World Christianity* (Orbis Books, 2009). He may be contacted at robert.gallagher@wheaton.edu.

David J. Hesselgrave (PhD, University of Minnesota) is emeritus professor of mission at Trinity Evangelical Divinity School. He served as a missionary to Japan with the Evangelical Free Church from 1950 to 1962 prior to his tenure at TEDS. He was the founding executive director of the Evangelical Missiological Society and the author of thirteen books and over eighty monographs including *Paradigms in Conflict* (Kregel, 2005) and the landmark *Communicating Christ Cross-Culturally* (Zondervan, 1991).

Rob S. Hughes (PhD candidate, Asbury Theological Seminary) is a postgraduate student in intercultural studies at Asbury Theological Seminary in Wilmore, Kentucky. His research has examined Lesslie Newbigin's pneumatology of mission, which was informed in part by Roland Allen's convictions as discussed in chapter 2. He may be contacted at rob.hughes@asburyseminary.edu.

John W. Mehn (DMin, Trinity International University) has served in Japan with Converge Worldwide (BGC) since 1985. His ministry has included church planting, equipping church planters, and leadership development. John serves as the chair of the leadership team of the Japan Church Planting Institute. He may be contacted at reproducingchurches@gmail.com.

Craig Ott (PhD, Trinity Evangelical Divinity School) is department chair and professor of mission and intercultural studies at Trinity Evangelical Divinity School, where he has served since 2002. He previously served as a church planter and theological educator in Germany for twenty-one years with ReachGlobal. His most recent publications include coauthoring of *Global Church Planting* (Baker Academic, 2011) and *Encountering Theology of Mission* (Baker Academic, 2010), and coediting of *Globalizing Theology* (Baker Academic, 2006). He may be contacted at cott@tiu.edu.

J. D. Payne (PhD, Southern Baptist Theological Seminary) is the pastor of church multiplication with The Church at Brook Hills in Birmingham, Alabama. He is the executive vice president for administration with the Evangelical Missiological Society and has written eight books including *Discovering Church Planting* (Paternoster, 2009); *Strangers Next Door: Immigration, Migration and Mission* (InterVarsity Press, 2012); and *Pressure Points: Twelve Global Issues Shaping the Face of the Church* (Thomas Nelson, forthcoming). He also coauthored *Developing a Strategy for Missions* (Baker, forthcoming). He blogs at jdpayne.org and may be contacted at jpayne@brookhills.org.

Joel Thiessen (PhD, University of Waterloo) is assistant professor of sociology at Ambrose University College in Calgary, Alberta, where he has served since 2008. His research centers on religion and culture in Canada based on face-to-face interviews with those who attend religious services weekly, mainly for religious holidays or rites of passage, or not at all. He may be contacted at jathiessen@ambrose.edu.

Mark S. Williams (PhD, Ateneo de Davao University, Philippines) is affiliate faculty of intercultural studies at Trinity Lutheran College in Everett, Washington, where he has served since 2011. He previously served as a research anthropologist in the southern Philippines for sixteen years with SIM. His publications include "Western Globalization versus Dar-ul Islam" in *Religions, Regionalism, and Globalization in Asia* (Ateneo de Manila University Press, 2010). He may be contacted at markswilliams59@yahoo.com.

INTRODUCTION

Methodological Stewardship: Always Evaluating, Always Adjusting

J. D. PAYNE

It has been one hundred years since the publication of Roland Allen's classic work *Missionary Methods: St. Paul's or Ours?* In honor of this historic event, the Evangelical Missiological Society selected the topic of missionary methods as its theme for the 2012 annual meeting held in Chicago, Illinois. This book represents some of the papers presented during that two-day gathering in September.

While we gathered only for a couple of days to reflect on missionary methods and Allen's historical influence, this meeting was a timely reminder of the need for the church to be in constant evaluation of the methods she uses to make disciples of all nations. Such is a good thing. Methods are the "how-to" components of our strategies. They are a necessity. Without them nothing would be accomplished for global disciple making. However, just because we are doing something on the field, *even if we are experiencing results,* does not warrant a refrain from the evaluation of our actions.

As Goes Your Theology, As Goes Your Missiology, As Go Your Methods

While disciple-making movements do not exist without methods, methods must maintain their proper place within the evangelical missions enterprise. If we fail to recognize this point, we are in danger of hindering the work of the Spirit through us as we make disciples of all nations. Methods are necessary, but not foundational. We do not begin to think about our missionary task by asking, "What works?" or "How do we . . .?" Rather, we begin with a biblical and theological foundation. It is out of this bedrock that our missiology flows, and from there our methods are formulated and applied to the field. While the process of arriving at our methods is usually a reflective process of an ongoing return to the Scriptures and our missiology in light of our contexts, as a heuristic tool I have portrayed this process in more of a linear fashion than what happens in reality.

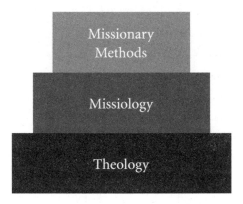

If our biblical and theological foundation is wrong, our missiology and methods are on tenuous grounds when it comes to the advancement of the kingdom among a population segment or people group. A poor foundation is likely to result in poor practice on the field. The church is a supernatural body that is empowered by the supernatural. Therefore, our missionary methods are to be shaped, influenced, and restricted by the divine revelation found in the Scriptures. Missionaries must be outstanding theologians and outstanding in the practical application of their methods to the field. To have one without the other is a liability to the kingdom.

Stewardship of Critique

Aggressive methodological evaluation is something that should be expected of missionaries. Placing our methods under a microscope is simply a matter of kingdom stewardship. The church is called to be faithful servants (Matt 25:14–30) and to bear much fruit (John 15:1–11). She has been given a commission from the Lord who expects results (i.e., make disciples). Ongoing prayerful critique is important to our field labors and church health. However, the church must be cautious in that such evaluation is not based on a methodology built upon a foundation of pragmatism (Craig Ott develops this further in the Conclusion). The missionary task is not like working on an assembly line whereby the factory employee produces a set number of widgets every workday. During the latter twentieth century, an evangelical pragmatism developed that resulted in many leaders seeking the latest and greatest methods to increase the numbers of people who were part of their churches. This divorce of our field-based methods from healthy missiology rooted deeply in a biblical and theological foundation resulted in numerous problems in the kingdom—the number of live bodies increased in our churches but not always with an equivalent increase in conversions and sanctification.

This methodological error among the church in North America was simply a variation on the problems made by the Anglican Church in the nineteenth and twentieth centuries—a matter that Allen strongly opposed. Rather than being influenced by a heavy dose of pragmatism, the Anglican Church allowed Western cultural preferences to be imported into non-Western contexts. Yes, a bit of pragmatism was there; after all, such traditional methods worked in the West. But the foundation supporting much of their methods included a heavy dose of paternalism.

As a product of their day, the Anglican Church had been influenced by colonialism and recognized that new believers and churches would not be able to support and manage the Western ecclesiological structures exported to the East. The result was that missionaries had to maintain control over such work in the new fields and, like a parent with a child, raise up the new churches to function in the East as the church functioned in the West. Having served in China during the Boxer Rebellion and having studied the New Testament to understand Paul's approach to missions, Allen strongly critiqued the missionary methods of his day. He recognized that over time the church's methods had gradually moved away from a biblical foundation.

Keeping the Magnets Together

While we can trace the origins of some of the problems of the church in North America and the Anglican Church of yesteryear to pragmatism and paternalism, a deeper issue was at stake. Though the manifestation of the problem revealed itself on a methodological level, the problem on the field was not simply that the church needed a new and better method, but a return to biblical moorings from which practice was to then be developed in view of context.

The biblical and theological foundation and missionary methods are like two magnets. When turned in the proper directions, they adhere to one another. However, if their poles are changed by an improper orientation, then they repel one another.

In every age, the church must keep the magnet of methodology in proper alignment with the polarity of biblical orthodoxy. The temptation is to allow our methods to shift with the whims of societies and cultures to such a degree that context takes priority. Such should never be the case. The Bible is explicit on what is necessary for someone to enter the kingdom of God; the nature of this God; the exclusivity of Christ's atoning work; and how a disciple should act in relation to his or her heavenly Father, other brothers and sisters, and those outside of the kingdom. The Bible contains an irreducible ecclesiological minimum that must be in place before any group of kingdom citizens is able to call themselves a local church. For us to compromise doctrine, neglect teaching people to obey the commands of Jesus that they may be thoroughly equipped for every good work, and use methods so difficult that few of the new believers and churches could ever imitate us as we imitate Christ (1 Cor 11:1; 1 Thess 1:6), is to call into question the methods we are using.

The scriptural boundaries for methodological flexibility are very wide. Such should not surprise us, for the Lord who allowed the cultures of the world to develop has also allowed for a wide range of approaches to make disciples of the peoples of those cultures. There is much freedom for methodological adjustment, as differing contexts demand different paradigms for gospel engagement. However, methodology must never become the foundational magnet by which our biblical and theological convictions are to align.

Aggressive Evaluation

Oftentimes evangelicals are some of the strongest conservatives when it comes to clinging to methods. We have a history of churches that, after embracing a particular method, will often cling to that paradigm long after its effectiveness has passed. We often invert the pyramid listed above, making methods our foundation and clinging to them with such tenacity that to change them is tantamount to changing doctrine. Such is not the way of wise stewards.

Ongoing evaluation is a necessity as we seek to develop and apply methods among the nations. Some methods may have a very long lifespan; others may be necessary only for a season. While the kingdom ethic we proclaim never changes, our contexts do change. And with changing context comes the reality of changing methods. Once it is determined that a more excellent way is necessary, we must exhibit the courage to make such necessary methodological adjustments—often a challenging task.

G. W. Peters was correct when he commented:

> A method which may be very effective at one time, at one place, among one people, may not be effective at another time, another place, another people. In fact, it may prove disadvantageous if not disastrous. Therefore, a method-bound movement cannot become an effective *world* movement. Neither can it last very long. It will soon be relegated to the outdated and the outworn. We do not need a renewal of the Gospel, but we do need continuous renewal of methodology to communicate the age old Gospel in an intelligible, meaningful, and purposeful manner.[1]

Peters' call for such a methodological renewal was promulgated at Lausanne in 1974. His exhortation, however, is timeless. As we consider missionary methods during our age, we should be asking questions such as:

1. Are our methods biblically grounded?
2. Are our methods ethical?
3. Do our methods avoid unhealthy pragmatism and paternalism?
4. Will our methods allow for the gospel to connect with the people?
5. Are our methods highly reproducible among the people?
6. Do our teams have the necessary resources to use our methods?

---

1   G. W. Peters, "Contemporary Practices of Evangelism," in *Let the Earth Hear His Voice: International Congress on World Evangelization, Lausanne, Switzerland,* ed. J. D. Douglas (Minneapolis: World Wide, 1975), 181.

Part of an aggressive evaluation of methods at any time among any people is the grasp of principles to assist us in such a time of adjustment. While not exhaustive, the following principles serve as a starting point for us to keep in mind:

1. **Methods Must Be Held Loosely.** Methods will change over time and from people to people. A tight grip on a particular method now is likely a prescription for problems later.
2. **Not All Methods Will Reach All Peoples.** Methods are contextually unique. What works among this people group may not work very well among that people group.
3. **Different Methods Have Different Results.** Methods do not produce the same results. We can saw a small tree in half with a steak knife or a chain saw. Both methods of sawing will accomplish the desired outcome, but one clearly reflects wisdom better than the other.
4. **Methods Are Best Developed in the Field.** We can learn from the stories of others. We can ponder the possibilities of our methods within a classroom. But our methods are best developed in context as we attempt to make application of our principles to the field.
5. **Methods Must Be Kept in Check with the Biblical Foundation.** Apart from being anchored in a biblical foundation, missionary methods can be developed to produce any number of unhealthy practices.

Methods Matter

This book is our attempt to serve as a catalyst for methodological evaluation and, where necessary, adjustment. This publication reminds the church of the importance of considering her methods. This work is divided into two sections. The first addresses biblical foundations for our methods. Robert Gallagher revisits Paul and Roland Allen, and challenges us to consider our present realities. Rob Hughes continues the Allen discussion by drawing attention to one of the matters for which Allen was famous: his understanding of the Spirit in missionary activities. John Cheong concludes this section by examining the incarnational model through the work of Stott, Hesselgrave, and Köstenberger.

The second section, and largest portion of this book, is comprised of chapters related to missionary practices. Gary Corwin examines a century of missions methodology particularly related to North American evangelical work. David Hesselgrave's chapter raises awareness of the fact that contextualized preaching requires sharing the difficult biblical truths (e.g., hell, judgment of God) of the Scriptures with our hearers.

One of the most challenging issues shaping the face of the church and missions today is that of oral learners. We presently live in a world with an estimated 4 billion such individuals. Most missionaries coming from Western churches are not only highly literate, but also are trained in many missionary methods that are often most effective among literate recipients. Anthony Casey's chapter brings to our attention the growth of orality issues as related to missionary practices today.

Another one of the most challenging issues applying pressure on the church today and shaping her missionary methods is that of the migration of the nations. We presently live in a world where 214 million people are living outside of their countries of birth, a number representing 3 percent of the world's population. Drawing from his research in Canada, Joel Thiessen challenges us to consider what it means to be a missionary in the West, where the waves of nations are splashing on our shores.

The last three chapters of this book provide insights into missionary methods being used in animistic societies, Japan, and among Muslims in the Philippines. Robert Bennett raises awareness of both productive and unproductive methods where animistic practices are commonplace. John Mehn's chapter examines church reproduction in a Japanese context. Mark Williams' work offers a case study of methods used among Filipino Muslims.

Craig Ott, my coeditor on this book, writes our conclusion. While summarizing the contents of this work, Ott also raises several very important matters for evangelicals to consider today when it comes to our missionary methods. His work is more than a conclusion to a book; it is a challenge for right thinking about missionary methods and the encouragement found in the spirit of mission—especially when we do not have all of the methodological answers to the challenges of our day.

Missionary Methods, One Hundred Years Later

During his day, Allen was a voice of one crying in the wilderness. He was well aware of this reality. For example, when his grandson asked him if he could read his writings, the senior Allen replied, "Oh, yes, you can read them by all means—but you won't understand them; I don't think anyone is going to understand them until I've been dead ten years."[2] While it was not quite a decade following Allen's death, this prediction was close. Allen observed the methods of his day, saw the limitations, examined the Scriptures, and made arguments for systemic shifts to bring about what he believed was a more excellent way. Whether or not we agree with Allen's conclusions is not the point I wish to make as we conclude this Introduction. However, one matter we should take away from Allen's work, one hundred years later, is his challenge to us that we should know our present methods and evaluate them in light of the Scriptures and our contemporary realities. Once we begin such a process of reflection and inspection, we may determine that what we are doing on the field is exactly what we should be doing. However, we may also come to find out that significant change is necessary.

May our discussions, evaluations, and adjustments of our methods today result in kingdom advancement. It is our hope that this book may make a contribution to that great gathering around the throne of God (Rev 7:9,10) where the Spirit and Word working across the ages—through the church's methods—bring about worship among all nations.

---

2   Hubert J. B. Allen, *Roland Allen: Pioneer, Priest, and Prophet* (Grand Rapids: Eerdmans, 1995), vii.

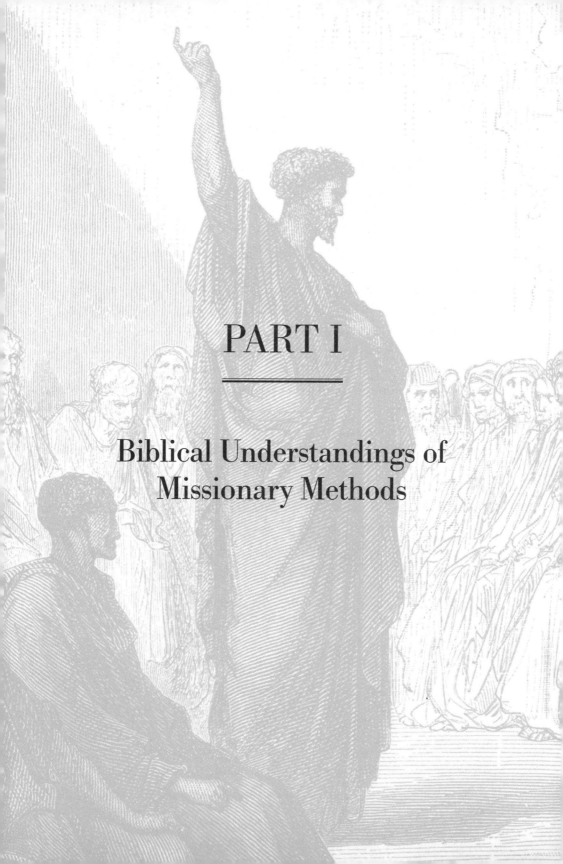

PART I

Biblical Understandings of Missionary Methods

1

Missionary Methods: St. Paul's, St. Roland's, or Ours?

ROBERT L. GALLAGHER

Introduction

This chapter examines various perspectives of Paul's missionary methods as recorded in the book of Acts and his epistles, as well as comparing and contrasting the findings with Roland Allen's claims in his book *Missionary Methods: St. Paul's or Ours?* This assessment clarifies implications for contemporary mission praxis and, conversely, suggests that an awareness of key missiological issues should aid in enhancing biblical studies.

To understand Paul's mission strategy, it is important to first define fundamental terms and establish a methodology of biblical interpretation. With these foundations established, crucial areas of Paul's missionary techniques are demonstrated: Paul was empowered by the Holy Spirit in speech and guidance, functioned in community with associates and other Christian workers, planted and distributed his partners with continued interaction—all to complete the task of the gospel as he preached systematically in prominent centers before moving on. Having described Paul's manner of operation, the final section discusses ways of mission inadequately addressed in Allen's work: the vital function of prayer and spiritual conflict in the expansion of Christ's kingdom.

Definitions

Mission may be defined as the total undertaking God has assigned the church for the salvation of the world. The end result of mission is God, through the church and beyond, reaching across barriers of culture, language, geography, ideology, and ethnicity to bring people to Christ by announcing the gospel in speech and social action. Evangelism may be defined as the activity of the church's mission, through which people are offered the gospel to accept Christ by faith as Savior and serve him in his kingdom community. Having defined these key terms, let us consider the approach to biblical interpretation.

Allen's Hermeneutical Approach

A critical review of Roland Allen's study, which has won such "wide assent and influenced policy and practice," is necessary.[1] Since this paper includes an appraisal of Allen as a foil for the discussion of Pauline methods, both the strengths and weaknesses of his contribution will be biblically assessed. This evaluation first needs to realize Allen's method of biblical hermeneutics. Analyzing the index of his biblical references in *Missionary Methods* shows that his use of the Scriptures was somewhat imbalanced. Allen referenced the Gospels four times, including only one reference to the Gospel of Luke. He cited Acts fifty-four times, which indicates that he had little concept of evaluating Acts in light of Luke's first volume. Therefore Allen could not recognize repeated mission tapestries throughout Luke-Acts as valuable insights to Luke's idea of Paul's missionary methods. Allen obviously failed to take advantage of the whole of Luke's narrative to help interpret the Pauline journeys.

Furthermore, all of Allen's biblical references from Acts were between chapters 13 to 22. They were distributed as follows: the first trip had twelve references, the second twenty-five, and the third ten. After Allen concludes the third mission in Acts 20, he recorded only two scriptures from chapters 21 and 22. In other words, Allen formed his theory of Paul's missionary tactics based largely on Paul's second journey and without any consideration of any missional value beyond Acts 20. Obviously Allen's definition of Paul's "mission" was restricted to the three traditional journeys. As defined, however, this paper views mission as "reaching across barriers

---

1   Kenneth G. Grubb, publisher's foreword to *Missionary Methods: St. Paul's or Ours?*, by Roland Allen, American ed. (1912; repr., Grand Rapids: Eerdmans, 1962), vi.

of culture, language, geography, ideology, and ethnicity to bring people to Christ," which would consider the following Pauline experiences as missionally relevant as well: his conversion (Acts 9:1–22; 22:3–16; 26:9–18); his prejourney evangelistic efforts in Damascus (Acts 9:19–22; 26:20), Jerusalem (Acts 9:23–30; 22:17–21; 26:20), and Syrian Antioch (Acts 11:25–30; 12:25); his activities and speeches beyond the third journey in Jerusalem (Acts 21:17–23:30); his witness before Governor Felix (Acts 23:31–24:27) and Governor Porcius Festus, King Agrippa, and Bernice (Acts 25:1–26:32) at Caesarea; and his journey to Rome via Malta and subsequent gospel presentation to the city's Jewish leaders (Acts 27:1–28:31).

Finally, Allen, in observing the letters of Paul to the Gentile churches, focused predominately on the Corinthian correspondence with forty-six biblical references, compared to 1 and 2 Thessalonians (twenty-two), Galatians (seven), 1 and 2 Timothy (six), Romans (five), Titus (three), Philippians (two), and Ephesians and Colossians with one mention each. Philemon was not cited. Allen not only placed considerable interpretative stress on a select number of Paul's letters to draw his conclusions, but also often gave his arguments a concentrated biblical weight in various subjects. For example, Allen's chapter on "Authority and Discipline" (pages 111–25) contains sixteen references to the Corinthian letters within seven pages (111–17), while page 68 holds nine references from 1 Thessalonians ("The Substance of St. Paul's Preaching"). When discussing Paul's first and second mission journeys, Allen similarly displayed a biblical convergence whereby pages 20 to 23 had eight references, six notations for both pages 10 to 12 and page 62, four for pages 66 to 67, and three for page 41. Analyzing the first three journeys showed an even more pronounced biblical concentration: pages 10 to 12 and page 62 (eight scriptures cited), and page 41 and pages 66 to 67 (both five). All this indicates that Allen supported his claims within a narrow range of Scripture. What then were the factors that shaped the British missionary's myopic view of biblical understanding?

Allen does not often mention his tradition—which guided him to order, ministry, and sacrament—yet Newbigin asserted that Allen took his sacramental theology for granted and, by default, used it as an exegetical lens to interpret the Bible. Thus, Allen approached the book of Acts and the Pauline corpus with a biased hermeneutical view that shaped his understanding and conclusions, which Newbigin emphasized in his foreword to *Missionary Methods*. He cautioned, "Allen was a missionary of the Society for the Propagation of the Gospel. He was a priest of the Church of England nurtured in the Catholic understanding of churchmanship. He was a High Churchman."[2] The bishop of the Church of South India continued:

> In Allen's thought—so far as I understand it—the central place given to the work of the Spirit in no way implied a lessening of the importance of the ordered life of the church as one divine society bound together in a single visible fellowship with the Lord and His apostles, and visibly united in the sacramental life.[3]

An Alternate Biblical Hermeneutic

Since the book of Acts was Allen's primary measure of Pauline mission methodology, this chapter will now explore an alternate biblical hermeneutic of interpreting Acts to draw missional conclusions and reexamine Allen's work, while serving as a model to elucidate the Lukan mission tapestries of prayer and spiritual conflict. William W. Klein, Craig L. Blomberg, and Robert L. Hubbard Jr. in *Introduction to Biblical Interpretation* believe that Luke was not only a trustworthy historian, but also composed theological realities "to teach his readers what he believed God was accomplishing in the world and what God was commanding believers to do in and through the events he narrated."[4] To correctly interpret the teaching of a pericope in Acts, we need to correlate that section with the writer's overall structure of Luke-Acts and the progressive themes throughout. If we splinter the book of Acts into pieces (systematic theological, devotional, narrative, or sermon fragments) and do not view the overarching narrative of the whole of Luke-Acts, we fail to embrace the author's complete theological purpose. Our bits and pieces of Acts are more easily accommodated to our all-persuasive cultural story, dictated by our personal pilgrimage, theological tradition, and mission context. Yet when we shape the Bible rather than letting the Bible shape us, the question becomes what we can learn from the Bible rather than what the Bible is teaching.

I. Howard Marshall reminds us, "Our aim is to discover what the text meant in the mind of its original author for his intended audience."[5] This goal is subverted

---

2   Lesslie Newbigin, foreword to Allen, *Missionary Methods*, ii.
3   Ibid., iii.
4   William W. Klein, Craig L. Blomberg, and Robert L. Hubbard Jr., *Introduction to Biblical Interpretation* (Dallas: Word, 1993), 345.
5   I. Howard Marshall, introduction to *New Testament Interpretation: Essays on Principles and Methods* (Grand Rapids: Eerdmans, 1977), 15.

when we do not interpret the biblical text as originally intended. This is evident in Allen's disregard for the theological motifs in the Gospel of Luke that will inevitably impact Acts. In particular, Luke's interest in the role of the Holy Spirit, the believing community of prayer, spiritual conflict in mission, the contextualized gospel message, and compassion to the outcasts should not be overlooked.

Following this historical-critical approach to interpretation, we seek the first author's theological message and the response that he desired from his original audience. Only then should we ask what this means for our own mission context. In the process of proper interpretation of historical narrative, how does the reader discern what was applicable only to the original culture, and what should be practiced in today's context? In other words, should biblical narratives of the church's actions and decisions in the book of Acts also serve as norms to guide today's church? In part, the interpreter must be observant of the text itself, which may hold clues as to whether or not an example should be implemented.

On the other hand, Gordon D. Fee and Douglas Stuart claimed, "Unless Scripture explicitly tells us we must do something, what is only narrated or described does not function in a normative (i.e. obligatory) way—unless it can be demonstrated on other grounds that the author intended it to function in this way."[6] Concerning the hermeneutics of historical narrative, Fee and Stuart maintained that the word of God in Acts can only be regarded as normative for contemporary believers if it can be shown what the narrative was intended to teach. They stated, "Historic precedent, to have normative value, must be related to intent. That is, if it can be shown that the purpose of a given narrative is to establish precedent, then such precedent should be regarded as normative."[7]

This paper challenges the hermeneutical proverb of Fee and Stuart and offers a less restrictive approach, while still directly involving the vital purposes of the narrative. To interpret Acts, we must study the whole book, which includes Luke's Gospel, as well as the history of the early church in Acts, to understand if specific incidents form recurring themes. If individual events form a consistent pattern, then we can conclude that the biblical writer was emphasizing a normative principle. If the arrangement varies from situation to situation, then the applications may

---

6   Gordon D. Fee and Douglas Stuart, *How to Read the Bible for All Its Worth*, 3rd ed. (Grand Rapids: Zondervan, 2003), 118–19. Also see Gordon D. Fee, *Gospel and Spirit: Issues in New Testament Hermeneutics* (Peabody, MA: Hendrickson, 1994), 91–92.

7   Ibid., 121.

change based on context. Luke-Acts encompasses constant patterns of ministry, which will be explained later in this essay.

What about variations in the mission process? For instance, should Christian leaders today follow Paul's strategy of preaching first in the local synagogue? Expecting repeated missionary methods within the text when the mission context changes is misguided. In Paul's early mission trips, he demonstrated a pattern of reasoning with the Jews in synagogues first;[8] yet when he moved to the Gentile communities of Lystra, Derbe, and Philippi, there were no synagogues (Acts 14:11,21; 16:13), so he resorted to preaching Jesus' resurrection in the marketplaces (Acts 17:17,18). Luke considered both models of evangelism as suitable applications of missionary principles since the operation varied depending on the situation and culture.

The fact that this pattern changes prevents us from concluding that any one specific episode presents a general strategy of mission. These observations thus negate the view that a particular episode should be normative as a missionary routine. To apply the specific form of evangelism today, one must discover contemporary situations that are similar to the first-century world. It must be observed, however, that in each of the aforementioned examples of preaching, a common focus was on the lordship of Christ. This consistent principle was not a coincidence in the ministry of the believers, and was a practice that the author intended to be applied at all settings and cultures, despite contrasting modes of operation.

In cavalier fashion, Allen challenged this interpretative process by declaring:

> Unless we are prepared to drag down St. Paul from his high position as the great Apostle of the Gentiles, we must allow to his methods a certain character of universality, and now I venture to urge that, since the Apostle, no other has discovered or practiced methods for the propagation of the Gospel better than his or more suitable to the circumstances of our day. It would be difficult to find any better model than the Apostle in the work of establishing new churches. At any rate this much is certain, that the Apostle's methods succeeded exactly where others have failed.[9]

---

8   See Acts 9:20; 13:5,14; 14:1; 17:1,2,10,17; 18:4,19; 19:8; cf. 18:26.
9   Roland Allen, *Missionary Methods: St. Paul's or Ours?*, American ed. (1912; repr., Grand Rapids: Eerdmans, 1962), 147.

Allen's persuasive writing style was sometimes manipulative and ahistorical, not considering any of the Spirit-inspired expansions of Christianity such as the monastic, Celtic, Orthodox, and Church of the East movements of the first millennium; the Catholic mission efforts such as the Franciscans, Dominicans, and Jesuits; the Protestant mission endeavors of the Puritans, Pietists, Moravians, and Methodists; or the undertakings of majority world churches in Christian history. Yet the British Anglican avowed repeatedly, "The fact remains that he [Paul] was the most successful founder of churches that the world has ever seen."[10]

Finally, in analyzing the missionary methods of Acts, we need to be aware that it is not Paul's view that we are studying. The Gentile author, Luke, obtained his information from various sources, including Paul, his friend and occasional travel companion. Contrarily, the Pauline letters provide a more direct understanding of the apostle's mission techniques since he himself provided the commentary. Two final cautions are needed: although the genre of Paul's epistles is fairly straightforward as letters, they were historically occasional, which can prove an interpretative challenge. Furthermore, didactic literature should not be conceived as superior to narrative when seeking sound doctrine or vice versa since both should be appreciated as complementary to one another.

In summary, remember that Allen's interpretations of Paul's movements in Acts were taken through an incomplete Lukan viewpoint. Allen's resulting conclusions were truncated by emphasizing only one section of Luke's structure and purpose, and by this methodology he defaulted towards concentrated pockets of Scripture to prove his contentions. Considering the entire Lukan narrative illuminates the repeated patterns within mission tapestries, as well as the author's original theological purpose and intended response of his audience.

Completing the Mission Task in Community

This chapter will now briefly reference the mission ways of Paul found in the New Testament by underlining the particular similarities with those discovered in Allen's *Missionary Methods*. Paul centered his ministry and coworkers in the prominent cities of the eastern Mediterranean including Damascus, Syrian Antioch, Iconium and Lystra, Derbe, Philippi, Thessalonica and Athens, Corinth, and Ephesus.[11]

---

10 Ibid., 93.
11 Ibid., 10–17, 126.

Upon arrival in a city, Paul and his companions would generally practice a systematic approach of preaching Jesus as the Messiah and establishing a base of operations. They would first attend the local synagogue and proclaim their risen Lord to the Jewish people. If there was no synagogue, such as in Philippi, they would search out the God-fearers—Gentiles who followed Judaism yet had not submitted to the rituals of full conversion (Acts 13:43; 16:13,14). After speaking to the synagogue and God-fearers, they preached to the general populace in the marketplaces.[12]

The Apostle Paul worked in community to distribute the salvation news of the Messiah. Contrary to the image of Paul as an individualistic preacher, he frequently coordinated his missionary activities with a group of cross-cultural workers. Paul's companions in the first two intercultural encounters were mostly Jewish, with the exceptions of Timothy and Luke; yet by the third mission Paul's traveling colleagues were predominantly Gentiles. As Allen repeatedly asserted, Paul had absolute confidence in the operation of the Holy Spirit within this multicultural cohort.[13]

In addition to Paul's community in mission, he used associates for the expansion of the gospel, including Jewish coworkers such as Lucius, Jason, Sosipater, Sosthenes, Mark, and Jesus Justus; as well as Titus and Tychicus who were Gentile Christians. These working partners provided special services; for instance, financial aid and collection, forwarding of church greetings, and communicating appeals of assistance. Altogether the apostle had a contingent of fifty-four male and thirteen female associate workers. Throughout Allen's text, he repeatedly affirmed the above observations by emphasizing that Paul willingly "practiced retirement." The first-century pioneer was pleased when his new converts made progress without his help, and he freely allowed them to exercise the authority and power that they had in Christ.[14]

Paul's vocational methods incorporated faith in the Spirit's work in cross-cultural and multitalented communities, as well as strategic involvement of other Christians in the vicinity. When Paul arrived in a city, he not only used his itinerant coworkers for missional tasks but also involved other local Christians. Allen similarly advocated the development of trust in national leadership and churches. He maintained that the majority of Western missionary practice was based on the distrust of the indigenous leader's integrity and "to check the free flow of native liberality." This attitude smacks of European superiority and a "fear of independ-

---

12   Ibid., 19–22.
13   Ibid., 121, 124–25, 141–150.
14   Ibid., 98–103.

ence" by importing organizations to generate "submission to foreign domination."[15] Allen confronted his audience:

> We think it quite impossible that a native church should be able to exist without the paternal care of an English overseer. If it were financially independent it might be tempted to dispense with his services, and then, we are persuaded, it would at once fall into every error of doctrine and practice.[16]

After Paul established himself in prominent centers by systematically preaching and employing his fellow workers and other Christians living there, he distributed his "fellow-soldiers" beyond his immediate sphere of influence to plant churches in the surrounding regions.[17] Along the Lycus River valley, for example, stood the three important towns of Laodicea, Colossae, and Hierapolis, where churches were established by Epaphras (Col 1:7; 4:12–17). Epaphras was most likely sent by Paul from Ephesus to preach the gospel in the valley even though the apostle had never visited the churches (Col 2:1). Allen endorsed this observed practice of Paul when he alleged, "From Ephesus the Gospel spread throughout all the neighbouring country so that many churches sprang up, the members of which had never seen St Paul's face, and he himself could write to the Romans that he had 'no more place in those regions' (Rom 15:23)."[18]

To establish a church in a particular region, Paul at times left behind a trusted coworker to strengthen the fledging believers. In comparing the "we" passages of Acts 16:12,13 and Acts 17:1, it would appear that Luke was left in Philippi for five years between the second and third mission journeys. Allen confirmed, "This has seemed to many a sufficient reason for arguing that St. Luke was left at Philippi all that time. In that case he must, without doubt, have been a pillar of strength to the church in that place." Allen refused, however, to acknowledge that Paul had a regular practice of establishing his fellow workers as ministers in the new churches which he founded, and only recognized the incident of Luke in Philippi as an isolated case based on "our ignorance of the movements of St. Luke." Allen disputes, "It is impossible to argue from an isolated and doubtful incident of this kind against the

---

15   Ibid., 60.
16   Ibid., also see 142–43.
17   Ibid., 12.
18   Ibid., 111.

whole course of St Paul's action elsewhere." Unfortunately, when Allen spoke of the "whole course," he was selective and imprecise in his choice of Paul's circumstances, and sometimes disagreed from silence to support his case.[19]

On this point, could it be that Allen's theological convention influenced his interpretation of these events so that he overcompensated to support his opinion of self-sufficient churches? In observing the training of Paul's converts, the British missionary viewed the process through an Anglican sacramental lens. To defend this hypothesis, observe Allen's contention:

> Visits paid at long intervals, occasional letters, even constant communication by means of deputies, is not at all the same thing as sending catechists or teachers to stay and instruct converts for a generation whilst they depend upon the missionary for the ministration of the sacraments. Nothing can alter or disguise the fact that St Paul did leave behind him at his first visit complete churches.[20]

Yet Paul did not leave all the churches he founded to develop on their own via occasional letters and visits, but planted faithful colleagues to advance the maturity of the community in their new faith, though not necessarily to administer the sacraments. This was evidenced when Paul left Priscilla and Aquila, and later Timothy, with the church at Ephesus to teach correct doctrine (Acts 18:18–21,24–26). Similarly, he left Titus, his long-time associate, in Crete to continue the ministry of building the numerous churches on the island (Titus 1:5,10,14). Paul continued communication with these congregations in a purposeful missionary strategy of personal visits, sending his cohorts to assess spiritual health, and writing letters to challenge and edify the believers.[21]

A final observed apostolic method was Paul's continual sharing of the gospel in a region until his missionary work was finished. In the letter to the church of Rome, Paul wrote that he had preached the gospel of Christ and planted churches, in terms of present-day countries, from Israel to Lebanon, in Syria, Turkey, and Greece, and on through Bulgaria, Albania, Serbia, Montenegro, Bosnia and Herzegovina, Slovenia, and Croatia (Rom 15:18,19). At the time of his writing he was planning

---

19   Ibid., 86.
20   Ibid., 87; also see 103, 105.
21   Ibid., 85–87.

to pass through Rome on his way to further mission in Spain where Christ was not known. Again in Romans 15:23,24 he verified the completion of his initial task, "But now that there is no more place for me to work in these regions, and since I have been longing for many years to visit you, I plan to do so when I go to Spain." Only after the mission endeavor was accomplished in a particular territory did Paul and his workforce venture to new projects in other locations.[22]

Allen's line of reasoning was that, since the apostle stayed a short time in places, this "conduced in no small measure to St Paul's success."[23] He continued:

> The facts are these: St Paul preached in a place for five or six months and then left behind him a church, not indeed free from the need of guidance, but capable of growth and expansion . . . The question before us is how he could so train his converts as to be able to leave them after so short a time with any security that they would be able to stand and grow.[24]

By quickly leaving the new converts, Allen believed that Paul gave the indigenous leaders an opportunity to rely on the Holy Spirit and embody their responsibility to be missionaries and local churches.[25] We will now give closer attention to this core argument of his book.

Empowered by the Spirit in Mission

Allen's main thesis in *Missionary Methods* was that the church of today could find solutions to their present difficulties by following Paul's principles of planting indigenous churches and trusting the Holy Spirit to work in new believers and their congregations. Many Western missionaries lack confidence in the Spirit to work in their converts, even when they trust his role in their own lives. Paul had faith in the Holy Spirit and viewed the Spirit as God's main missionary—a Person living and working through inexperienced followers. Allen repeated that the Apostle Paul "believed that He [the Spirit of Christ] would perfect His Church, and that He would establish, strengthen, and settle his converts. He believed, and acted as if he believed. It is that faith which we need today. We need to subordinate our methods,

---

22   Ibid., 89.
23   Ibid., 93.
24   Ibid., 84–85.
25   Ibid., 93–94.

our systems, ourselves to that faith."[26] Allen debated throughout his text that this "is one of the most obvious lessons which the study of St Paul's work teaches us."[27]

In *Missionary Methods* Allen mentioned the Holy Spirit eighty-nine times. Except for twenty-three general references to the Spirit, he mostly denoted the Spirit's work in mission as the concept of trusting him in the lives of the new converts and churches (on some nineteen occasions, or about 21 percent of his total references).[28] Allen discussed other functions of the Spirit with much less emphasis, including guidance (thirteen times), indwelling (twelve), unity (three), teaching (two), and gifts (one). He also included far less significant recognition of the Spirit's attributes, such as power (fourteen times), presence (three), life (one), and eternity (one); together with four cautions regarding the rejection of the Spirit.

Undebatably, Allen was influential with his emphasis on the Holy Spirit and mission, yet his awareness of the Spirit's role and person was repetitive, narrow, and largely philosophic. Conceivably this restriction was due to his situation in China where he was troubled by activity-driven Western missionaries whose theological traditions dictated an inflexible church system that stifled the Spirit's missional objectives in the indigenous congregations.[29] This disturbing circumstance became a concentrated passion that negated a more comprehensive pneumatological interpretation.

One must examine the work of the Holy Spirit in the mission journeys of Paul in a more holistic manner to compare the findings with Allen's contained efforts. This will involve considering the tapestry of the Spirit in Luke-Acts following the hermeneutical methodology outlined in this chapter's introduction. In other words, before considering the role of the Spirit in the Pauline excursions of Acts, the student of Paul's missionary methods needs to scrutinize Luke's understanding of the Spirit in the whole of his corpus. Only then can one interpret why Luke recorded particular features of the Spirit within the Pauline mission journeys before drawing any contemporary application.

Luke recognized that the Holy Spirit was the Trinitarian God who called Paul to cross-cultural ministry (Acts 13:1–4). Luke understood God's Spirit as a Person who orchestrated Christ's mission in his conception, commissioning, speech, and ministry to the marginalized. Parallel to the Spirit working in Jesus' undertaking

---

26   Ibid., 149.
27   Ibid., vii.
28   Ibid., vii, viii, 6, 91, 121, 124–25, 144, 149–50.
29   Ibid., 141–50.

was his role in the lives of the early disciples through revelation and empowerment. The book of Acts records the continued role of the Spirit of Jesus in the ministry of the early church as he strengthened and appointed church leaders while imparting wisdom, faith, and joy (Acts 20:28).

The remainder of this section analyzes the three foremost purposes of Luke's theological message concerning the Holy Spirit and mission. Luke viewed the role of the Spirit as filling the believing community so that they would be guided to opportunities of empowerment "to testify to the resurrection of the Lord Jesus" (Acts 4:33). First, the Spirit filled the followers of God on twenty-four occasions in Luke-Acts. In Luke's Gospel there was a marked concentration around the Messiah's birth with the Spirit filling John the Baptist and his parents (Elizabeth and Zechariah), Simeon, and Jesus himself, as he began his earthly ministry "full of the Holy Spirit" (Luke 3:22; 4:1,18). Luke then moved his attention from the beginning of Christ's mission to the inauguration of the church's ministry when approximately 120 men and women were filled with the Holy Spirit at Pentecost (Acts 2:1–4). Similar to Luke's first volume, Acts also demonstrated that individuals and communities in mission continued to receive the fullness of the Spirit, such as Peter, the seven servers including Stephen, and Cornelius and his family and friends.

The Lukan episodes of the Spirit's filling within the time of Paul are especially significant for this chapter. Again, the biblical author repeated an ongoing theme of Luke-Acts: that the Spirit rested upon people who spread the good news of the Messiah. The two prominent missionaries to the Gentiles, Saul/Paul (Acts 9:17; 13:9) and Barnabas (Acts 11:24), were both empowered by the Spirit to preach Christ. And as a result, communities also received the Spirit, such as the Pisidian disciples (Acts 13:52) and the twelve followers of John the Baptist at Ephesus (Acts 19:2–7). At the start of the Gentile undertaking, Luke summarized the ministry of Jesus to emphasize this point: "God anointed Jesus of Nazareth with the Holy Spirit and power, and . . . he went around doing good and healing all who were under the power of the devil, because God was with him" (Acts 10:38). In simpler terms, Luke stressed that the Messiah's teaching and miracles came by the Holy Spirit's power and not his divinity, and that after the resurrection his followers received the identical Spirit to carry on the work that he began.

Another repeated Lukan manifestation of the Spirit of God was that of guidance. The recognition of the baby Jesus as the Messiah was directed by the Spirit (Luke 2:26,27), as was the induction of Christ's ministry (Luke 4:1,14). Later, when the

Spirit of Jesus came upon the early believers, they were correspondingly guided in their journey from Jerusalem to Rome to spread the message and perform miracles. The following include a number of instances in the book of Acts where the Spirit led Jesus' supporters in mission: Philip and the Ethiopian eunuch, Peter with Cornelius, and the decision of the Jerusalem Council.

The Spirit's role in guiding the expansion of the faith continued in the life of Paul. As the Syrian Antioch leaders were worshiping God, the Holy Spirit said, "Set apart for me Barnabas and Saul [Paul] for the work to which I have called them" (Acts 13:2). The church prayed, fasted, and laid hands on them, and the Holy Spirit sent them forth into cross-cultural encounters. In the midst of the second missionary trip, as Paul, Silas, and Timothy journeyed through Asia Minor, the Holy Spirit showed the way they were to travel (Acts 16:6,7). In Acts 19:21 and 20:22, Paul sensed the Holy Spirit's compulsion to go to Jerusalem and Rome. Then, in 20:23,24 and 21:4, Paul received the Spirit's warning of future imprisonment and hardship. Similarly, Agabus, through the Spirit, also cautioned Paul about suffering in Jerusalem under the Roman oppressors (21:10–14). The Spirit, through the committed communities, guided the apostle toward future events.

Lastly, the Lukan role of the Holy Spirit majored on the believers being filled and led by the Spirit to speak the inspired words of God. Some twenty-two times the Gentile writer recorded the followers of Christ expressing Spirit-motivated words beyond their own capabilities to progress God's intentions. Again we see a concentration of this phenomena around the birth of Christ with Elizabeth and Zechariah prophesying, followed by Jesus' first recorded sermon (Luke 4:18,19), and the disciples speaking before rulers (Luke 12:11,12). The rest of the eighteen registered occasions were in Acts where the Spirit of God motivated individuals to speak, such as Jesus after his resurrection, Peter to the Sanhedrin, Stephen confronting the Synagogue of the Freedmen and Sanhedrin Council, Cornelius and associates in their exaltation of God, and Agabus' warning prophecy of imminent famine; and where the Spirit-filled community of the Way, likewise, were witnesses of Christ (Acts 1:8), such as with the Pentecost disciples and the church at Jerusalem (Acts 2:17,18; 4:31,33).

Yet again, this reiterated Lukan theological message of the Spirit's role in mission to speak God's thoughts was conspicuous within the record of Paul. The Holy Spirit not only filled and guided Paul's ministry, but also spoke God's thoughts through and to him. Paul's warning and judgment to Elymas (Acts 13:9,10), John's twelve disciples' speaking in tongues and prophecy as they received the Spirit through Paul's ministry, and the cautioning prophecies by the churches at Macedonia (20:22,23) and Tyre (21:4) of Paul's impending suffering, in addition to Agabus' warning (Acts 21:10–14), were all performed through the Spirit of God. Certainly, within the Pauline journeys of Acts, the Spirit's role to cause inspired speech in the propagation of the Christian faith was of utmost importance to Luke, even though it would seem in Allen's estimation to be of little consequence. The next section of this essay turns to survey two other mission methods of Paul found in the Gospel of Luke and book of Acts that were also inadequately discussed in Allen's *Missionary Methods:* prayer and spiritual conflict.

Prayer in Mission

To properly study the theme of prayer and mission, and adequately recognize any missionary method found in the Lukan testimony of the Pauline tours, we need to consider the whole of Luke's body of writing to interpret the significance of those incidences in question. With this in mind, this chapter will now succinctly travel through Luke's Gospel and Acts, tracing the motif of prayer in the context of Jesus' and the church's salvation history, before analyzing the Pauline sections of prayer.

Luke emphasized prayer more than any other Synoptic writer through the use of prayer terms and motifs. For instance, Luke included the prayer motif at key junctions in his narrative of Jesus. The Son of God prayed at his baptism (3:21) and after a day of working miracles (5:15,16). Before choosing the Twelve, Jesus spent the night on the mount in prayer (6:12), and previous to Peter's confession of faith and his first prediction of the passion, the Messiah prayed alone (9:18). Jesus traveled to the mount of transfiguration to pray (9:29), and he prayed with thanksgiving after the mission of the seventy disciples (10:17–21). His example led his followers to ask him to teach them to pray (11:1), and Jesus prayed during his agony on the Mount of Olives (22:39–46) and during his crucifixion (23:34–46).

This interest in the spiritual practice of prayer continued in the book of Acts where Luke associated prayer with the most important events in the life of the church. It was while praying that the disciples received the Spirit, who empowered them to speak the word of God with courage and impact (2:42; 4:31). Prayer was the special obligation of the Twelve (6:4), and accompanied the ordination of the church's ministers (6:6). Through prayer the Samaritans received the Holy Spirit

(8:15,17) and Cornelius was converted (10:2,4,9,31). Prayer preceded the miracles of the apostles (9:40) and the freedom of Peter from prison (12:5).

Looking at the life of Paul, the idea of prayer and God's mission continued its resounding course. Paul followed a regular custom of prayer, whether at the temple in Jerusalem (22:17) or beside a river at Philippi (16:13,16). Prayer and fasting were employed at the commissioning of Paul and Barnabas, the church's first missionaries (13:3), as well as the selection of church leaders after Paul's first Gentile mission (14:23). Like Peter, Paul and Silas were praying when they were miraculously released from the Macedonian prison (16:25). The father of Publius, the chief official of Malta, was healed of fever and dysentery after Paul prayed (28:8). Finally, Paul, in a posture of adoration, kneeled in prayer to the sovereign God as he departed from the Ephesian elders at Miletus (20:36) and the believers in Tyre (21:5).

Luke not only emphasized the role of prayer, for him prayer was the means whereby God directed his mission of salvation to alienated humanity. Through prayer God guided the mission of Jesus, the early church, and Paul during decisive moments. Prayer communicated the divine presence and inspiration of the Holy Spirit to the early believers and, in doing so, apprehended the dynamic power of the Spirit for salvation history. In other words, Luke conceived of prayer as an important means by which God orchestrated the course of redemptive history. Prayer functioned as an important tool through which the divine plan of salvation was made known, and Paul enacted a special part in that Lukan story as God's instrument of bringing salvation to the non-Jewish peoples.

Allen referred to prayer only ten times in his book, and not once did he connect prayer with Paul's missionary methods. In his text the only reference to Paul and prayer concerned the preaching in Philippi where the apostle "preached at the prayer-place."[30] Allen spoke of prayer three times in relation to demonic gods,[31] with the majority of his other prayer references supporting his exhortation that new churches not be defined by Western systems and rituals, raising the possibility that a new convert's "attendance at a house of prayer may take the place of prayer."[32] Additionally, the Englishman argued that Paul never instructed his newly founded churches in a form of prayer, and thus missionaries should not import to new congregations a scheme of prayer such as the Anglican Prayer Book with its complete systems of theology and worship. Not doing so would then enable the fledgling

---

30   Ibid., 23.
31   Ibid., 36, 44, 130.
32   Ibid., 55–56.

church to develop its own practices of prayer rather than "to hear prayers read for them in the church by a paid mission agent."[33]

Spiritual Conflict in Mission

This paper will now examine the mission tapestry of spiritual conflict in Luke-Acts to comprehend Luke's overall understanding and thus attempt to explain what the Pauline incidences of power encounter express about the apostle's missionary methods. That is, in considering spiritual warfare, one should consider Luke's theological message in his record of satanic activity within his total history of Jesus and the early church. Once again, to receive Luke's complete meaning, the whole of Luke-Acts needs to be observed rather than an individual slice that only considers Paul's missionary journeys.

In Jesus' case, he first battled Satan in Luke 4:1–13, and continued this confrontation throughout the Gospel of Luke in a number of episodes of demonic deliverance: the unclean spirit at the Capernaum synagogue, Legion of Gerasenes, the boy with the violent spirit, and the man with a dumb spirit. Women were also liberated from demons, such as Peter's mother-in-law who was stricken by a spirit named "fever," the female disciples of Jesus who had been freed from spirits and disabilities, and the stooped woman who had been bound by a demon of infirmity for eighteen years. In the book of Acts, Jesus' task of demonic deliverance was maintained through the church: Peter's shadow in Jerusalem, Philip and the unclean spirits of Samaria, and Peter and John with Simon the magician.

Even from the first encounter of Christ and Satan in the wilderness, Luke emphasizes that the victory belonged to the Son of God. When Jesus conquered afflicting spirits, he proclaimed that the kingdom of God had come (Luke 11:20). This theological missive of God's victorious kingdom continues from Luke's Gospel through his history of the first-century church. Turning to the Pauline missionary methods of Acts, we notice that the former Pharisee was also successful over the demonic world with Elymas, the Jewish false prophet (Acts 13:6–12); a woman possessed by a spirit of divination (Acts 16:16); many who were healed from evil spirits through cloths he had touched (Acts 19:11,12); and the seven sons of Sceva who tried to exorcise in Jesus' name (Acts 19:13–17). Paul summarized his victory over satanic forces before Agrippa and Festus when he proclaimed that, by God's

---

33   Ibid., 161.

resolve, he brought people "from darkness to light, and from the power of Satan to God" (Acts 26:17,18).

Moreover, the power encounters in Luke-Acts served as a reminder to the original audience that the gospel could never be thwarted, no matter what kind of demonic opposition came against them. At every stage of the primitive church's geographic expansion, they encountered territorial warfare, which they repeatedly overcame. This happened in the initial expansion from Jerusalem to the region of Samaria, the first Gentile mission to Cyprus and the cities of the Anatolian plateau, the opening deployment of Paul to Europe, and the expansion of the gospel throughout Asia Minor. In summary, Luke placed Paul's missionary resolve of encountering demonic powers within a broader framework to validate the invincibility of God's kingdom through Christ. We now turn to Allen's understanding of the missionary purposes of spiritual conflict in Paul's journeys.

In Allen's chapter on "Miracles" he claimed, "Miracles hold an important place in the account of St Paul's preaching."[34] The British author believed that Paul's use of miracles revealed constant principles, which should guide our mission practice today; however, he reluctantly concluded, "We have powers sufficient to gather hearers; we have powers sufficient to demonstrate the Divine Presence of the Spirit of God with us . . . if only we will use our powers to reveal the Spirit."[35] This statement again indicates an exegetical praxis hindered by Allen's theological convention.

Although Allen did not take into consideration the overall purpose of spiritual conflict in Luke-Acts, the "miracles" section of *Missionary Methods* contains a concentration of seven references (out of a total of less than twenty in the book) to Christ's victory over demonic forces as the chief evidence of miracles. Allen stated, "Paul healed the sick and cast out devils,"[36] citing the expulsion of evil spirits at Philippi and Ephesus.[37] These instances demonstrated God's salvation to the heathen who were "released from the bondage of sin and the power of the devil."[38] Allen continued:

> There can be no doubt that this power of working marvels ["healing all who were oppressed of the devil"], this striking demonstration of the authority of Jesus over evil spirits, was in the early Church

---

34   Ibid., 41.
35   Ibid., 48.
36   Ibid., 46.
37   Ibid., 41.
38   Ibid., 45.

considered to be a most valuable weapon with which to confute opponents and to convince the hesitating. "It was as exorcisers," says Professor Harnack, "that the Christians went out into the great world, and exorcism formed one very powerful method of their mission propaganda." . . . Christians appealed to exorcism as proof of the divinity of Christ and of His superior authority over all the heathen gods and demons.[39]

Allen concurred that exorcism was a powerful mission method, yet was reluctant to encourage the practice for today, even though "such [exorcisory] powers were highly valued in the Church." Allen considered that "their importance can be easily overrated and it is manifest that St Paul saw this danger and combated it."[40] In this chapter, Allen mistakenly correlated the events of the Lukan Acts with that of Paul's Corinthian teaching on the gifts of the Holy Spirit without distinguishing the two very different perspectives. To prove his assertions, Allen quoted the Acts record of Paul's supernatural manifestations throughout his chapter on miracles, and only towards the end switched to Paul's epistles to accommodate his negative view regarding contemporary application of the miraculous.

Allen was correct in asserting that Paul "does not give the gift of miracles the highest place among the gifts of the Spirit," and that "best of all was the spirit of charity." Indeed what was most important to Paul was not the power of the miraculous but "the Spirit who inspired the life."[41] Allen does not take into consideration, however, that Paul was correcting a community of Corinthian believers who were misusing the operation of the gifts of the Spirit in their congregation; whereas, on the other hand, Luke was describing the expansion of the first-century church to a community who needed encouragement and hope in the midst of persecution and hopelessness.

Conclusion

What do the findings of this paper mean for contemporary missionary methods? Are there any adjustments needed for today's missions? It would seem that Paul's

---

39   Ibid., 47, quoting Adolf Harnack, *Expansion of Christianity in the First Three Centuries,* vol. 1 (London: Williams & Norgate, 1908), 131.

40   Allen, *Missionary Methods,* 47.

41   Ibid., 47–48.

purposefulness in mission suggests that his focused attention on his churches was not only to bring them to a healthy condition of maturity for their own sake, but more toward a development that would produce an effective witness of the risen Christ. Paul certainly was concerned to have churches of order and security, yet his dynamic mission strategy propelled him toward an aggressive desire of God's mission for his churches.

Paul's missionary methods, however, were not independent of the Spirit of God. They were more than strategies of human construct. Under sovereign direction, the Holy Spirit was the orchestrator of Paul's mission program and a continuance of the ministry of Jesus (Acts 16:5,6). The mission of the church is the work of the Spirit, and each generation needs to resubmit its ecclesiastical traditions to the examination of the Spirit of Christ, acting not by applying a set of methods to work church growth, but out of obedience to the ways of the sovereign Spirit of God, who is Lord of the church.

Works Cited

Allen, Roland. *Missionary Methods: St. Paul's or Ours?*, American ed. Grand Rapids: Eerdmans, 1962. First published 1912.

Fee, Gordon D. *Gospel and Spirit: Issues in New Testament Hermeneutics.* Peabody, MA: Hendrickson Publishers, 1994.

———, and Douglas Stuart. *How to Read the Bible for All Its Worth*, 3rd ed. Grand Rapids: Zondervan, 2003.

Grubb, Kenneth G. Publisher's foreword to *Missionary Methods: St. Paul's or Ours?*, by Roland Allen, vi. American ed. Grand Rapids: Eerdmans, 1962. First published 1912.

Harnack, Adolf. *Expansion of Christianity in the First Three Centuries,* vol. 1. London: Williams & Norgate, 1908.

Klein, William W., Craig L. Blomberg, and Robert L. Hubbard Jr. *Introduction to Biblical Interpretation.* Dallas: Word, 1993.

Marshall, I. Howard. Introduction to *New Testament Interpretation: Essays on Principles and Methods*15. Grand Rapids: Eerdmans, 1977.

Newbigin, Lesslie. Foreword to *Missionary Methods: St. Paul's or Ours?,* by Roland Allen, i–iii. American ed. Grand Rapids: Eerdmans, 1962. First published 1912.

2

Roland Allen's Understanding of the Spirit's Centrality in Mission

ROB S. HUGHES

As the theme of this book was chosen in recognition of the one-hundredth anniversary of the publication of Roland Allen's *Missionary Methods: St. Paul's or Ours?*, it is important to include in its discussion a concise examination of some of Allen's writings which are particularly relevant for contemporary missiological reflection and practice. While Roland Allen's career as a missionary was brief, the works which he produced as he reflected upon his experiences as a missionary in China have been highly influential in the field of missiology, and they bring with them practical ramifications for mission today. It is this author's understanding, through the short time that he has spent with Allen's writings, that Allen's grasp of the centrality of the Holy Spirit in mission, like that of Lesslie Newbigin, provides an understanding of mission which is essential for the church today, particularly in today's globalized and increasingly postmodern contexts.

Lesslie Newbigin, in his foreword to Roland Allen's *Missionary Methods: St. Paul's or Ours?*, writes of Allen's works, "The very heart and life of his message was that the mission of the church is the work of the Spirit."[1] Similar to Newbigin's assessment, John E. Branner writes, "The gift of the Holy Spirit to believers was something which was to govern Allen's entire concept of mission, particularly that of

---

1   Lesslie Newbigin, foreword to *Missionary Methods: St. Paul's or Ours?*, by Roland Allen, American ed. (1912; repr., Grand Rapids: Eerdmans, 1962), ii.

the indigenous church."[2] He adds, "The basis of Allen's understanding of the work of the Holy Spirit was that He is the Spirit of mission. He is a witnessing Spirit, a sending Spirit. It was Christ who gave the commission and it is the Spirit of Christ within who enables the believer to obey."[3]

Overview of Allen's Key Writings

Allen's key writings, which grew out of his missionary experiences in China from 1895 to 1903, include *The Spontaneous Expansion of the Church* and *Missionary Methods: St. Paul's or Ours?* David M. Paton has collected other significant writings of Allen in three books: *The Ministry of the Spirit, Reform of the Ministry,* and *The Compulsion of the Spirit: A Roland Allen Reader.* More recently, Allen's grandson J. B. Hubert Allen has written a biography of him, *Roland Allen: Pioneer, Priest, and Prophet,* and J. D. Payne has offered *Roland Allen: Pioneer of Spontaneous Expansion.* Lastly, of particular worth for the purposes of this chapter is Allen's other substantial writing, a book entitled *Missionary Principles,* which discusses "the Holy Spirit as the Spirit of Missions."[4]

In a review of one of David Paton's collections of Allen's writings, Hans Kasdorf has provided a summary of Allen's major assertions in eight points. As an appropriate introduction and overview of Allen's thought, he writes as follows:

> When we speak of St. Paul's missionary method, Allen contends, we can do so only by acknowledging among other things the following essentials about the Spirit's work:
>
> 1. Paul was controlled by the Holy Spirit and not by the "Western spirit . . . of superiority towards all Eastern people" (p. 6).
> 2. Converts should be encouraged to exercise spiritual gifts "freely and at once" (p. 10).
> 3. We missionaries must have "faith in the Holy Ghost (who is) in our converts" (p. 11).

---

2   John E. Branner, "Roland Allen: Pioneer in a Spirit-centered Theology of Mission," *Missiology* 5, no. 2 (April 1977): 181.

3   Ibid., 181.

4   Roland Allen, *Missionary Principles* (Grand Rapids: Eerdmans, 1964), 12.

4. We also need to exercise confidence that new Christians can "overcome apparently insuperable difficulties by the power of the Holy Ghost" (p. 19)—difficulties inherent in their culture and social structure.

5. The secret of church expansion is not rooted in the presence of the missionary, but in the "Grace of the Holy Spirit given to all Christians" regardless of age or race (p. 35).

6. New Christians have the right to live their own lives directed by the Holy Spirit without being dictated to by the foreign missionary (pp. 38–48).

7. The Lord gives the gift of the Spirit by the laying on of hands, and the Spirit gives spiritual gifts for the work of the ministry. Therefore, the church should ordain and free the national "voluntary clergy" without formal theological training for church ministry (pp. 71–75; 100–107). The power of the Spirit and not the policy of the church is what counts. "When we turn from considerations of Spirit to considerations of policy and expediency, we are in danger of losing the path which leads to the revelation of truth" (p. 81).

8. Obedience to the Spirit may make it necessary "to break a tradition." What that means, Allen explains, is to free missionaries from settled work in a church to itinerant or pioneer evangelism in new areas (pp. 115; 122–123).[5]

Kasdorf's summary captures the main elements of Allen's key works, writings that were concerned with Western missionaries' being so consumed with the methods and tasks of missionary work (and their own investment in this work) that they both neglected the primacy of the Spirit and failed to trust the Spirit to guide and equip their converts. As a result, Western missionaries, despite good intentions, actually held back what the Spirit wanted to accomplish in creating indigenous churches throughout the earth. Allen himself states the essence of this point in the final chapter of *Missionary Methods* where he writes:

---

5   Hans Kasdorf, "Review of *The Compulsion of the Spirit: A Roland Allen Reader*, edited by David Paton and Charles H. Long," *Missiology* 12, no. 3 (July 1984): 115, 122–23.

Now if we are to practice any methods approaching to the Pauline methods in power and directness, it is absolutely necessary that we should first have this faith, this Spirit. Without faith—faith in the Holy Ghost, faith in the Holy Ghost in our converts, we can do nothing. We cannot possibly act as the Apostle acted until we recover this faith. Without it we shall be unable to recognize the grace of the Holy Spirit in our converts, we shall never trust them, we shall never inspire in them confidence in the power of the Holy Spirit in themselves. If we have no faith in the power of the Holy Spirit in them, they will not learn to have faith in the power of the Holy Spirit in themselves.[6]

Roland Allen's Understanding of the Spirit's Centrality in Mission

In pursuit of a brief but deeper examination of these themes and their contemporary application, this chapter will now turn to two substantial but lesser-known works of Allen: "Mission Activities Considered in Relation to the Manifestation of the Spirit" and *Missionary Principles.* These works have received less attention than *Missionary Methods* and *The Spontaneous Expansion of the Church,* yet they embody Kasdorf's eight summary principles with clarity and hold application that is particularly relevant for the current context of the newly emerging and globalized postmodern West.

Mission Activities Considered in Relation to the Manifestation of the Spirit

The first work, which was written for presentation at a 1926 missionary conference held in Shanghai, asks the provocative question, "Why is it that the Christian Movement in China has impressed people chiefly as a movement of activities rather than as a spiritual force?" By "activities," Allen refers to those things "which we

---

6   Roland Allen, *Missionary Methods: St. Paul's or Ours?,* American ed. (1912; repr., Grand Rapids: Eerdmans, 1962), 152.

universally employ in all our missions everywhere."[7] He writes, in a deliberately lengthy fashion, as follows:

> It would be tedious to make out a complete list of them, but they include such things as the organization and direction of schools for the education of the people, of clubs for the welfare of young men and women, of institutions for the improvement of social conditions in towns and villages, of agitations for the removal of amelioration of evils such as opium smoking, or child marriage, or foot-binding, or forced labour, or overcrowding, of hospitals for the cure of the sick, of lectures on public health, of schemes for the improvement of agriculture and such like, an endless list.[8]

In contrast to this tedious list, a spiritual force, in this case, is defined simply as "the power of the Spirit of Jesus, or of the Holy Spirit."[9] From this point, Allen then outlines his argument as follows:

> The question implies four definite statements: (1) that the activities are so prominent that they absorb attention; (2) that the missions appear to exist for them; (3) that there is a spiritual force which might appear, and be made manifest; (4) that this force is obscured. We may also, I think, say that the question suggests that the revelation of the spiritual force is, in the mind of the author of the question, a matter of importance, and its obscurance a source of regret.[10]

Allen thus asserts that the overwhelming amount of "activities" in missionaries' lives obscures the role and work of the Holy Spirit. He then reports that when he posed the question above at the Shanghai conference, the conference attendees suggested the "solution" to the problem contained therein was simply "an exhortation to piety of life" in missionaries whose lives had become too busy.[11] Allen rejected this "solution" as insufficient, writing:

---

7   Roland Allen, "Mission Activities Considered in Relation to the Manifestation of the Spirit," in *The Ministry of the Spirit: Selected Writings of Roland Allen,* ed. David M. Paton (London: World Dominion, 1960), 89.

8   Ibid., 89–90.

9   Ibid., 90.

10   Ibid., 90–91.

11   Ibid., 91.

Is it true that missionaries generally are so immersed in activities that they neglect their prayers and forget the Spirit which
should inform all their activities? The missionary body is a large
one composed of many different individuals of many different
types, and in so large a body some may be, and probably are, so
afflicted; but the great majority are sincerely desirous of being
guided by the Spirit and of expressing the Spirit in all their activities; and behind them is a great host of Christian people who pray
for them and subscribe money to help them, earnestly desiring
the manifestation of the Spirit. I do not think, then, that we can
possibly accept this answer as complete, or sufficient.[12]

Instead, he suggests that the missionaries' "activities" act to "obscure the Spirit
in three ways":

1.   They may obscure it because they are made too prominent;
2.   They may obscure it because they are used in such a way as
     to obscure it;
3.   They may obscure it because they are in themselves of such
     a character to obscure it.[13]

Allen then devotes the remainder of his text to elaborating on just how this
obscuring happens, and its ramifications. He argues that as missionaries depend
upon "means," rather than on the Spirit, their converts, too, learn to depend upon
these activities and are left ignorant of how to rely on the Spirit.[14] The result is both
a weakening of the church and a failure to develop indigenous leadership. He writes:

The activities of the foreigners and of their trained agents oppress
them spiritually whilst they assist them. They learn to rely upon
the activities of the foreigners or of the committees, at the best
to follow and support them when they lead, at the worst to wait
for them to act. They cannot act naturally, freely, in the Spirit.[15]

---

12   Ibid., 91–92.
13   Ibid., 92.
14   Ibid., 99.
15   Ibid., 101.

In contrast to this weakened church that is held captive by missionary activity, Allen advocates instead for an indigenous church. He writes, "If then we want to see a manifestation of the Spirit in a form which can be understood, it must be in the unfettered activity of Christians under their own natural conditions."[16] He then adds:

> I believe that this is the key to the problem which we have before ourselves. The spiritual force, the Holy Ghost, will be manifested to the people of any country to which we go when they see that Spirit ministered by us manifested in the spontaneous activity of their own countrymen.[17]

If local Christians are allowed to experience the leading and the power of the Spirit in their own way, unhampered by missionary activity and Western forms, then the potential arises for Christianity to be unleashed as "a spiritual force" rather than as a flurry of activity. Allen asserts:

> It is here that we see the importance of the establishment of little native churches which are obviously and unmistakably not under our control, but fully equipped with their own ministers and possessing full spiritual authority to direct their own life. We should spend our strength in establishing as many of these as possible. The establishment of such churches would at once strike at the root of the difficulty which is presented to us. The people would see in those churches Christians possessed by the Spirit and showing forth the Spirit being in some way different from other people who had not received the Spirit and acting in some way differently from other people.[18]

As these indigenous churches grow, Allen asserts, the mission activities' role would lessen in comparison, and the life of the local churches would become the primary expression of Christianity in the culture.[19]

As one reads Allen's description of the indigenous church and considers the Chinese context of his initial question, one must note the historical circumstances

---

16   Ibid., 111.
17   Ibid., 111–12.
18   Ibid., 112.
19   Ibid.

which brought about the exact situation for which he called. As Western missionaries were forcibly expelled from China for most of the twentieth century, their grasp on their converts was released, and Chinese Christians were forced to depend upon the Holy Spirit, rather than on the missionaries, for guidance. As a result, looking at the state of Christianity in China nearly ninety years after this Shanghai conference, one sees what is perhaps the largest truly indigenous church in the world, one which is remarkably characterized by the centrality of the Spirit, rather than by a flurry of "activity." The reality that attests to the effects of the removal of the Western missionaries and their activities in China serves as a prime "case study" for the effects of allowing the Spirit to move unencumbered in the creation of a thriving, Spirit-led, indigenous church.[20]

Missionary Principles

Allen's second work to be examined, *Missionary Principles,* is also written in response to a dilemma: "the failure of the command to preach the Gospel to all nations."[21] Regarding this dilemma, Allen writes:

> We are sometimes surprised that men who call themselves the servants of Christ appear to be wholly unmoved by the command of Christ to preach the gospel to all nations. The command is clear; it is repeated again and again. Christians do not question its authority; they do not doubt that Christ gave it; they do not doubt His right to give it; they simply disobey it. The command does not come home to them. It does not appear to have any binding force.[22]

Why is this the case? Allen asserts, "When we so think or speak we are treating the command of Christ as if it were a law of the same order as the laws of Judaism or of any other legal system." The gospel, however, is different from this kind of law. He writes, "The commands of the Law are external, the commands of the Gospel are internal. The commands of the Law are given from without, the commands of

---

20   As a similar example, one could also cite the rise of African indigenous (or independent) churches during roughly the same time period.
21   Allen, *Missionary Principles*, 7.
22   Ibid., 15.

the Gospel are implanted."[23] Allen affirms the Old Testament promise that God will write his law "on their hearts" (Jer 31:33), as fulfilled in the New Testament. These laws are written on Christians' hearts through the Spirit, who indwells them. Allen writes, "Christ first gives the Spirit and then the command. He first comes to us, and then commands us to go." While this may at first seem to be a minute distinction of chronology, Allen hails this point as "the essential characteristic of the Gospel" and the "very existence and character of our religion."[24] He writes as follows:

> It is by this that Christianity is separated from all other religions. It stands apart, in a class by itself, distinct from all others, not merely in the fullness of its truth and the height of its moral teaching, but in its essential character. Christ did not merely impart a doctrine more true, more exalted than Moses, or Confucius, or the Buddha or any others who had preceded Him. He did not merely introduce a new understanding of the Nature of God and of the manner of approach to Him. He imparted His own Spirit, He implanted His own Divine Life in the souls of His people. The others gave commands; they taught with more or less truth what men ought to be and do, and their systems may be compared one with another because they are in the same order. But it is impossible to compare a system of directions with a Spirit. It is impossible to put into the same class commands and motives. They gave commands: Christ gives motive power. They told men what they ought to do: Christ imparts the Spirit from which the command emanates.[25]

As Christ imparts his Spirit, which Allen characterizes as a "missionary Spirit," He also imparts this Spirit's love for lost people. Allen writes:

> The Spirit of Christ is the Spirit of Divine Love and compassion and desire for souls astray from God. The command appeals to that Spirit. But to turn from the Spirit and to appeal to the command, is to transpose the whole order and meaning of the Gospel. It is to

---

23   Ibid., 16.
24   Ibid., 26.
25   Ibid., 26–27.

appeal to the dead for life, to expect from an external command the virtue of an internal motive.[26]

He then adds, "The Spirit which Christ imparts is the Spirit of which this command is the proper expression. He is the Spirit of the command. The command is a missionary command, the Spirit is a missionary Spirit."[27] "Missionary zeal," Allen asserts, "depends upon the knowledge of the Holy Spirit."[28] It also depends, however, on an awareness of the missionary need, "of the existence and the need of souls astray from God."[29] A lack of missionary zeal, therefore, is caused by either ignorance, for which the solution is the provision of information, or "a restraint of the Spirit of Christ," a problem whose solution is "spiritual renewal."[30] He writes:

> Missionary zeal is grounded in the nature and character of the Holy Ghost. It begins with an act of reception. When men open their hearts to Christ and He enters to dwell there, then enters the spirit of missionary zeal. Missionary zeal is a form of charity; and charity is not a gift of the Spirit which one may have, another not have. It begins with an act of reception, and it is to be sustained not by renewed applications of external stimuli, whether in the form of orders, commands, or exciting stories and appeals, but by repeated acts of reception, repeated acts of surrender.[31]

Allen's thesis, therefore, is that missionary zeal comes with surrender to God, as it is intrinsic to God's character and to the Spirit living inside Christians. He writes:

> The Spirit which impels to missionary labour is the Spirit of Christ. All missionary desire and effort proceed from the presence of Christ in the souls of His people. He is the only source. He is also the end. From Him proceeds the impulse; in Him it finds its fulfillment; to Him it moves.[32]

---

26   Ibid., 31–32.
27   Ibid., 36.
28   Ibid., 44.
29   Ibid., 44–45.
30   Ibid., 45.
31   Ibid., 55–56.
32   Ibid., 67.

Allen then discusses the means by which mission is carried out. This discussion, though practical, is also grounded in the impulse of the Spirit. He asserts:

> The end is spiritual, the means also must be spiritual. The impulse is of Christ, the end is Christ, the means are in Christ. Christ is the source, the end, the worker. If it is true that we cannot even think of missionary work except as the Divine Missionary inspires us, it is also true that we cannot effect anything except as Christ uses us as agents for working out His purpose. All that we can do is to bring to Christ surrendered wills and hearts and minds to co-operate with Him. He is the only source of spiritual power. Missionary life begins with an act of reception; missionary zeal grows upon knowledge of the Spirit so received; missionary work is the expression of that Spirit in activity. Such expression is necessary for us.[33]

As missionaries work in fulfillment of the command, they are dependent upon the Spirit not only for zeal, but also for power. The Spirit of Christ is central not only for inspiration, but also for efficacy. Allen highlights the significance of this recognition, writing, "It makes a great difference whether we constantly realize that it is the Spirit which is the effective force."[34] In regards to the Spirit's role in the missionary's requests for material provision, he states:

> It makes a great difference in our appeals to others. If we habitually realize that it is the Spirit which is the effective force, it is the Spirit for which we appeal. If what we want is Spirit, it is Spirit for which we shall ask. If we habitually think that material offerings are of no value whatever for our work, except as expressions of Spirit, we cannot possibly appeal for them as if they were of some value in themselves, apart from the Spirit which offers them. If our appeals are expressed in material terms, it is because we think materially.[35]

---

33 Ibid., 103–4.
34 Ibid., 107.
35 Ibid., 110.

Allen's assertion, which comes daringly close to gnostic dualism, essentially insists upon a dependence on the Spirit for everything, including the missionary's material needs. In the sentences following this assertion, Allen criticizes missionary fundraising attempts that adopt the methods of "purely secular work, like company promoters" or "like tramps" who appeal to various other motives in potential donors, irrespective of the ethics of these motivations, as long as they produce the required funds.[36] In contrast, missionaries are to trust the Spirit for their material needs. His core point, which alleviates any fear of Gnosticism, reads as such:

> Only by spiritual means can spiritual results be effected. But the Spirit works through the material. Even so it was the Lord of Glory manifested Himself. He took a material body and so fulfilled it with His Spirit that it became to all ages and to all the world the manifestation of the Godhead which no man hath seen nor can see. So it was that He instituted a religion of sacraments. There is in Christ no ignoring of the outward material form. The whole world is sacramental and Christ is sacramental and the religion of Christ is sacramental.

> Because Christ is sacramental missions are sacramental. We act as Christ acted. His Spirit works in us and manifests Himself in us as He manifested Himself in His own Body.

> This is the power which God has given us, the power of making material things into the vehicles of spiritual force. We see this every day.[37]

Allen's final assertion regarding missionary means, one which is the natural extension of the sacramentalism discussed above, is that we, being made up of body and soul, and possessing a mixture of material and spiritual possessions, are to offer ourselves and our belongings to God. He writes:

> So it was with our Lord, so it is with us. As His spiritual offering was the offering of a Body, so our spiritual offering is the offering of ourselves, all that we are and all that we have, body and soul,

---

36   Ibid., 110–11.
37   Ibid., 120–21.

affections and possessions. So clothed, the Spirit of Christ can work out through us that for which the Spirit is given to us, the Revelation of Christ to the world.[38]

Thus, the fully surrendered Christian offers himself or herself fully to the God who indwells with a missionary Spirit, imparting compassion for the lost and missionary zeal, both of which are used to spread the message of Christ as the Spirit works through material means.

Summary and Application

Allen's missionary experiences at the turn of the century involved frustration with overly materially focused missionary activities which neglected the spiritual, an omission which resulted in a lack of spiritual power and freedom in the people whom the missionaries sought to reach. He wrote to provide a corrective to this focus and to help give rise to indigenous, Spirit-empowered churches. Allen wrote of the impoverishing effects of Westerners' lack of understanding of the Spirit's centrality and sought to bring correction.

Allen's writing seeks the release of the Spirit to witness through Christians, something which occurs through their offering themselves as sacrifices for the Spirit's use. Allen asserts that at conversion the Spirit comes to indwell Christians, and that the Spirit is indeed a missionary Spirit. As such, the Spirit would impart both missionary zeal and compassion in Christians, but ignorance of people's need for Christ or the suppression of the Spirit's reign can impede this missionary zeal (as can distraction with overly consuming "missionary activities"). Allen thus urges Christians to fully surrender themselves to Christ, trusting him to provide for material and spiritual needs, as the Spirit is released through them to spread the news of Christ to the world.

In critique of Allen's view, one must certainly hail his grasp of the centrality of Christianity's uniqueness in its provision of God's Spirit indwelling believers, yet his discussion of this contrast with law makes one wonder about the role of obedience in the Christian life. Allen seems to write of disobedience in terms of suppression of the Spirit, but does Scripture not call for Christians to be obedient to external

---

38   Ibid., 134.

commands as well? While Allen's main point is indeed central, the nuancing of Christian obedience, even from the point of spiritual indwelling, needs to be clarified.

In essence, though, those who seek to engage contemporary Western and non-Western cultures with the gospel can learn a great deal from Allen regarding the centrality of the Holy Spirit in mission. Allen aptly describes the lack of spiritual understanding in the West and writes of some of the consequences of the resultant failure to trust the Spirit. In this writer's opinion, much of the "disconnect" which Allen noticed between Western missionaries who were consumed with activities and the turn-of-the-century Chinese people, who were looking for a "spiritual force," came as a result of the Western missionaries' Enlightenment-influenced worldview. Both Paul Hiebert and Lesslie Newbigin have written influential works in this regard.[39] As the Enlightenment brought a "closed universe" understanding of reality into Western culture, its influence tended to blind Western Christians to many of the more spiritual and less material aspects of their faith. This lack of emphasis on the work of the Holy Spirit carried over into their missionary work, which, to non-Westerners, appeared more as "a movement of activities" than a "spiritual force."[40] This author's hope for Western missionaries, and for the Western church in general, is that as Westerners (1) come into more contact with non-Westerners through the rise of globalization, and (2) begin to see the Enlightenment's "closed universe" understanding of reality being challenged through the rise of postmodernism, both those within the church and outside of the church will begin to see again some of the more spiritual, less material aspects of reality which are reflected in a biblical worldview.[41] One can hope that as the Enlightenment's understanding of reality is challenged, Western Christians will be more easily able to grasp the Holy Spirit as the spiritual force which Allen described, and will, from a posture of greater understanding and trust, allow their missionary efforts to be both inspired and empowered by "the Spirit of Christ within who enables the believer to obey."[42]

This shift, if embraced, can (1) help Western believers to become more faithful and empowered in their missionary call, as they rely on the Spirit instead of merely

---

39   Paul G. Hiebert, "The Flaw of the Excluded Middle," *Missiology* 10, no. 1 (January 1982): 35–47; and Lesslie Newbigin, *Foolishness to the Greeks: The Gospel and Western Culture* (Grand Rapids: Eerdmans, 1986).

40   Allen, "Mission Activities," 89.

41   This author is not asserting that a fully postmodern understanding of reality can be equated with a biblical one, but only that the postmodern critique of the Enlightenment's understanding is both accurate and helpful in this regard.

42   Branner, "Roland Allen," 181.

immersing themselves in activities which "obscure the Spirit"; and (2) help Western missionaries to connect with non-Westerners in a spiritual rather than primarily material fashion, bringing them a Christianity which exists not as a movement of activities but as a spiritual force grounded in the love of God.[43] As this happens, and as Western missionaries learn to trust the Holy Spirit's working in their converts, one can anticipate the rise of a variety of truly indigenous churches, both in Western and in non-Western settings in North America and abroad. In addition, one can also anticipate the rise of a more creative and empowered missionary force which is deeply obedient to the missionary call.

Works Cited

Allen, Roland. "Mission Activities Considered in Relation to the Manifestation of the Spirit." In *The Ministry of the Spirit: Selected Writings of Roland Allen,* edited by David M. Paton, 86–113. London: World Dominion, 1960.

———. *Missionary Methods: St. Paul's or Ours?,* American ed. Grand Rapids: Eerdmans, 1962. First published 1912.

———. *Missionary Principles.* Grand Rapids: Eerdmans, 1964.

———. *The Spontaneous Expansion of the Church.* Grand Rapids: Eerdmans, 1962.

Branner, John E. "Roland Allen: Pioneer in a Spirit-centered Theology of Mission." *Missiology* 5, no. 2 (April 1977): 175–84.

Hiebert, Paul G. "The Flaw of the Excluded Middle." *Missiology* 10, no. 1 (January 1982): 35–47.

Kasdorf, Hans. "Review of *The Compulsion of the Spirit: A Roland Allen Reader,* edited by David Paton and Charles H. Long." *Missiology* 12, no. 3 (July 1984): 370–71.

Newbigin, Lesslie. *Foolishness to the Greeks: The Gospel and Western Culture.* Grand Rapids: Eerdmans, 1986.

———. Foreword to *Missionary Methods: St. Paul's or Ours?,* by Roland Allen, i–iii. American ed. Grand Rapids: Eerdmans, 1962. First published 1912.

Paton, David M. *The Ministry of the Spirit: Selected Writings of Roland Allen.* London: World Dominion, 1960.

———, ed. *Reform of the Ministry: A Study in the Work of Roland Allen.* London: Lutterworth, 1968.

———, and Charles H. Long, eds. *The Compulsion of the Spirit: A Roland Allen Reader.* Grand Rapids: Eerdmans, 1983.

---

43   Allen, "Mission Activities," 89–92.

3

Reassessing John Stott's, David Hesselgrave's, and Andreas Köstenberger's Views of the Incarnational Model

JOHN CHEONG

Introduction

The idea that the divine meaning of the cosmos was embodied in the life of Jesus . . . has played a remarkably central part in the history of Christian belief, so much so that Christianity can be characterized as the religion of the incarnation [which] powerfully expresses . . . the way God acts savingly, with deep implications for the way Christians are to follow in mission.[1]

According to Ott, the Incarnation as a model for mission has been argued as a basis for missionary identification, holistic ministry, liberation, contextualization, inculturation of the church, and manifesting the life of Christ. Ott summarizes the views as follows[2]:

---

1   Ross Langmead, *The Word Made Flesh: Towards an Incarnational Missiology* (Lanham, MD: University Press of America, 2004), 29.
2   Craig Ott and Stephen J. Strauss, *Encountering Theology of Mission: Biblical Foundations, Historical Developments, and Contemporary Issues*, with Timothy C. Tennent (Grand Rapids: Baker Academic, 2010), 117–23.

1. As cultural identification, missionaries should fully adopt the culture of the intended people just as Jesus identified with humanity (i.e., 1 Cor 9:19–23; Phil 2:5–8; Heb 4:15; 12:14,15).

2. As holistic ministry, it is living out the gospel in word and deed. Liberation theologians especially identified it "not merely with humanity in general, but particularly with the poor, oppressed and marginalized of society."[3]

3. As contextualization or inculturation, it is the ground for contextualizing the gospel and the church.

4. As mediating the life of Christ, it is being like him to the people one serves (i.e., Gal 2:20a; 1 Cor 11:1; 2 Cor 4:10).

Langmead observes that the term "incarnational" as used in mission has been imprecise though evangelical missiologists' embracing of it as a model for mission can be traced to John 1:4; 17:18; 20:21; Gal 2:19,20; Eph 5:1,2; Phil 2:1–11,21; 1 Pet 2:21.[4] Its acceptance as a missionary model and method, especially (1) and (2), is seen in Stott who understands John 17:18 and 20:21 as key. There, "Jesus . . . made his mission the *model* of ours, saying '*as* the Father sent me, *so* I send you.'"[5]

Also, this model covers "everything the church is sent into the world to do," as "all authentic mission is incarnational mission."[6] Stott adds, "As our Lord took on our flesh, so he calls his Church to take on the . . . world."[7] *Inter alia,* when Stott discusses the Incarnation as the model of mission, it is the aspect of cultural identification with the people, not that the church is to pattern every aspect of its work after that of Jesus.[8] For example, the church would be

---

3   Orlando Costas, *Christ Outside the Gate: Mission Beyond Christendom* (Eugene, OR: Wipf & Stock, 1982).

4   Langmead, *The Word Made Flesh*, 3. For missiological views, see Sherwood G. Lingenfelter and Marvin K. Mayers, *Ministering Cross-culturally: An Incarnational Model for Personal Relationships* (Grand Rapids: Baker, 1986), 26; Ken McElhanon, "Don't Give Up on the Incarnational Model," *Evangelical Missions Quarterly* 27, no. 4 (October 1991): 390–93; S. Mondithoka, "Incarnation," in *Dictionary of Mission Theology: Evangelical Foundations,* ed. John Corrie (Downers Grove, IL: InterVarsity Press, 2000), 177–81; and Alan Neeley, "Incarnational Mission," in *Evangelical Dictionary of World Missions,* ed. A. Scott Moreau, Charles van Engen, and Harold Netland (Grand Rapids: Baker, 2000), 474.

5   John R. W. Stott, *Christian Mission in the Modern World* (Downers Grover, IL: InterVarsity Press, 1975), 23.

6   Ibid., 30; and John R. W. Stott, *The Contemporary Christian: Applying God's Word to Today's World* (Downers Grover, IL: InterVarsity Press, 1992), 342.

7   Stott, *Christian Mission,* 25.

8   Stott, *The Contemporary Christian,* 357–58.

under the authority of Christ (we are sent, we did not volunteer); renouncing privilege, safety, comfort and aloofness, as we *actually enter into other people's worlds*, as he entered ours; humbling ourselves to become servants, as he did; bearing the pain of being hated by the hostile world into which we are sent (John 17:14); and sharing the good news with people where they are.[9]

However, Hesselgrave cautions against Stott's incarnationalism as the model for mission because it wrongly focuses "on continuity between Christ's incarnate earthly ministry and the contemporary ministry of the church today."[10] To buttress his point, Hesselgrave employs key arguments from Köstenberger's *The Missions of Jesus and the Disciples according to the Fourth Gospel*. Because of this, I shall mainly examine the latter and only refer to Hesselgrave where needed. Though there are other aspects of the incarnational model beyond John 20:21, I mostly evaluate Köstenberger's and Stott's understanding of it vis-à-vis John's mission theology,[11] as their views of it have greatly influenced evangelicals. This chapter assesses the viability of the model while interacting with some New Testament exegetes who have engaged it in John's Gospel.

Missional Themes in John's Gospel

In this section, three missional themes in John's Gospel will be studied to examine his understanding of the incarnation and its relationship to mission: the theme of "sending," the use of the adverb "just as" in John, and the work of the Holy Spirit.

---

9   Ibid., 265 (italics mine).

10   David Hesselgrave, *Paradigms in Conflict: 10 Key Questions in Christian Missions Today* (Grand Rapids: Kregel, 2005), 144–45.

11   Theologians have also debated whether the Incarnation is a valid model for mission. Those who accept it include David J. Bosch, "Reflections on Biblical Models of Mission," in *Towards the 21st Century in Christian Mission: Essays in Honor of Gerald H. Anderson*, ed. James M. Philips and Robert T. Coote (Grand Rapids: Eerdmans, 1993, 188–90); Costas, *Christ Outside the Gate*, 6–17; Donald Senior and Carroll Stuhlmueller, *The Biblical Foundations for Mission* (Maryknoll, NY: Orbis Books, 1983), 290–91, 331; Stott, *Christian Mission*; and with reservations, Eckhard J. Schnabel, *Jesus and the Twelve*, vol. 1 of *Early Christian Mission* (Downers Grove, IL: InterVarsity Press, 2004), 1574–75; and Eckhard J. Schnabel, "As the Father Has Sent Me, So I Send You (John 20:21): The Mission of Jesus and the Mission of the Church," *Missionalia* 33, no. 2 (2005): 282. The objectors include D. A. Carson, *The Gospel according to John*, Pillar New Testament Commentary (Grand Rapids: Eerdmans, 1991), 566; and Andreas J. Köstenberger, *The Missions of Jesus and the Disciples according to the Fourth Gospel* (Grand Rapids: Eerdmans, 1998), 212–17.

Greater attention will be paid to the first two while the last will be briefly treated due to space limitations.

Sending

Mission is at the heart of the fourth Gospel, and an understanding of it is linked to knowing what Jesus' mission is in John.[12] In John's Gospel, Jesus' identity and mission is expressed in terms of being sent, beginning from 1:1–18 through the end.[13] Some forty-four verses refer to God as "one who sends" and of Christ as "one who is sent."[14] The goal of Jesus' mission is clearly stated in 3:17 (cf. 6:38,39; 12:49,50) and is "decisive for understanding how Jesus 'is sent,' [and] determining *the* mission on which the community's mission is grounded and modeled."[15] Mission thus is "frequently used to express Jesus' identity as 'the one whom the Father (or God) sent' and, correlatively, to express the Father's identity as 'the one who sent me.'"[16] McPolin notes four types of "sending" in John's Gospel[17]:

> John the Baptist is "sent" by God to testify about Jesus (1:6–8; 3:28). Jesus himself is sent by the Father to testify about the Father and to do his work. The Paraclete is sent forth by both Father and Son to give testimony about Jesus. And finally, the disciples are sent by Jesus to do as he did.[18]

---

12   Köstenberger, *Jesus and the Disciples,* 45, 207. Exegetes debate whether John's Gospel was written for mission or to encourage the community, centering on the ambiguity of the Greek text of 20:21; for example, L. Legrand, "A Johannine Mission Model," *Indian Theological Studies* 43, nos. 3–4 (2006): 253–65; and Köstenberger, *Jesus and the Disciples,* 3. For this article, it assumes that John's Gospel purpose is missional.

13   Francis DuBose, *The God Who Sends: A Fresh Quest for Biblical Mission* (Nashville: Broadman, 1983), 49; and Michael Waldstein, "The Mission of Jesus and the Disciples in John," *Communio: International Catholic Review* 17, no. 3 (1990): 311. Jesus constantly refers to himself as the one whom God has sent in 5:38; 6:29; 10:36; 17:3, while those referring to God as the sender are 4:34; 5:23,24,37; 6:38,39,44,57; 7:16,18,28–29; 8:16,18,26,29; 9:4; 11:42; 12:49; 13:20; 14:24; 15:21; 16:5; 17:8,21,23,25 [Albert Curry Winn, *A Sense of Mission: Guidance from the Gospel of John* (Philadelphia: Westminster, 1981), 22]. Thus, the "sense of having been sent into the world by God lies at the very core of Jesus' self-understanding" (Winn, *A Sense of Mission,* 22). The word "send" registers forty-one times in John (translated from *pempo* and *apostello*) [José Comblin, *Sent from the Father: Meditations on the Fourth Gospel* (Maryknoll, NY: Orbis Books, 1979), vii]. Thus, the center of John's Christology can be seen in the verb "send" vis-à-vis the Son's relationship to the Father (Winn, *A Sense of Mission,* 29).

14   DuBose, *The God Who Sends,* 49.

15   Senior and Stuhlmueller, *Biblical Foundations,* 290, 295.

16   Waldstein, "The Mission of Jesus," 311.

17   Cited by Senior and Stuhlmueller, *Biblical Foundations,* 292.

18   See also Calvin Mercer, "Jesus the Apostle: 'Sending' and the Theology of John," *Journal of the Evangelical Theological Society* 35, no. 4 (1992): 457; and Senior and Stuhlmueller, *Biblical Foundations,* 292.

Each "sending" builds on the previous work of the other so that we can say that these "missions are interrelated."[19] Sending has "a legal presumption that an agent will carry out his mission."[20] Schnabel elaborates:

> The sending of the disciples as Jesus' envoys and representatives confers authority on the disciples and on their message [and] since the sending by the Father still continues (note the perfect *apestalken* in 20:21), the disciples are given a share as participants in the mission of Jesus.[21]

Jesus is not only sent but also sends in 17:18 and 20:21. Through Jesus (the sent one), the world will encounter the Father (the sender). Jesus thus repeatedly spoke of his mission to speak the words the Father sent him to speak (5:23,24; 7:16; 8:26; 12:49; 14:24). At its heart, this is evangelism [i.e., when Jesus prayed for the disciples that they not be taken out of this world but sent into it (17:15,18)].[22]

> In all these cases, the Father remains as the source of mission . . . Thus mission cannot be a continuing process; rather it is a participation in God's mission. The Johannine Jesus reveals as both the expression of God's mission and the *prototype* for the disciples' mission.[23]

Jesus' sending highlights four aspects of his mission: (1) to bring glory to the Father (7:18; 8:50,54; 11:4,40); (2) to do the works of the Father (4:34; 5:19,36); (3) to speak the words of the Father (7:16; 12:48–50; 14:24); and (4) to represent the Father (12:44–45; 13:20; 14:9).[24] Structural *similarities* exist between Jesus' mission and the disciples: (1) Their sending by Jesus corresponds to Jesus' sending by the

---

19   Senior and Stuhlmueller, *Biblical Foundations,* 292. Conceptually *shaliah* has structural similarities between the rabbinic *shaliah* and the early Christian *apostolos* (Schnabel, *Jesus and the Twelve,* 271); i.e., of an envoy with *delegated* authority and power to represent the sender in a mission. Köstenberger notes that in keeping with this motif, "the disciples are designated as Jesus' successors, taking their place in a long string of predecessors that ranges from the OT prophets to John the Baptist and climaxes in Jesus" [Andreas J. Köstenberger, *John,* Baker Exegetical Commentary (Grand Rapids: Baker, 2006), 433].

20   Andreas J. Köstenberger and Scott R. Swain, *Father, Son and Spirit: The Trinity and John's Gospel* (Downers Grove, IL: InterVarsity Press, 2008), 90.

21   Schnabel, "As the Father," 283.

22   Winn, *A Sense of Mission,* 87.

23   S. Johnson Samuel, "The Johannine Perspective on Mission in Christ's Praxis," *Bangalore Theological Forum* 20, no. 3 (1988): 10 (italics mine).

24   Schnabel, *Jesus and the Twelve,* 213.

Father; consequently, the disciples should know Jesus as intimately as Jesus knows the Father (15:15; 17:7,8,25). (2) They should be completely dependent upon Jesus, as the Son was dependent upon the Father (4:13,14; 15:7,8,16). (3) They shall bring glory to Jesus and do his will as Jesus did the Father's will (4:3; 5:30,38). (4) They shall be obedient to Jesus and keep his word (14:21,23,24; 15:14,20; 17:6). (5) They shall make Jesus known and testify of him as Jesus did the same for the Father (12:44,45; 13:20).[25]

In reference to 17:18, Morris notes that "the emphatic *eme* and *kago* stress" that Jesus' mission "forms the pattern for the mission of the apostles" in 17:18.[26] At the same time, structural *dissimilarities* also exist between Jesus' mission versus the disciples' mission where Jesus understood that his doing the Father's will (4:34; 5:30; 6:38–40) defined his identity and mission; here sending is linked to Jesus' identity and mission.[27] At the same time, 17:18 and 20:21 link his relationship to the Father and his mission to that of his followers.[28]

Köstenberger, however, believes that the concept of "sending" and its similarities speak not of "the ways in which Jesus came into the world (i.e., the Incarnation), but *the nature of Jesus' relationship with his sender* (i.e. one of obedience and utter dependence), [that] is presented in the Fourth Gospel as the model for the disciples' mission."[29] He arrives at this through a semantic field analysis of the "sending" passages and finds *two* categories used in John: obedience/fulfillment or representation/witness.[30] However, a closer examination of the "sending" passages show that it can be understood in *three* ways when interpreted within their pericope: obedience/dependence, representation/witness, or a middle category that combines the two aspects.

---

25   Schnabel, "As the Father," 272.
26   Leon Morris, *The Gospel according to John,* New International Commentary of the New Testament (Grand Rapids: Eerdmans, 1990), 647.
27   Schnabel, "As the Father," 275–79.
28   DuBose, *The God Who Sends,* 50.
29   Köstenberger, *Jesus and the Disciples,* 217.
30   Ibid., 2–3, 17. Köstenberger believes this approach overcomes the limits of the "word study" method. Though he does an exhaustive semantic field analysis, he ignores the larger corpus of John's mission theology in 1–3 John and Revelation. Also, his analysis relies on Saussurean semiotics (Köstenberger, *Jesus and the Disciples,* 26), which is problematic when he associates "representation" as direct imitation. For the epistemological limits in understanding the nature of words or signs, see Paul G. Hiebert, *Missiological Implications of Epistemological Shifts* (Harrisburg, PA: Trinity Press International, 1999) 36–60, 68–94. Space limits further discussions, but see Langmead, *The Word Made Flesh,* 36–39, as to how the Incarnation should be understood, not in Saussurean but Piercian semiotics of metaphors.

Obedience/dependence aspect only	Obedience/dependence and representation/ witness	Representation[31]/witness aspect only
4:34–38; 6:38,39,44; 7:33; 8:42; 10:36(?); 12:49,50; 16:5.	7:16–18; 8:26,28,29; 11:42–45; 14:24; 17:3,4.	1:6–8; 3:17,34; 5:23,36–39; 6:29,40; 7:28,29; 8:16–18; 9:3,4; 10:36(?); 12:44,45; 13:16,20; 14:26; 15:21,26; 17:18,21,23,25; 20:21.

TABLE 1: CATEGORICAL MEANINGS OF "SENDING" IN JOHN'S GOSPEL

Assessment: From Table 1, one concludes that the representation/witness aspect is more prevalent than obedience/dependence. In some cases, the two categories overlap. Thus, if the disciples' mission is compared to Jesus,' representation/witness must be included and not limited to obedience/dependence. The fact that "sending" in John may combine the two meanings in some cases means that *Jesus not only obeys the Father but also represents him.* Even Köstenberger concedes this point.[32]

Why is representation/witness important to the disciples' mission and not merely obedience/dependence? For John, the key is God's love linked to the sending of Jesus (3:16,17) and the disciples (17:23–26).[33] This love should lead others to share God's eternal life through faith in Christ. The disciples' mission in John's Gospel is structurally conceived to parallel Jesus' mission. As Jesus was sent into the cosmos, the disciples are likewise (4:38; 17:18; 20:21).[34] From this, one concludes that the disciples' sending in mission is linked to representing/witnessing Jesus.

Representation/witness also relates to *identification.* Here John highlights Jesus' incarnation in his ability to identify with individuals in intimate conversations. This stands in contrast to Hesselgrave's proposal of Paul as the better paradigm for "representational mission."[35] There, it is only most applicable towards Paul's public, proclamatory ministry but not personal one-on-one encounters, which

---

31   Hesselgrave, *Paradigms in Conflict,* 152, uses "representation" vis-à-vis Paul as the model missionary, not Jesus. Here I show that it includes Jesus as well, in a complementary not oppositional sense to incarnationalism.

32   Köstenberger, *Jesus and the Disciples,* 120.

33   DuBose, *The God Who Sends,* 135.

34   Samuel, "The Johannine Perspective," 12; R. Kysar, "As You Sent Me: Identity and Mission in the Fourth Gospel," *Word and World* 21, no. 4 (2001): 373; and Senior and Stuhlmueller, *Biblical Foundations,* 289.

35   Hesselgrave, *Paradigms in Conflict,* 150–59.

is more clearly modeled by Jesus. John's Gospel shows the most occurrences of Jesus having intimate conversation with individuals. In the Synoptics, individual encounters are rare, as Jesus usually addressed crowds or the disciples collectively, but in John they are "more frequent and more developed (3:1–21; 4:7–26; 9:2–39; 11:17–40; 12:23–36)."[36] Paul, "except for the lone exception of Philemon, addresses his letters to communities [or] crowds."[37]

John 4 is a prime example, if not *model* for evangelism where the "sending" of Jesus to meet the Samaritan woman is implicit in the *dei* in 4:1. Even if one shies from using the word "model" to describe Jesus' "strategies" in communicating with the woman, it is implicitly an evangelistic model, if not method.[38] Here is a clear exception to the limits of Köstenberger's semantic field analysis. Such encounters clearly demonstrate one of the aspects of the incarnational model that missiologists refer to as a prime example narrative-wise; John 4 not only illustrates the theme of obedience/fulfillment but also the identificational nature that representation/ witness are models for us to emulate.[39]

While almost all references to "sending" in John relate to Jesus' mission, key verses that apply to the disciples' mission in 17:18 and 20:21 are the most important and "forms an important bridge between the missions of Jesus and of the disciples."[40] John's sending theology culminates here, allowing us to draw conclusions on the correspondences between Jesus' mission and the disciples.'

For example, Köstenberger notes John's sending theology indicates "no separate class of 'missionaries' [as] all believers are sent."[41] In addition, the original disciples also function in John's Gospels as "representatives and models for later generations of believers [so that] what is *primarily* true for Jesus' original followers, extends *derivatively* also to later believers."[42] Also, "Jesus' prayer anticipates the disciples' commissioning in 20:21 (cf. 4:38; 13:20; 15:26,27) [and] Jesus' relationship to the Father as his sender is now presented as the pattern for the disciples' relationship to Jesus as their sender."[43] Carson notes that it is

---

36   Legrand, "Johannine Mission Model," 257–58. Even when Jesus speaks to individuals in the Synoptics (Mark 2:1–12; 5:1–20; 7:24–30; 9:14–29; 10:17–24), "a crowd stands in the background" (Legrand, "Johannine Mission Model," 257).

37   Ibid., 258. Curiously Legrand overlooks 1 and 2 Timothy and Titus, where Paul also had a solo audience in mind.

38   Schnabel, *Jesus and the Twelve,* 242–47.

39   Mondithoka, "Incarnation," 180.

40   Köstenberger, *Jesus and the Disciples,* 84.

41   Ibid., 198.

42   Ibid., 152.

43   Köstenberger, *John,* 496.

probably wrong to think of the disciples simply replacing Jesus now that he is returning to his Father [as the] perfect tense in "As the Father has sent (*apestalken*) me" suggests . . . that Jesus is in an ongoing state of "sentness[.]" Christ's disciples do not take over Jesus' mission; his mission continues and is effective in their ministry (14:12–14).[44]

"Just As"

According to Stott, another argument for the incarnational model is the meaning of "as" (*kathos*) in 17:18, 20:21.[45] Köstenberger contends that *kathos* may be translated "in like manner" or "in the same way as" and its meaning connotes an analogous relationship, not a direct imitation of Jesus.[46] Here, Köstenberger's contention concerning the correspondence between Jesus and the disciples in *kathos* must thus be examined.

William Danker notes four main uses of *kathos* in the New Testament: comparative, extent/degree, causative, and temporality. However, only the comparative and causative are found in John; the former occurs in 1:23; 3:14; 5:23; 6:58; 7:38; 8:28; 10:26; 14:27; 15:9; 17:18; 20:21; and the latter is seen in 17:2.[47]

If exegetes see *kathos* as comparative, then the analogous sense is held, but if it is considered causative, then the modeling aspect is favored.[48] Other uses of *kathos* in John (i.e., extent/degree) would have to be interpreted in the context of his Gospel. Space does not permit fully examining all passages except for 13:14,15; 15:9–13; 17:11–18,20–23; and 20:21.

13:14,15: Here is the clearest example of *kathos* that means "direct imitation." In addition, Jesus links a discipleship marker here: to *go* bear fruit in 15:16 in mission, an act that Jesus had modeled for the disciples to see and do in his name to serve others (15:15,17). This going is a spiritual progression in relationship to God, then to the world (15:18–16:3), where Jesus prays for their mission (17:18) and eventual

---

44   Carson, *The Gospel*, 649.

45   Stott, *Christian Mission*, 23.

46   Köstenberger, *Jesus and the Disciples*, 186; and Köstenberger and Swain, *Father, Son and Spirit*, 174–75. For example, there is neither a perfect one-to-one correspondence between Jesus and the disciples in every citation as well (e.g., in 17:16, the sense that Jesus is not "of the world" cannot similarly be applied to the disciples).

47   Frederick William Danker, ed., *A Greek-English Lexicon of the New Testament and Other Early Christian Literature*, 3rd ed. (Chicago: University of Chicago Press, 2000), 493–94.

48   Morris, *Gospel according to John*, 649; and Raymond E. Brown, *The Gospel according to John*, (Vol. 29A) Anchor Bible (New York: Doubleday, 1970), 269.

commissioning (20:21). Köstenberger notes that if *kathos* is seen as "model" in the sense of an "example" in 13:34, it is tenable, but it is entirely not the same for the rest of John's Gospel, as "Jesus is presented as a model of service to believers *to one another,* not to the unbelieving world."[49] However, it is too limiting to hold that "everyone" in 13:34 excludes the world in John's Gospel. Jesus loved the disciples (13:1–3) so that he could model this love for them to love one another (13:34,35) and that this love, in turn, would be the foundation for their mission to the world.

15:9: Stott comments that this verse

> surely means that the Father's love for him was a model of his love for his people. Similarly, "as the Father sent me, so send I you" seems to make his commission a model of ours ... [so] that authentic Christian mission is incarnational mission. It necessitates entering other people's worlds, as Christ entered ours, and giving ourselves in service.[50]

Köstenberger remarks that 15:9 should be regarded as

> the kind of love Jesus showed the disciples. In 17:18, it is the way Jesus sent his disciples; he set them apart (cf. for his own setting apart, 10:36); he imparted to them the Spirit (cf. for Jesus' impartation with the Spirit, 1:34–36; 3:34); and he sent them out. In 20:21 the point seems to be that the same kinds of parameters guiding the sender-sent relationship between the Father and Jesus now also are to govern the relationship between Jesus and his disciples.[51]

In comparing the two, Köstenberger centers on the ethical implications, while Stott proposes a more concrete example of identification. If 15:9 is read alone in John, it cannot bear the weight of Stott's description as to what *kathos* can mean. But seen in the full context of John's Gospel, it is possible. The near context of 15:1–17 is about obeying Jesus and *remaining in the example of Jesus,* which matches one of the missiological definitions for incarnational ministry.

---

49   Köstenberger, *Jesus and the Disciples,* 215.
50   John R. W. Stott, "An Open Letter to David Hesselgrave," *Trinity World Forum* 16, no. 3 (1991): 1.
51   Köstenberger, *Jesus and the Disciples,* 186.

<u>17:11–18, 20,21</u>: Chapter 17 must be compared to 13:33,34 as there are links between the two. Waldstein writes that "the root of this movement [in mission] lies in the movement of love that characterizes the Father in relation to the Son."[52] The love of the Father to the Son is also the base for the unity of the disciples in mission and is constructed on the model of 13:34,35.[53]

In comparing 13:34,35 and 17:21–23, the disciples' mutual love and unity for one another are foundational for their mission and their re-presentation of Jesus to the world that must be accompanied by an actual going (cf.15:16) in order for fruit to be borne.[54] This is consistent in John with the progress of the disciples, whom Jesus intends to send out into the world by chapters 20–21.

Table 2 reveals the structural parallelism between these passages.[55] For 17:21–23 especially, the *kathos* clause in each block not only holds up for the believers the model of Jesus' unity and the Father, *kathos* has a comparative and causative force here—that heavenly unity is both the model and source of the unity of believers.[56]

13:34,35	17:20,21	17:22,23
that you love one another	*that* all may be one	*that* they may be one
as I have loved you	*as* you, Father, are in me and I in you	*as* we are one, I in them and you in me
that you too may love one another	*that* they too may be in us	*that* they may be completed into one
In this all will *know* that you are my disciples, if you have love for one another.	so that the world may *believe* that you sent me	so that the world may *know* that you sent me and that you loved them as you loved me

TABLE 2: A COMPARISON OF SOME PARALLEL STRUCTURES IN JOHN

52   Waldstein, "The Mission of Jesus," 326.
53   Ibid., 329.
54   Köstenberger, *Jesus and the Disciples*, 189.
55   George R. Beasley-Murray, *John*, World Biblical Commentary (Waco, TX: Word, 1987), 303; and Morris, *Gospel according to John*, 640–41.
56   Brown, *Gospel according to John*, 769.

In 17:21–23, this unity strengthens community and evokes faith in others, "so that the world may believe that you have sent me" (v. 21) and so that "the world will know that you sent me and have loved them even as you have loved me" (v. 23).[57] This unity is achieved through "the imitation of the divine relationship." A natural conclusion of 17:22 is that the church is God's presence in the world—the divine amid the unsaved and the community of believers as the continuing incarnation of the Word (1:4).[58] At the same time, the church is a human instrument of God's agency in the world, witnessing to his presence "thanks to the activity of the Spirit among them."[59] Thus, "the whole relationship of Christ with God is the model by which we understand our relationship to God."[60]

As "in the case of Jesus (cf. 3:16), their love is to be followed by works (14:12), going (15:16), witnessing (15:27), and the proclamation of a message (17:20; 20:23)."[61] John 17 is in continuity with 3:16,17 because in the sending of the disciples into the *world* (17:18), their unity is destined to be fruitful for the *world* "so that the world may know that you sent me" (17:21,23).[62] This unity is based on the loving relationship found between the Father and Son.[63] Köstenberger notes that "together with love (13:34,35; 15:12,13; 17:26), unity constitutes a vital prerequisite for their mission (see 17:23)."[64] In such indwelling, the "believers' complete unity results from being taken into the unity of God, and, once unified, believers will be able to bear witness to the true identity of Jesus as the Sent One of God."[65] The trajectory in John's Gospel leading up to 17:18 means that the association Jesus has with his disciples is not a mere spiritual union but a tangible and visible one linked to mission. It continues, if not in imitation, in many aspects of his life for the

---

57   Kysar, "As You Sent Me," 374.

58   Ibid.

59   Ibid., 376.

60   Ibid., 374.

61   Köstenberger, *Jesus and the Disciples,* 190.

62   Waldstein, "The Mission of Jesus," 325.

63   Kysar, "As You Sent Me," 374. Carson, *The Gospel,* 568, remarks: "This is not simple a 'unit of love.' It is a unity mediated, predicated on adherence to the revelation the Father mediated to the first disciples through his Son, the revelation they accepted (17:6,8) and then passed on ('those who believe in me *through their message,*' 17:20). It is analogous to the oneness Jesus enjoys with his Father . . . Similarly, the believers . . . are to be one in purpose, in love, in action undertaken with and for one another, in joint submission to the revelation received . . . They are 'in' the Father and his Son, so identified with God and dependent upon him for life and fruitfulness, that they themselves become the locus of the Father's life and work *in them* (cf. 14:12; 15:7). All of this is to the end *that the world may believe that you have sent me.*"

64   Köstenberger, *John,* 497.

65   Ibid., 499.

disciples.[66] Though there is a differentiation "between God's incarnation in Jesus and God's indwelling in the Christian—in other words between natural Sonship and general Christian sonship . . . *no sharp differentiation is apparent in [the unity] in [17:21–23]*."[67] (italics mine)

The kind of incarnational identification with Jesus that his sending signifies culminates in v. 23—*that our being in him and his love leads to a missional witness to the world.*[68] Most astounding is the privilege the disciples have in answering Jesus' prayer—by dwelling in unity. However, "the fact that Jesus prays to the Father for this unity indicates that the key to it lies within God's power."[69] In this sense, the disciples participate in the ongoing revelation and redemptive aspect of showing the Son to the world. As we become one, accomplished by the power of the Spirit that indwelt the disciples, the unity of the Father and the Son is revealed. Here, our unity becomes not only an essential identity as a church. It is also a reflection of the unity between the Father and Son in a missional witness of Jesus and the focus of that sending to go into the world in 17:18.[70]

20:21: Brown explains the force of *kathos* here as follows:

> The Father's sending of the Son serves both as the model [the comparative aspect of *kathos*] and the ground [the explanatory aspect of *kathos*] for the Son's sending of the disciples. Their mission is to continue the Son's mission; and this requires that the Son must be present to them during this mission, just as the Father had to be present to the Son during his mission.[71]

Here, Beasley-Murray observes:

---

66   Brown, *Gospel according to John*, 776. He also adds that "some type of vital, organic unity seems to be demanded by the fact that the relationship of Father and Son is held up as the model of unity . . . [in that] the Christians are one with one another and with the Father and the Son because they have received of this life" (776).

67   Ibid., 779.

68   DuBose, *The God Who Sends*, 69; and Köstenberger and Swain, *Father, Son and Spirit*, 151.

69   Brown, *Gospel according to John*, 776.

70   DuBose, *The God Who Sends*, 70. In this sense, "Jesus' union with the Father forms the basis of the believers' union in their mission [thus] the disciples are taken into the love and unity of the persons of the Godhead as responsible agents and representatives of Jesus the sent Son" (Köstenberger and Swain, *Father, Son and Spirit*, 152).

71   Brown, *Gospel according to John*, 1036.

In the person of the Son, in his words and deeds, the Father is himself present, his words declared and his actions performed. The time has now come for the disciples to go forth into the world as the representatives of the Lord.[72]

The phrase "as the Father has sent me" implies a sending in the past that continues to the present. Such is "the force of the Greek perfect tense [such that] the form of the fulfillment of Christ's mission was now to be changed, but the mission itself was still continued and still effective."[73] Thus, "the apostles were commissioned to carry on Christ's work, and not to begin a new one."[74] For Jesus, whose "sense of mission was inseparable from his self-identity," this stamp of his identity marks his missional purpose upon our image in 20:21 after linking the disciples' identity and purpose by his name in 17:11.[75] Thus, as the church sends others out into mission to witness God's love, we also reflect a part of who God is by nature as a sender. The commissioning of 20:21 then leads us to the "declaration of mission and the bestowal of the Spirit." What is presupposed in 20:21 is 14:12–14 as the disciples go forth in their mission and seek the help of their Lord, "in response to their prayers he will do through them 'greater things' . . . in the powerful mission that he continues!"[76]

The explicit correspondence of Jesus' mission and the disciples in 20:21 can be summarized: (1) That Jesus desires to continue his mission and presence *through the giving of his Spirit* to the disciples. (2) That the missional message they proclaim is equal in force to that which Jesus spoke of—the forgiveness of sins from the basis of Jesus' own authority to forgive or retain sins (20:23) and shepherd Christ's flock.[77]

Assessment: The idea of imitation in the *kathos* passages show that both univocal (i.e., one-to-one) and metaphorical senses are present (13:34,35; 17:21–23; 20:21) as well as the comparative and causative force elsewhere (e.g., 17:20,21) and possibly in 20:21.[78] As a concept, the Incarnation can be appropriately used in some sense of

---

72   Beasley-Murray, *John,* 379.
73   Ibid.
74   Brown, *Gospel according to John,* 349–50.
75   DuBose, *The God Who Sends,* 13.
76   Beasley-Murray, *John,* 380.
77   Köstenberger, *Jesus and the Disciples,* 110, 176; and Köstenberger and Swain, *Father, Son and Spirit,* 161.
78   Brown, *Gospel according to John,* 769. By stating that *kathos* has an analogical sense in John, Köstenberger shows a flawed or inconsistent dependence on Saussurean semiotics, as this system means that any word studies must have a univocal meaning, while an analogical sense of a word rests on Piercian semiotics (that there is an inexact correspondence between the sign, the significance, and the signifier).

imitation as a *model,* where some aspects of Jesus' life can be and should be imitated in John's mission theology. It is too limiting to state there is *nothing* that one can imitate of Jesus in reference to the *kathos* passages examined.[79] While 17:18 and 20:21 alone cannot mean nor carry *all* the weight that missiologists may load onto it *if it is always meant in the primary sense of incarnationalism* (i.e., representing or imitating Jesus; e.g., Hesselgrave[80]), the *kathos* passages can carry them in the *secondary or derivative sense.* However, John's mission theology overall indicates that his *full corpus* can bear that weight.

Conclusions

At this point, three questions may be asked to conclude our examination of John's missional theology of the Incarnation and how it informs our assessment of it as a model of mission.

Is There Continuity or Discontinuity in 20:21?

For missiologists, there are always aspects of the Incarnation that are discontinuous to the mission of the disciples and to us as well. There is agreement that "Jesus' unique identity functions as the foundation for his unique mission," that the central mission in John is Jesus' mission and not the disciples, "every other mission is derivative of his: the Baptizer's, the Spirit's and the disciples.'"[81] Missiologists and theologians can also agree that the disciples participate in Christ's revelatory and redemptive work in a mostly secondary sense (but disagree on possibilities of the primary sense).[82]

See also earlier footnote 32.

79   There are other aspects of *kathos* that the disciples should imitate Jesus that a word study does not reveal. For example, they are sent to reap (4:34–38), hold to Jesus' teachings (8:31–32; 12:24–26), wash one another's feet (13:13–15), share in the suffering of the master (13:16; 15:20) (Köstenberger, *Jesus and the Disciples,* 146), bear fruit (15:16, 26,27), and feed his sheep (21:15–19). For 4:38, Köstenberger notes that the disciples' reaping where they did not sow disavows them "any part in making their own mission and maintaining a clear distinction between the eras of Jesus' predecessors, of Jesus, and of the apostolic mission" [Köstenberger, "The Greater Works of the Believer according to John 14:12," *Didaskalia* 6 (Fall 1994): 39)]. With regard to 21:19, Köstenberger observes the following: Peter also dies "the same kind of death Jesus died—though . . . without any atoning significance [so in this manner], he also functions as a representative for subsequent believers, whom Jesus likewise calls to 'shepherd' his people" (Köstenberger, *Jesus and the Disciples,* 159–60). Similarly, John is also described as a representative. In summary, John's Gospel shows us that there are different ways of following or imitating Jesus.

80   Hesselgrave, *Paradigms in Conflict,* 144–45.

81   Köstenberger, *Jesus and the Disciples,* 50, 141.

82   Ibid., 81.

Even if the disciples' mission may be derivative to Jesus' in 20:21, "the mission of Jesus is presented as a model for the mission of the disciples."[83] The disciples are

> Jesus' envoys whom God reveals himself to the world. Sentences such as "whoever sees me sees him who sent me" (12:45), and "no one comes to the Father except through me" (14:6) that were valid for Jesus are now valid for the disciples. The disciples are given the task of making God and his Messiah visible. And they are to show people the way to God the Father and his Son. The content of the disciples' mission is determined by the content of Jesus' mission.[84]

However, the "sending of the disciples is not an end in itself, and it does not serve the promotion of their own image [but] are signposts to the Son and to the Father and thus signposts to salvation and to eternal life."[85]

Is Jesus' Sending from the Father Equivalent to Ours?

The sending aspect of the disciples on mission in 17:18 and 20:21 cannot be reduced to mere obedience (contra Hesselgrave and Köstenberger) nor as *non*-imitation.[86] There is *some* sense of imitation while understanding our human limitations versus Jesus' divinity.[87] For "just as the Son represented the Father, so Jesus' followers are to represent the Son as they are indwelt and enabled by the Spirit."[88] The sending of the Spirit to be with the disciples is key—sending them into the world to carry forth the mission of Jesus. It is an overstatement to say that the "disciples cannot and are not commanded to reproduce Jesus' incarnation or even model their own mission after it."[89] There is usually an analogous comparison and in some cases a call for direct imitation.

---

83   Schnabel, "As the Father," 282.
84   Ibid.
85   Ibid.
86   See Hesselgrave, *Paradigms in Conflict*, 154; and Köstenberger, *Jesus and the Disciples*, 107.
87   Köstenberger, *Jesus and the Disciples*, 115–16.
88   Köstenberger and Swain, *Father, Son and Spirit*, 107.
89   Köstenberger, *Jesus and the Disciples*, 220.

How Do We Define the Incarnational Model?

As a missionary method, the Incarnation has been touted as a prescriptive model. Hesselgrave however critiques incarnationalism as something we cannot do, as we are not Jesus, and by so doing robs the uniqueness of Jesus' identity.[90] However, Hesselgrave finds that an imprecision in its definition has fostered debates whether it can be used in any sense of a model or imitation.[91] Missiologists have also played a part in this by their imprecise theological expositions as to how much of Jesus' ministry actually implies imitation versus that of general obedience. Interestingly, Köstenberger admits there are imprecise definitions of the incarnational model.[92] Theologians have, however, misunderstood the missiological literature regarding the incarnational model.

In missiology there are four senses of the incarnational model: (1) direct imitation of Jesus, (2) insider identification, (3) contextual translation, and (4) principalized obedience/discipleship) into one (i.e., direct imitation).[93] In his writings, Köstenberger only engages with (1) and (4). If we take the above possibilities for incarnational ministry, we see that Köstenberger mostly objects to (1), firmly opposes (2) without any interaction in *The Missions of Jesus and the Disciples according to the Fourth Gospel* and his other writings, entirely misses (3), and valorizes principalized obedience.

To clarify the discussion, Langmead suggests three groups of meaning for incarnational mission: (1) following Jesus as the pattern for mission, (2) participating in Christ's risen presence as the power for mission, and (3) joining God's cosmic mission of enfleshment in which his self-embodying dynamic is evident from the

---

90   Hesselgrave, *Paradigms in Conflict,* 150, 153.

91   Köstenberger, *Jesus and the Disciples,* 13, citing Prescott-Erickson. Generally, "model" may mean "analogy," "imitation," or "principle." For Köstenberger, the word "model" is fraught with danger and may connote an equal comparison between Jesus' unique incarnation and mission that defined his identity and purpose versus ours. Thus, he prefers "analogy." Evangelicals tend to stress a principle model of following Jesus while the Anabaptists stress imitation aspects of discipleship (Langmead, *The Word Made Flesh,* 61–92). Neeley, "Incarnational Mission," 474, observes that evangelicals "tend to accentuate the divinity of Christ so disproportionately that the ultimate result is a kind of Christological docetism in which the human nature of Jesus is virtually eliminated or is little more than a façade for his divinity." Köstenberger's writings on Jesus' mission seem to bear this tendency, where we see little of Jesus' humanity. However, whatever one's theological system, any *true* incarnational model in a mission theology must engage with Jesus' life in his totality—his birth, life, death, and resurrection (Langmead, *The Word Made Flesh,* 18–19). Otherwise the stress is simply on the *with* (identification aspects that includes "solidarity with the poor" in suffering) but not the *for* (advocacy aspect) (ibid., 220).

92   Köstenberger, *Jesus and the Disciples,* 213.

93   Lingenfelter and Mayers, *Ministering Cross-culturally,* 26; McElhanon, "Don't Give Up," 390–93; Mondithoka, "Incarnation," 177–81; and Neeley, "Incarnational Mission," 474.

beginning of creation. Langmead also makes a distinction between "incarnation" as a *process* and as an *event*.[94]

Köstenberger's writings, however, mostly defend the latter but ignore this continued dynamic in mission. In addition, when he objects to insider identification, he generally dismisses it without serious examinations of Jesus' identifications *with people* in John's Gospel through the examples of the latter's intimate encounters with them.[95]

Lastly, there is also an incarnating dynamic in mission where "the life of the Christian witness, in all of its imperfection, is intended to incarnate the present love of God . . . to share with them '*not only* the gospel of God *but also* our own selves . . .' (1 Thess 2:8)."[96] This is modeled in Jesus' relationship to the Father through the ways his enfleshment plays out in his life and witness in carrying out the Father's mission. However, incarnational mission can only be done when it is "enabled and guided by the continuing presence of Christ through the Holy Spirit [so that] Christ is present and 'becomes flesh' wherever his mission is being continued."[97] In this way, it can be "understood as *at the one time* experiencing the transforming presence of Christ *and* following Jesus in embodying it in Christian community and mission." [98]

Which Is the Better Missionary Model—Jesus' or Paul's?

When Hesselgrave critiques Stott, he uses "representation" in reference to Paul as the model missionary, not Jesus.[99] In this article, I show that it includes Jesus as well, in a complementary not oppositional sense to incarnationalism; representation/witness also relates to *identification*. We have already seen how Jesus is the better paradigm for "representational mission" in contrast to Hesselgrave's proposal of Paul when modeling intimate identificational encounters with people. When one views the "either/or" debates in missiology that pit Paul against Jesus, it is better to understand them as complementary aspects of missionary methods that demonstrate aspects

---

94   Langmead, *The Word Made Flesh*, 8.
95   For example, he inexplicably writes that "missionaries will never be able to become [insiders], no matter how hard they try. Therefore, they should not pretend that they can." Andreas J. Köstenberger, "Anguish over Austria: Rising above Pragmatism," *Evangelical Missions Quarterly* 31, no. 1 (January1995): 69.
96   Daryl Guder, "Incarnation and the Church's Evangelistic Mission," *International Review of Mission* 83 (1994): 424.
97   Langmead, *The Word Made Flesh*, 52–53.
98   Ibid., 55.
99   Hesselgrave, *Paradigms in Conflict*, 152.

of Christian representation/witness. For example, while church planting methods are better seen in Paul, personal encounters and incarnational identification are more illustrative in Jesus' ministry.

In conclusion, effective incarnational missiology should not say "Look at us and you will see Jesus" but "Look beyond us to Jesus."[100] The Incarnation as a model in John's Gospel is viable because

> Christianity is "incarnational"; this adjective refers both to the reality of God's saving action and its manner. Christian mission, similarly, is incarnational in both senses: *bodily experiencing a new reality in Christ and sharing it through embodiment as Jesus did.*[101]

As we become embodied vessels of God in mission, in that sense we are an "incarnating dynamic."[102] This can be understood in the *Stuttgart Statement on Evangelism:*

> We cannot share the gospel without sharing ourselves. We live by the gospel of an incarnate Lord; this implies that the gospel has to become incarnated in ourselves, the "evangelists." This is not to suggest that, in our evangelism, we proclaim ourselves, but that those whom we wish to invite to faith in Christ will invariably look for signs of that faith in us.[103]

In such participation, "if mission defines who Christ is, and if Christ sends us as he was sent, then mission defines who we are."[104] This is the great privilege of doing incarnational mission with Christ through the power of his Spirit.

---

100   Patrick Fung, cited in Langmead, *The Word Made Flesh,* 197.
101   Langmead, *The Word Made Flesh,* 9 (italics mine).
102   Ibid., 20.
103   Cited by Guder, "Incarnation," 424.
104   Winn, *A Sense of Mission,* 53.

Works Cited

Beasley-Murray, George R. *John*. Word Biblical Commentary. Waco, TX: Word, 1987.

Bosch, David J. "Reflections on Biblical Models of Mission." In *Towards the 21st Century in Christian Mission: Essays in Honor of Gerald H. Anderson*, edited by James M. Philips and Robert T. Coote, 175–92. Grand Rapids: Eerdmans, 1993.

Brown, Raymond E. *The Gospel according to John*. Vol. 29A. Anchor Bible. New York: Doubleday, 1970.

Carson, D. A. *The Gospel according to John*. Pillar New Testament Commentary. Grand Rapids: Eerdmans, 1991.

Comblin, José. *Sent from the Father: Meditations on the Fourth Gospel*. Maryknoll, NY: Orbis Books, 1979.

Costas, Orlando E. *Christ Outside the Gate: Mission Beyond Christendom*. Eugene, OR: Wipf & Stock, 1982.

Danker, Frederick William, ed. *A Greek-English Lexicon of the New Testament and Other Early Christian Literature*. 3rd ed. Chicago: University of Chicago Press, 2000.

DuBose, Francis. *The God Who Sends: A Fresh Quest for Biblical Mission*. Nashville: Broadman, 1983.

Guder, Daryl. "Incarnation and the Church's Evangelistic Mission." *International Review of Mission* 83 (1994): 417–28.

Hesselgrave, David. *Paradigms in Conflict: 10 Key Questions in Christian Missions Today*. Grand Rapids: Kregel, 2005.

Hiebert, Paul G. *Missiological Implications of Epistemological Shifts*. Harrisburg, PA: Trinity Press International, 1999.

Käsemann, Ernst. *The Testament of Jesus: A Study of the Gospel of John in the Light of Chapter 17*. Translated by Gerhard Krodel. Philadelphia: Fortress, 1968.

Köstenberger, Andreas J. "Anguish over Austria: Rising above Pragmatism." *Evangelical Missions Quarterly* 31, no. 1 (January 1995): 64–70.

———. "The Greater Works of the Believer according to John 14:12." *Didaskalia* 6 (Fall 1994): 36–45.

———. *John*. Baker Exegetical Commentary. Grand Rapids: Baker, 2006.

———. *The Missions of Jesus and the Disciples according to the Fourth Gospel*. Grand Rapids: Eerdmans, 1998.

———, and Scott R. Swain. *Father, Son and Spirit: The Trinity and John's Gospel.* Downers Grove, IL: InterVarsity Press, 2008.

Kysar, R. "As You Sent Me: Identity and Mission in the Fourth Gospel." *Word and World* 21, no. 4 (2001): 370–76.

Langmead, Ross. *The Word Made Flesh: Towards an Incarnational Missiology.* Lanham, MD: University Press of America, 2004.

Legrand, L. "A Johannine Mission Model." *Indian Theological Studies* 43, nos. 3–4 (2006): 253–65.

Lingenfelter, Sherwood G., and Marvin K. Mayers. *Ministering Cross-culturally: An Incarnational Model for Personal Relationships.* Grand Rapids: Baker, 1986.

McElhanon, Ken. "Don't Give Up on the Incarnational Model." *Evangelical Missions Quarterly* 27, no. 4 (October 1991): 390–93.

Mercer, Calvin. "Jesus the Apostle. 'Sending' and the Theology of John." *Journal of the Evangelical Theological Society* 35, no. 4 (1992): 457–62.

Mondithoka, S. "Incarnation." In *Dictionary of Mission Theology: Evangelical Foundations,* edited by John Corrie, 177–81. Downers Grove, IL: InterVarsity Press, 2000.

Morris, Leon. *The Gospel according to John.* New International Commentary of the New Testament. Grand Rapids: Eerdmans, 1990.

Neeley, Alan. "Incarnational Mission." In *Evangelical Dictionary of World Missions,* edited by A. Scott Moreau, Charles van Engen, and Harold Netland, 474–75. Grand Rapids: Baker, 2000.

Ott, Craig, and Stephen J. Strauss. *Encountering Theology of Mission: Biblical Foundations, Historical Developments, and Contemporary Issues.* With Timothy C. Tennent. Grand Rapids: Baker, 2010.

Samuel, S. Johnson. "The Johannine Perspective on Mission in Christ's Praxis." *Bangalore Theological Forum* 20, no. 3 (1988): 8–16.

Schnabel, Eckhard J. "As the Father Has Sent Me, So I Send You (John 20:21): The Mission of Jesus and the Mission of the Church." *Missionalia* 33, no. 2 (2005): 263–86.

———. *Jesus and the Twelve.* Vol. 1 of *Early Christian Mission.* Downers Grove, IL: InterVarsity Press, 2004.

Senior, Donald, and Carroll Stuhlmueller. *The Biblical Foundations for Mission.* Maryknoll, NY: Orbis Books, 1983.

Stott, John R. W. *Christian Mission in the Modern World.* Downers Grove, IL: InterVarsity Press, 1975.

———. *The Contemporary Christian: Applying God's Word to Today's World.* Downers Grove, IL: InterVarsity Press, 1992.

———. "An Open Letter to David Hesselgrave." *Trinity World Forum* 16, no. 3 (1991): 1–2.

Waldstein, Michael. "The Mission of Jesus and the Disciples in John." *Communio: International Catholic Review* 17, no. 3 (1990): 311–33.

Winn, Albert Curry. *A Sense of Mission: Guidance from the Gospel of John.* Philadelphia: Westminster, 1981.

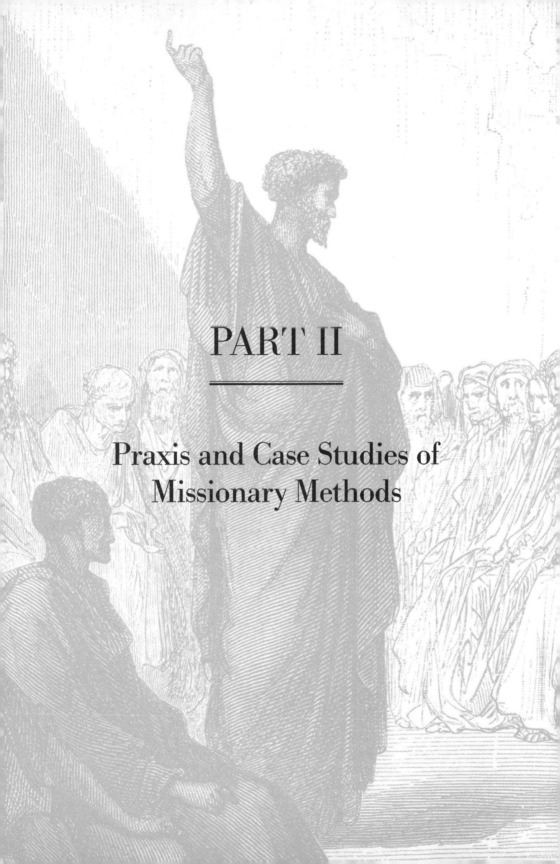

PART II

Praxis and Case Studies of Missionary Methods

4

From Roland Allen to Rick Warren: Sources of Inspiration Guiding North American Evangelical Missions Methodology 1912–2012

GARY R. CORWIN

While biblical revelation is always the foundational inspiration for engaging in missions in all times and seasons, it has not always been the primary methodological inspiration. It certainly was for Roland Allen, however, as the missionary methods of the Apostle Paul were not only a historical biblical narrative to learn from, but also *the* model to be followed by all the Lord's servants since.

In the one hundred years since Allen's famous *Missionary Methods: St. Paul's or Ours?,* there have been a number of other thought and/or cultural paradigms that have risen to significantly impact missions methodology for varying lengths of time. The category lines for these could certainly be drawn in a variety of ways, but the following provide at least a sense of what some of the inspirational paradigm streams may be:

The Power Stream
- *The Colonial Context*
- *Pax Americana*
- *Setting Global Agendas*

The Science Stream
- *Social Science Missiology*
- *Church Growth*
- *Technology*

The Organizational Stream
- *Professionalization of Missions*
- *Corporatization of Missions / Managerial Missions*
- *Business as Mission*

The Ecclesiastical Stream
- *Theological Precision Missions*
- *Amateurization of Missions*
- *Megachurch Missiology*

The Biblical Model Stream
- *The Gospel Mandate: Paul as Model*
- *Holistic Mission: Jesus as Model*

It should come as no surprise to thoughtful readers that not all of the inspirational paradigm categories above are of equal impact or longevity. However, though they have not all been equally beneficial, they have each played a role in influencing the direction and intensity of missions from North America over the last century. We turn now to look at each of them more specifically The Power Stream

The Power Stream

Whenever cultural forces occupy the same geographical space, there is normally a jockeying for prominence, position, and influence. When the power position of those cultural forces is out of balance, it is almost axiomatic that one side becomes the master and the other the mastered. This is true even when the relationships may be largely benign as, by and large, those of the missionary enterprise in the last two centuries have been. It is a function of that basic power relationship that very few of the points of interaction are left untouched or untainted by that circumstance.

That is not to say, therefore, that little that is good can come out of it, but it is to say that many things, including missions methodology, are profoundly affected.

The Colonial Context

The subject of colonialism is one that has received a great deal of attention in many academic disciplines, including missiology. According to missiologist Jonathan Ingleby it can be defined this way:

> Colonialism refers to the occupation and possession of territory by which an empire or nation state attempts to establish a permanent outpost beyond its borders. Accordingly, the idea of colonialism usually has a civilizational component, not simply the occupation of territory, but also cultural and religious transformation. The almost universal use of the term as a pejorative refers not only to the use of force against indigenous peoples, but also the imposition of a "foreign" world-view on them. Because the spread of world Christianity has largely taken place in the modern era, it has been difficult to disassociate it from colonial history.[1]

It is also true however, as Ingleby acknowledges, that the missions enterprise "often described itself in 'colonial' language ('the spread of civilization,' 'advance,' 'progress,' and the like)."[2]

There can be little doubt that the mind-set described above also had a profound impact on missionary methods. The cultural patterns and preferences of missionaries were greatly influenced by their own backgrounds, loyalties, and tastes. They shared many of the assumptions about indigenous peoples and civilization held by those tied more directly to the colonial government apparatus. As a result there was often an imposition of Western practices and patterns at the expense of local options in things like "church order, family customs and styles of leadership, even including buildings and clothing."[3]

---

1   Jonathan C. Ingleby, "Colonialism/postcolonialism," in *Dictionary of Mission Theology: Evangelical Foundations,* ed. John Corrie (Downers Grove, IL: InterVarsity Press, 2007), 62.
2   Ibid.
3   Ibid.

Missionaries thus fathered a "colonial" mindset which disregarded the legitimate claims of the context and encouraged attitudes of paternalism and dependency. This danger was identified early on in the modern missionary movement (consider the attempts of leaders such as Henry Venn and Rufus Anderson to popularize self-governing, self-financing and self-propagating churches) but the problem persisted.[4]

What has been said of Venn and Anderson in their work in the middle years of the nineteenth century also included the work of others, both contemporary and later. One contemporary, A. J. Crowther, the famed Nigerian missionary and church leader trained at Fourah Bay College in Sierra Leone, worked with Venn in the Church Missionary Society and pioneered missions outreach along the Niger River, becoming the first Anglican bishop of the Niger territories. Subsequent influential advocates of similar views included among others John Nevius, Roland Allen, and Melvin Hodges, whose writings and influence we shall discuss briefly in a later section.

Pax Americana

This Latin term that means "American Peace" is inspired by earlier examples of enforced peace through overwhelming military and economic power such as that exhibited in the *Pax Romana* of the Roman Empire and the *Pax Britannica* of the British Empire. Unlike either, however, it was and is not primarily a colonizing endeavor, but rather an influencing endeavor leveraged by the power of economic largesse and military protection. While it has been used in reference to various times and contexts including post–Civil War North America, and internationally in the period between the World Wars of the twentieth century, it is used most often in reference to the period since the end of World War II in 1945.[5]

---

4   Ibid., 63.
5   Wikipedia, s.v. "Pax Americana," http://en.wikipedia.org/wiki/Pax_Americana (accessed March 9, 2012) is a helpful, if not prestigious, summary of the term's usage over the last century and more. Its dominant usage as referring to the period since the end of World War II, however, is evident in articles such as Christopher Layne and Benjamin Schwarz, "Twilight of Pax Americana," *Los Angeles Times*. September 29, 2009, http://articles.latimes.com/2009/sep/29/opinion/oe-schwarz29 (accessed November 17, 2012); and Christopher Layne, "The End of the Pax Americana: How Western Decline Became Inevitable," The Atlantic, http://www.theatlantic.com/international/print/2012/04/the-end-of-pax-americana-how-western-decline-became-inevitable/256388/ (accessed November 17, 2012).

While different from the *Pax Britannica* in not being primarily a colonizing endeavor, the *Pax Americana* nevertheless has in numerous contexts been an inspirational source for many of the same, less admirable aspects of missions methodology—many of the things that are perhaps most easily summarized under the rubric of cultural insensitivity. As Lord Acton so accurately articulated, "Power corrupts, and absolute power corrupts absolutely."[6] The fact that American missionaries have during this period usually been far more wealthy than those among whom they were working, and that they are identified with a powerful and highly influential nation, has often impacted relationships in negative ways, even where nothing but the best of intentions have been present. For those interested in reading further on this subject, the 1950s book *The Ugly American* and Jonathan Bonk's *Missions and Money* are probably as good a place as any to see how some of these dynamics play out.[7]

Setting Global Agendas

More subtle than either the colonial contexts or the *Pax Americana,* the international agendas and the consultations, conferences, and networks that have developed from them have in too many cases been a reflection of the rich and powerful maneuvering the less powerful to pursue their priorities and cooperate in their plans. The fact that Western cultures and particularly the American one are so individualistic and entrepreneurial are certainly instrumental factors in this being so, sometimes to beneficial effect in spite of everything, but often producing considerable negative impact as well. Fortunately, more recent years have witnessed an increasingly more level playing field characterized by developing mutual plans together, rather than the poorer and the weaker simply serving as pawns in the process of achieving the purposes and plans of the richer and the more powerful.

An interesting measure in this regard is to simply compare those present, and those giving plenary addresses at the most important global evangelical missions conferences of the last one hundred years—Edinburgh 1910, Lausanne I (1974), Lausanne II in Manila (1989), and Lausanne III in Cape Town (2010). The measurable progress that has been made in North/South and East/West power parity in

---

6   http://www.acton.org/research/lord-acton-quote-archive.
7   William J. Lederer and Eugene Burdick, *The Ugly American* (New York: Norton, 1958); and Jonathan Bonk, *Missions and Money* (Maryknoll, NY: Orbis Books, 1991).

the global church (or perhaps better described as godly interdependence) as seen through these events is encouraging, but clearly still a work in process.

The Science Stream

It would almost be un-American if American evangelical missions methodology did not reflect a significant degree of influence from the experimental, inquisitive, and pragmatic nature of the American people that has provided the underpinning for scientific inquiry and its practical application throughout our history. The reality is that it has indeed reflected significant influence historically and continues to do so presently. This reality is visible in the emergence and widespread influence of social science missiology in missions practice generally, in the application of Church Growth theory more particularly, and in the important role that technological innovation has always played in missionary endeavors from North America.

Social Science Missiology

Social science missiology is a relatively recent adaptation of the last several decades in which various disciplines and aspects of the social sciences have been employed to serve missions purposes.[8] As the social sciences themselves are a relatively recent academic specialization, the integration of them as a resource in addressing the tasks of missiology is in effect an innovation employing an innovation. Enoch Wan describes the particulars:

> Specialization and integration in the social sciences are relatively recent developments in the larger academic disciplines in comparison with studies of the humanities (e.g., philosophy, literature) and the natural sciences (e.g., physics, chemistry). That they are *social* evidences the people component; that they are *sciences* shows commitment to certain methodological presuppositions across each of the fields. While there are several ways of classifying and categorizing disciplines in the social sciences . . . in their

---

8   While there is little doubt that widespread employment of the social sciences in the service of missions is a relatively recent phenomenon, it must be acknowledged that much earlier examples recognizing their potential usefulness do exist. See, for example, Darrell L. Whiteman, "Anthropology and Mission: The Incarnational Connection," in *Mission and Culture*, ed. Stephen B. Bevans (Maryknoll, NY: Orbis Books, 2012), 59–98.

relationship to mission and missiology they include anthropology, communication, economics, education, linguistics, modernization theory, politics, psychology, religion, research, and sociology.[9]

Overarching the benefits to be gleaned from particular social science disciplines is the synergistic benefits that integration of insights from those disciplines provide when viewed in conjunction with the insights that Scripture and history bring to the table. Examples of the actual utilization of these various disciplines in missionary preparation are varied and numerous:

> For example, many missions departments in Bible schools and seminaries have anthropologically trained faculty and offer courses in missionary anthropology. With increasing regularity, missionary candidates are screened by psychological testing prior to their acceptance by the organization and field appointments. Missionaries receiving language learning training are exposed to descriptive and applied linguistics. Many are trained in communication studies to enhance their ability to share Christ with non-Christians in culturally relevant ways.[10]

Likewise, in field ministry locations around the world, missions practitioners are employing various tools and methods of the social sciences to address serious issues and to help answer questions like these suggested by Wan:

> What are the social structures and undergirding cultural values that drive people of a given culture? How do they see the world and communicate their thoughts and feelings about their perceptions to others? How do people associate with each other and what rules govern role and status in a given society? What social and cultural dynamics are involved in religious conversion? How are people motivated, and how do they make decisions? What are the means of social change in a culture? What is the impact of urbanization on traditional religion and worldview? Many more

---

9   Enoch Wan, "Social Sciences," in *Evangelical Dictionary of World Missions*, ed. A. Scott Moreau (Grand Rapids: Baker Books, 2000), 885.

10   Ibid.

such questions could be stated. All focus on the human realities with which every culture must grapple.[11]

One of the most vigorous and distinctive applications of an interdisciplinary use of the social sciences in missiology and missions methodology has been in what is known as the Church Growth Movement. To it we now turn.

Church Growth

According to C. Peter Wagner, one of Church Growth's best known and most prolific advocates, it can be defined this way:

> Church Growth is that discipline which investigates the nature, expansion, planting, multiplication, function, and health of Christian churches as they relate to the effective implementation of God's commission to "make disciples of all peoples" (Matt 28:19,20). Students of church growth strive to integrate the eternal theological principles of God's Word concerning the expansion of the church with the best insights of contemporary social and behavioral sciences, employing as the initial frame of reference the foundational work done by Donald McGavran.[12]

Wagner goes on to point out that its "defining focus . . . is evangelism" and that which most clearly separates it from related groups is its explicit recognition of its founder, Donald A. McGavran.[13]

It is beyond the scope of this paper to say much about McGavran, but suffice it to say that his experience as a Disciples of Christ missionary in India provided the springboard for the movement. Growing in his frustration with the slow progress of missionary endeavor as he observed it, he undertook a vigorous effort to determine a better way to go about it. The result, after much research and analysis (based in large measure on the research of Methodist bishop Wascom Pickett's on "Christian

---

11   Ibid., 886.
12   C. Peter Wagner, "Church Growth Movement," in *Evangelical Dictionary of World Missions*, ed. A. Scott Moreau (Grand Rapids: Baker Books, 2000), 199.
13   Ibid.

mass movements" in India), was the publishing of *The Bridges of God* in 1955. With this event, the Church Growth Movement was born.[14]

The impact of this movement on modern missiology has been profound, spreading worldwide through the influence of its disciples, its fountainhead at Fuller Seminary, and through the major evangelical institutions where courses in church growth are taught. On missions methods per se the influence has been particularly pronounced with regard to evangelistic expectations: that believers in many cultures are far more likely to come to faith in Christ in groups through community decisions than as individuals going against the grain of their society.

Reflection on these kinds of "people movements" or "mass movements," as they are known, led in turn to what may be the most discussed and controversial aspect of Church Growth thought and practice—the homogeneous unit principle. As McGavran put it quite succinctly, this principle stresses that "human beings like to become Christians without crossing, linguistic, class, or racial barriers."[15] This writer has heard it expressed even more colloquially, though certainly less precisely, as "Birds of a feather flock together." Wagner describes the primary assumption involved:

> The homogeneous unit principle assumes that the focus and presentation of the gospel which has reaped an evangelistic harvest in a given people group might not have the same effect on other people groups, not because of the theological core of the gospel message, but because of irrelevant cultural trappings often attached to the gospel message by missionaries. Missionaries untrained in cultural anthropology tend to imagine that churches planted in any culture will look and sound and act like their own churches. The disastrous results of such cultural nearsightedness are extensively chronicled in missiological history.[16]

Critics of the homogeneous unit principle (HUP) have expressed concern about it having racial or class overtones. A fair reading of McGavran as a whole, however, would tend to alleviate that concern, though one can picture particular settings, particularly some urban ones (as McGavran acknowledges), where strict

---

14   Ibid.
15   Donald A. McGavran, *Understanding Church Growth* (Grand Rapids: Eerdmans, 1970), 163.
16   C. Peter Wagner, "Homogeneous Unit Principle," in *Evangelical Dictionary of World Missions*, ed. A. Scott Moreau (Grand Rapids: Baker Books, 2000), 455.

adherence to the HUP would certainly be counterproductive. In conclusion it is reasonable to say, as Wagner summarizes, "The homogeneous unit principle is a serious attempt to respect the dignity of individuals and the social units to which they belong, and to encourage their decisions for Christ to be religious decisions rather than social decisions."[17]

Technology

Ralph Winter used to speak of pursuing a "wartime" lifestyle rather than a "simple one." In doing so he was suggesting that while it is a good thing for God's people, and especially for missionaries, to live simply, that should not preclude the use of the most advanced technology available to achieve God's purposes. As in wartime, world evangelization efforts deserve the best equipment and technological means that can be accessed to get the job done. While there have been exceptions from time to time, that point of view has dominated missions methodology in the modern era.

Whether one looks at the pioneering work in jungle aviation, the use of about every band and frequency in radio communication for both internal communications and globe-circling evangelism and discipleship by groups like HCJB and Trans World Radio, satellite television programming, or more recent applications of Internet and other digital communication tools, technology has long been a boon to missions endeavor and a key factor influencing missions methodology. The impact has not always been entirely positive, however.

> Whereas in the past missionaries have often been distant in terms of time and geography, with E-mail they are just a click of a mouse button away. Some churches and individuals have sought to communicate more often with the missionaries and expect more and "better" reporting from them with less delay. With the current "faddishness" of E-mail some missionaries find themselves swamped with E-mail requests awaiting immediate response. The senders of E-mail . . . knowing that their messages arrive virtually as they send them, often expect answers back in the same way and in the same day.

---

17   Ibid.

Mission administrators then raise several crucial questions: Do the benefits justify the investment in the equipment and training costs? Are the technologies contextually appropriate? Will the use of new technologies facilitate the reaching of the mission field or not? Many technologies are available and affordable, but irrelevant or distracting.[18]

The astute reader will notice how dated the above quotation from the year 2000 sounds, technology having generated so many new tools and possibilities available today, adding to the general concerns about distractibility and counterproductive activity—skyping, online communication of ministry events, etc. Clearly, technology has been and will continue to be a great boon to missions methods, but it is equally true that it will almost always come with inherent temptations to misuse, as well as with unintended consequences.[19]

The Organizational (or Business) Stream

Similar to the science stream in terms of its pervasive influence, it would be most surprising if the American love affair with the organizational methods of business did not rub off on the missions enterprise. After all, as Calvin Coolidge famously said, "The business of America is business." The fact is that business methods and models have indeed rubbed off on the missions enterprise, both to good and not-so-good effect.

Unlike most of the streams we are looking at, however, many of the elements in the organizational stream that have impacted missions have been subtle in their influence. They are often, therefore, more easily recognized on a personal or anecdotal level than through documentary resources. In whatever ways they are recognized, however, there can be little doubt that they have been significant in their influence on missions methods.

---

18   Edgar J. Elliston, "Technology," in *Evangelical Dictionary of World Missions,* ed. A. Scott Moreau (Grand Rapids: Baker Books, 2000), 935.

19   For a fuller discussion of this subject, see Ron Rowland, "The Contribution of Technology to Missiology," in *Missiology and the Social Sciences: Contributions, Cautions and Conclusions,* Evangelical Missiological Series 4, ed. Edward Rommen and Gary Corwin (Pasadena: William Carey Library, 1996), 84–101.

Professionalization of Missions

In using the term "professionalization of missions" the intent is to convey the idea that missions agencies evolved from being primarily "Mom and Pop" operations to becoming much more professional in the sense of having and using best practices from the business world in areas such as finance, personnel systems, leadership development, accountability, and board structure. As with any evolutionary process, change in these areas took place over time, but momentum really seemed to build from the 1970s onward.

Probably no one was more instrumental in this process than Ted Engstrom. In addition to his own leadership roles with Youth for Christ and World Vision (which he is personally credited with turning from near bankruptcy to one of the largest Christian relief and development agencies), Engstrom had an enormous influence, particularly through his writings, on church and parachurch agencies of all kinds to be more effective in their administrative operations using sound business practices and principles. Over the course of his long and fruitful life (1916–2006) he wrote more than fifty books with titles like *The Making of a Christian Leader: How to Develop Management and Human Relations Skills* (1978), *The Pursuit of Excellence* (1982), and *The Best of Ted Engstrom on Personal Excellence and Leadership* (1988). He was also a key founder of the Evangelical Council for Financial Accountability.

Though Engstrom was a key man in this development, he was by no means alone in it. Many other business leaders who were as serious about following Christ as they were about being successful in business used their knowledge and experience to assist missions agencies and their leaders to be as effective in managing their organizations as they were in evangelism, teaching, or other direct ministry. By way of example, we shall mention only Ken Hansen, Ken Wessner, and Bill Pollard, all of whom have played key roles in the leadership of Servicemaster Corporation, and all of whom were very active over many years in consulting, leading seminars, and/or writing to assist various missions agencies with administrative and leadership issues. This writer personally remembers a seminar led by Ken Hansen in the late 1980s or early 1990s for global SIM leadership that was among the best he has experienced. The missions enterprise from North America owes much to such people.[20]

---

20   Rob Moll, "Ted W. Engstrom Dies at 90," *Christianity Today*, July 17, 2006, http://www.christianitytoday.com/ct/2006/julyweb-only/129–13.0.html?start=1 (accessed March 17, 2012).

Corporatization of Missions / Managerial Missions

As with most good things in life, when a good thing is taken too far it can be problematic. This seems clearly to be the case with regard to the business world's influence on the missions enterprise. The problems that have arisen have come not so much in the arena of how missions administration ought to function (the systems improvements described above have been almost universally helpful), but over what should constitute agency priorities and whether goals which are not easily quantifiable, or not accomplishable within a predictable amount of time, are worth focusing upon. That is not to say that this approach, too, has not had benefit (e.g., encouraging more systematic and energetic attention to least reached peoples), but it is to say that it also has a major downside.

Samuel Escobar, a leading Latin American missiologist, has been an outspoken critic of this approach, which he terms "managerial mission."

> The term managerial missiology refers to a trend within evan-gelical missiology that emphasizes the management of mission practice. It developed in North America during the last third of the twentieth century. It came from a cluster of institutions con-nected to the Church Growth school and movements such as AD 2000 and Beyond. It is an effort to reduce Christian mission to a manageable enterprise.
>
> Every characteristic of this missiological trend becomes un-derstandable when perceived within the frame of that avowed quantifying intention. Concepts such as "people groups," "un-reached peoples," "homogeneous units," "10–40 window," "adopt a people" and "territorial spirits" . . . express both a strong sense of urgency and an effort to use every available instrument to make the task possible. One way of achieving manageability is precisely to reduce reality to an understandable picture, and then to project missionary action as a response to "a problem" that has been described in quantitative form.[21]

---

21   Samuel Escobar, "Managerial Missiology," in *Dictionary of Mission Theology: Evangelical Foundations,* ed. John Corrie (Downers Grove, IL: InterVarsity Press, 2007), 216.

Escobar has rightly taken to task the tendency toward a "quantification is everything" bias in this approach. There are other concerns with it as well. The strong "closure" emphasis ("we must get the job done so Christ will return"), for example, which Escobar also mentions, seems to overstep the prophetic meaning of some of Christ's statements (e.g., Matt 24:14; Mark13:10) and suggest an almost mechanical control of God's timetable through human effort.[22] The great losers in these too-often-unbalanced approaches are the loss of focus on the teaching task in "making disciples," the loss of clarity in communication, as well as loss of attention to the "loving our neighbors as ourselves" task inherent in the Great Commandment (Matt 22:34–40).[23]

There is at least one other aspect in the corporatization of missions that should be mentioned before moving on. It is the increasingly common tendency to inflate the value of corporate background and skills as preparation for missions-related staff positions in churches, and for board and administrative leadership of mission agencies. While there are certainly important aspects of these roles for which such preparation is quite helpful, the diminishing weight being placed on pastoral and missions training and experience for these roles would certainly seem to indicate a shift in emphasis. Time will tell whether a healthy balance is being achieved.

Business as Mission

While it is not possible within the scope of this paper to say much about it, we must at least mention the much newer, and potentially profoundly positive contribution of the business world to missions described as "business as mission." It is both rapidly developing and rapidly growing in its impact on missions methods around the globe. Tom Steffen said the following in his introduction to *Business as Mission: From Impoverished to Empowered,* a volume he coedited with Mike Barnett for the Evangelical Missiological Society in 2006:

---

22   For an excellent discussion of the "closure" issue, see Craig Ott and Stephen J. Strauss, *Encountering Theology of Mission: Biblical Foundations, Historical Developments, and Contemporary Issues,* with Timothy C. Tennent (Grand Rapids: Baker Academic, 2010), 186–90.

23   For discussion of these potential dangers, see Gary R. Corwin, "Just Where Are the Frontiers?" *Evangelical Missions Quarterly* 28, no. 2 (April 1992): 118–23; Gary R. Corwin, "Editorial Response: In Pursuit of Good Communication in Mission," *International Journal of Frontier Missions* 9, no. 4 (October 1992): 117–18; and Gary R. Corwin, "Sociology and Missiology: Reflections on Mission Research," in *Missiology and the Social Sciences: Contributions, Cautions and Conclusions,* Evangelical Missiological Series 4, ed. Edward Rommen and Gary Corwin (Pasadena: William Carey Library, 1996), 19–29.

"To put it bluntly," wrote Doug Pennoyer, Dean of the School of Intercultural Studies, Biola University and President of the EMS, when announcing the call for BAM papers, "Business as mission (BAM) is a work in progress. It is a field that needs definition, theological clarity, and missiological focus. Our call for papers for our regional conferences is timely, and the culminating discussions and presentations at the national level puts us in a place to make a pivotal contribution in a sea of some confusion and even controversy" . . . While this volume will certainly not bring total clarity to the topic, it will provide some needed definition and precision while at the same time identify areas that will demand further discussion, clarification, and maturity.[24]

Beyond what can be said here, the reader is encouraged to explore further information on this rapidly evolving contribution to missions methods. There are several helpful resources described in the notes.[25]

The Ecclesiastical Stream

The way that both local churches and denominations have engaged with missions through the years has had a significant influence on missions methods. Because the nature of that engagement has evolved over time, that influence has evolved as well. It has, however, remained significant, whether one is looking at the decisions that have flowed from commitments to theological distinctives and denominational goals, or the impact of ubiquitous short-term missions endeavors, or the wide reach of the even newer phenomenon of megachurch missiology. We shall look now at each in turn.

---

24   Tom Steffen, introduction to *Business as Mission: From Impoverished to Empowered,* ed. Tom Steffen and Mike Barnett, Evangelical Missiological Series 14 (Pasadena: William Carey Library, 2006), 15–16.

25   C. Neal Johnson and Steven Rundle, *Business as Mission: A Comprehensive Guide to Theory and Practice* (Downers Grove, IL: InterVarsity Press, 2009); Mark L. Russell, *The Missional Entrepreneur: Principles and Practices for Business as Mission* (Birmingham, AL: New Hope, 2009); and Steven L. Rundle and Tom A. Steffen, *Great Commission Companies: The Emerging Role of Business in Missions* (Downers Grove, IL: InterVarsity Press, 2003).

Theological Precision Missions

Denominations exist because there are theological or practical commitments that a group believes are distinctive and important enough to warrant a separate institutional base from which to advance those commitments. Sometimes these commitments focus on issues that truly are of primary importance, and sometimes the issues involved are of secondary importance at best. Determining which is often in the eye of the beholder. In either case, these commitments will very often have the effect of skewing decisions about missions involvement and priorities in a particular direction.

Because of its distinctive commitments, any denomination or church body will almost never gather for their annual meeting without asking the question, "How many more churches like us have been established around the world?" Their missions-focused personnel will know this question is coming, and will almost instinctively orient their activities in the period leading up to it to produce a result that provides a positive answer to that question. In terms of missions methods this means that focus will almost always be skewed toward more receptive areas for evangelism and church planting, than to less receptive ones. While there are certainly exceptions to this among denominational missions both past and present, as agencies have responded to issues of need or to relational connections, the general tendency seems beyond question.

Interdenominational missions by contrast have tended to be driven by a different question, "What peoples or groups are being overlooked or underserved by current missions strategy?" That is not to say that these agencies are not also susceptible to the pressure to produce results to please their constituencies, but their constituencies are generally as much concerned with seeing efforts taking place among the least-reached or "resistant" peoples as they are to seeing measurable results in terms of churches planted or new believers won to Christ. That bias generally leads most of them to engage the least reached as their primary strategy, although many specialty interdenominational missions (e.g., campus focus, theological education, radio, aviation) often operate on different criteria altogether.

Amateurization of Missions

Ralph Winter coined the phrase a decade and a half ago to describe the tsunami of short-term missions that were becoming such an integral and important part of the missions enterprise from North America. He used the term by way of a warning that the flood of inexperienced and untrained individuals participating might do significant harm to the long-term progress of the gospel around the world. He cited the "Student Volunteers" of a century prior (the backbone of a movement lauded by most missions historians) as an example of what can go wrong:

> College educated "Student Volunteers" took one look at the level of education of many African pastors and declared them unqualified. They pushed real leaders out of the pulpits. Serious setbacks resulted in most fields. It took twenty, thirty, forty years for the volunteers to relearn much of what earlier missionaries had already discovered . . .

> Is "amateurization" always what happens when a new movement to the field takes place? . . . Even "short-termers" have their problems. Can a little knowledge be a dangerous thing?

> It did happen before. But we are reluctant to admit it. Popular interest in mission is so scarce that we mission professionals are inclined to accept "interest"—warts and all.[26]

Not all missiologists are as pessimistic as Dr. Winter seems to be above, however. Harold R. Carpenter, writing in response to Winter, makes the point that the primary problem may be something other than amateurization:

> Ralph Winter has raised a critical issue in contemporary missions . . . However, some of his assumptions and terminology are open to question. (1) Is it a fair assumption to call the 20,000 young people who went to the field between 1886 and 1936 amateurs? Most of them had as much or more preparation than the missionaries of the "Great Century." (2) Were the results of the Student Volunteer's ministry as negative as Ralph paints them? Some of the great names of missions come from the group of Student Volunteers, and in terms of results almost no century in history has produced the quantitative results of this century.

---

26   Ralph D. Winter, "The Re-amateurization of Missions," *Occasional Bulletin* 9, no. 2 (Spring 1996), http://emsweb.org/images/stories/docs/bulletins/winter_reamateurization_2_1996.pdf.

> Winter's concerns are valid, but I would suggest that the issue
> is more one of commitment than of preparation. Short-termers
> make some valuable contributions to missions, but a mission-
> ary can not really be effective without learning the language and
> culture of a people. This requires a long-term commitment and
> ministry. Are we really talking about re-amateurization of mis-
> sions or a lack of commitment to life-long service?[27]

Whatever one concludes on whether it is truly an "amateurization" of missions or something else, it is certainly clear that short-term missions have greatly
impacted the way missions from North America are thought of, and have both aided
and complicated the way missions is carried out around the globe. In conclusion,
A. Scott Moreau has summed up well the positives and negatives of the movement:

> On the down side, the explosion in short-term missions has not
> yet resulted in a corresponding increase in long-term missionar-
> ies. Even worse, short-term missions may very well be resulting
> in inoculation against long-term commitment for the coming
> generation. It is also true that increasingly the goal of short-term
> missions has shifted from participation in the Great Commission
> or exploration of long-term possibilities to personal fulfillment.
> Without proper preparation, they can also strengthen stereotypes
> that play into the Western myth of White Man's Burden, enabling
> participants to see their intended audience as objects who are ever
> needy rather than people who have something to share. They can
> build dependency and leave local initiatives stifled until the next
> short-term team comes through.
>
> On the up side, more than one million people every year are being
> exposed in some way to new cultural settings and ways of living.
> When properly prepared, many of them gain a more realistic
> view of what missionary life involves, and through their efforts
> accelerate ministry or other work in significant ways. Those in
> their teen years can be changed for the rest of their lives even if
> they do not themselves become long-term workers. Mature adults

---

27   Harold R. Carpenter, "Response," *Occasional Bulletin* 9, no. 2 (Spring 1996), http://emsweb.org/
images/stories/docs/bulletins/winter_reamateurization_2_1996.pdf.

can offer encouragement and wisdom in situations when needed. Professional health personnel can save lives and enable restoration to physical health. Business people can help local businesses start or grow in ways that will be important to their economies.[28]

Only time will tell which kind of impact will ultimately be dominant.

Megachurch Missiology

The last several decades have seen the development of a new and significant force in the missions enterprise from North America—the engagement of influential megachurches in global missions in ways unique to their particular ethos and experience. This new engagement often finds its impetus to a great degree in the assumption that their experience of growth in numbers and influence is replicable elsewhere around the world by following the same principles and methods. Or, like the huge growth in short-term missions, the assumption is simply that we can do missions directly at least as well as the agencies that have too long held a near monopoly in connecting to the churches and needs of other peoples and nations, and in generating creative methodology to do this well.

While it is beyond the scope of this paper to even attempt mentioning all the forms these efforts take, a brief look at three models that come quickly to mind will serve to provide some sense of the variety and scope of these endeavors. The first of these is the global network of the Willow Creek Association, an outreach of the Willow Creek Community Church of South Barrington, Illinois, and its founding pastor, Bill Hybels. It describes itself this way:

> Founded in 1992 by Bill Hybels, the Willow Creek Association (WCA) is a not-for-profit organization that exists to maximize the life-transformation effectiveness of local churches. We do this by stirring up and calling out the core leadership of churches around the world, encouraging them to follow their "holy discontent" as they build life-changing communities of faith. We then equip these leaders with next-step solutions to impact spiritual transformation of their people, their communities, and the world.

---

28   A. Scott Moreau, "Epilogue: The Drama of Today's Short-term Missions," in *Engaging the Church: Analyzing the Canvas of Short-term Missions,* ed. Laurie A. Fortunak and A. Scott Moreau (Wheaton, IL: Evangelism and Missions Information Service, 2008), 230.

At the core of the ministry is [the] deeply held belief that God's ordained plan to redeem and restore this world for Christ is through the church. In fact, we believe that is the hope of the world.

For nearly 20 years, the WCA has developed a respected history of excellence and innovation in serving local churches and their leaders. In that time, the WCA has inspired and trained more than one million church leaders and has created and distributed millions of church resources into tens of thousands of churches representing more than 90 denominations. With more than 10,000 Member Churches in 35 countries, WCA leadership training events are now held in more than 250 cities in 50 countries each year.[29]

The Association's appeal for new members adds further insight on the nature of its methodology:

Participating in the Willow Creek Association provides transformational experiences and resources that will strengthen you and your church in kingdom-important ways:

- Enlarge your own heart and capacity as a leader
- Sharpen your understanding of God at work in your setting
- Discover proven solutions God is using in churches around the world to accomplish His purposes
- Create the resource mix and flow that matches your unique situation
- Experience encouraging training through a variety of channels
- Join conversations with others from whom you can learn and share[30]

The second megachurch model is that of "City to City," a ministry of Redeemer Church and its founding pastor, Tim Kellar, in New York City. It forthrightly describes itself this way:

---

29   Willow Creek Association, "Who We Are," http://www.willowcreek.com/about/ (accessed March 21, 2012).

30   Willow Creek Association, "Membership," http://www.willowcreek.com/membership/ (accessed March 21, 2012).

> Redeemer City to City is the new organizational name for the Redeemer Church Planting Center (RCPC) and Redeemer Labs.
>
> Our mission is to help leaders build gospel movements in cities. We hope to build a global movement of leaders and practitioners who build upon and adapt our "DNA" to create new churches, new ventures, and new expressions of the gospel of Jesus Christ for the common good.[31]

Its work is global and ambitious, and very much connected to reproducing its own model in the great cities of the world. They work very hard at it and are experiencing considerable success. We will leave it to the reader to pursue more detail as desired.

The final, and perhaps most ambitious, megachurch model we shall look at is that of Rick Warren and Saddleback Church that operates out of a number of locations in southern California. Its "PEACE Plan" is its unique contribution and is self-described this way:

> The PEACE Plan is a massive effort to mobilize Christians around the world to address what Pastor Rick calls the "five global giants" of spiritual emptiness, corrupt leadership, poverty, disease, and illiteracy by promoting reconciliation, equipping servant leaders, assisting the poor, caring for the sick, and educating the next generation.
>
> PEACE is a movement to mobilize Christians
>
> in churches working together to . . .
>
> Plant churches that promote reconciliation
> Equip servant leaders
> Assist the poor
> Care for the sick
> Educate the next generation[32]

---

31   Redeemer Presbyterian Church, "Redeemer City to City," http://www.redeemer.com/about_us/ church_planting/ (accessed March 21, 2012).
32   Saddleback Church, "The PEACE Plan," http://www.saddleback.com/aboutsaddleback/ signatureministries/thepeaceplan/ (accessed March 21, 2012).

More specifically, those who visit their website are invited to "sign up" and become part of helping to make these things happen. Various resources are offered to help those who do to keep track of the projects they are already involved with, to find a church elsewhere in need of help, to become part of an existing work or to start a new one, to get training and resources, to see what others in their community are doing, and to easily find works that they are passionate about and able to support in various ways.[33] Figures for how many are taking advantage of these opportunities were not readily available.

The Biblical Model Stream

Of all the streams of thought and activity influencing missions methods today and over the last two centuries, none have been more dominant, or borne the weight of authority more powerfully, than those based upon the biblical models. While various nuances of approach can be noted within them, these models boil down basically to two—the Pauline apostolic model and the holistic mission model. The former seeks to follow the evangelism and church planting and nurturing methods of Paul, and the latter seeks to fashion itself more directly after the incarnational word-and-deed ministry of the Lord Jesus. The historical reality is that each of these models often look a lot more like each other in their actual application than the strongest advocates of each would like to admit. There is often considerable heat generated, however, in how the two camps characterize the work of the other.

The Gospel Mandate: Paul as Model

The Apostle Paul was keenly aware of his special calling as a minister of the gospel of Jesus Christ to the Gentiles. He preached the gospel boldly to them. He lived in the light of it at great personal sacrifice. And he defended it against perversion both in his writings and in personal debate. He also pursued his ministry using methods that have since been the primary model for establishing indigenous churches (i.e., those "that fit naturally into their environment").[34] John Mark Terry rightly traces pretty much all attempts to establish indigenous churches back to the Apostle Paul as their source.

---

33   Saddleback Church, "The PEACE Plan: Why Sign Up?" http://www.thepeaceplan.com/FAQ/why-signup(accessed May 3, 2013).

34   John Mark Terry, "Indigenous Churches," in *Evangelical Dictionary of World Missions,* ed. A. Scott Moreau (Grand Rapids: Baker Books, 2000), 483.

Missionary efforts to establish indigenous churches are attempts to do missions as the apostle Paul did. A brief recital of Paul's missionary methods demonstrates this fact. Paul served as an itinerant missionary, never staying more than three years in any city. Paul's approach to evangelizing regions was to plant churches in cities from which the gospel would permeate the surrounding areas. He never appealed to the churches in Antioch or Jerusalem for funds with which to support the new churches. Rather, he expected the churches to support themselves. Paul appointed and trained elders to lead all the churches he planted. He gave the churches over to the care of the Holy Spirit, but he also visited them and wrote to them periodically.[35]

Terry goes on to trace the development of "indigenous church" thinking with brief descriptions of the key principles advocated by a series of its champions: Henry Venn (1796–1873) and Rufus Anderson (1796–1880) advocating the necessity of establishing "three-self" churches capable of self-support, self-government, and self-propagation; John L. Nevius (1829–93) and "The Nevius Plan" that was adopted and had such great success in Korea; Roland Allen (1868–1947) whose books *Missionary Methods: St. Paul's or Ours?* (1912) and *The Spontaneous Expansion of the Church* (1927) have been so impactful in the twentieth century; and Melvin Hodges of the Assemblies of God, whose book *The Indigenous Church* (1953) updated and popularized for many what had gone before.

Terry concludes his article with a helpful listing of indigenous principles that reflect a composite of the thinking of those discussed above. We conclude this section with it:

Missionaries who seek to establish indigenous churches should keep these principles in mind as they begin their work: (1) Missionaries should plant churches with the goal in mind. This means that the desired outcome—an indigenous church—should influence the methods employed. (2) There will always be a dynamic tension between supracultural doctrines and variable cultural traits. (3) Church planters should expect the churches to support themselves from the beginning. (4) Bible study groups should be

---

35   Ibid., 483.

encouraged to make basic decisions even before they organize as churches. (5) Missionaries should encourage new congregations to evangelize their communities and seek opportunities to begin new churches. (6) Missionaries should always use reproducible methods of evangelism, teaching, preaching, and leadership. (7) Missionaries should give priority to developing nationals to serve as church leaders. (8) Missionaries should view themselves as temporary church planters rather than permanent pastors. (9) Missionaries should resist the temptation to establish institutions and wait for the national church to take the initiative. (10) Missionaries must allow the national churches to develop theologies and practices that are biblical yet appropriate in their cultural settings.[36]

Holistic Mission: Jesus as Model

"The aspiration for a more comprehensive view of mission became evident in evangelical circles as early as the Wheaton Congress of 1966."[37] So says Rene Padilla, a leading Latin missiologist and an early advocate for what is today commonly known as "holistic mission." He goes on to trace the increasing energy behind the concept, noting the role of John Stott at Lausanne I (1974) with the Lausanne Covenant's affirmation of the duty of sociopolitical involvement, as well as summarizing Stott's opening address on "The Biblical Basis of Evangelism":

> "The mission of the church arises from the mission of God" and should, therefore, follow the incarnational model of Jesus Christ. On that basis, he argued that "mission . . . describes everything the church is sent in to the world to do," as those who are sent by Jesus Christ even as the Son was sent by the Father, that is "to identify with others as he identified with us" and to serve as "he gave himself in selfless service for others."

> The affirmation that the actual commission itself must be understood to include social as well as evangelistic responsibility seems to

---

36   Ibid., 485.
37   C. R. Padilla, "Holistic Mission," in *Dictionary of Mission Theology: Evangelical Foundations,* ed. John Corrie (Downers Grove, IL: InterVarsity Press, 2007), 157.

suggest a real integration of the vertical and the horizontal dimensions of mission, which is at the very heart of *holistic* mission.[38]

Doug McConnell, reflecting on the growing acceptance of holistic mission thinking, points to the shift that took place between the first and second Lausanne Congresses. Both the Lausanne Covenant (1974) and the Manila Manifesto (1989) "focus on evangelism, yet the latter emphasizes the issue of the whole gospel, demonstrating the wide acceptance of social concern as an integral part of the Good News of Christ."[39] McConnell also expands and sharpens the definition of holistic mission:

> Holistic mission is concerned with ministry to the whole person through the transforming power of the gospel. While holistic mission affirms the functional uniqueness of evangelism and social responsibility, it views them as inseparable from the ministry of the kingdom of God. Therefore, holistic mission is the intentional integration of building the church and transforming society.[40]

Concern over the integration of evangelism and social concern under the rubric of "missions" has generally not existed because of a low view of social concern as an inappropriate and unnecessary response of believers who are faithful and obedient in following Christ. On the contrary, the traditional agencies that emphasize evangelism and church planting do so in spite of their own significant labors to improve the social conditions of people in the areas of health, education, clean water, agriculture, etc. The point of concern, therefore, comes not over whether all these things ought to be done, but over whether they all constitute the special task of missions. The fear, invariably, is over whether this broadening definition of missions, to basically include all that Christ has commanded us to do, will in the end diminish the most central missions task that is evangelism and church planting among all peoples. The sad evidence that this may in fact be happening is that many of the newer agencies that claim their commitment to holistic mission are actually "halfistic," ministering to human need but avoiding verbal proclamation of the gospel like the plague.

---

38   Ibid., 157.
39   Douglas McConnell, "Holistic Mission," in *Evangelical Dictionary of World Missions*, ed. A. Scott Moreau (Grand Rapids: Baker Books, 2000), 449.
40   Ibid., 448.

McConnell states that "holistic mission is the commitment to all that the church is called to do, which includes the Great Commission (Matt 28:18–20) and the Great Commandment (Matt 22:37–40)."[41] Others, including this writer, would suggest that the commitment he describes is broader than missions. It is the commitment of all obedient followers of Christ. The uniquely missionary task is encompassed in the command to "make disciples" as outlined in the Great Commission.

Conclusion

Missions methods over the last one hundred years have received, and sometimes suffered the impact of, a great many influences. We have looked at five streams of influence that have flowed together to help shape missions from North America into the broad river that we know today—the power stream, the science stream, the organizational stream, the ecclesiastical stream, and the biblical model stream. While the river is sometimes fast flowing and energetic, and sometimes slow and muddy, it does keep flowing and it does seem to "self-correct" (or should that be "Spirit-correct") by the Lord's grace and the Spirit's oversight. There is another very powerful stream flowing now that is likely to bring more new life and correction to the river's flow than anything else currently bringing influence to bear—the "globalization of missions" stream.

However confused or misguided missions from the West may be or become, the huge and growing stream of energetic missions coming from the Global South and East is changing, and will continue to change, both the ministry landscape everywhere and the methods being used even by the Global North. Hopefully that change will not simply be an abdication of personal responsibility through "proxy missions," in which the Global North only sends money and not its youth, but a genuinely interdependent time in which all the gifts of God distributed around the globe, in personnel and resources, work together to achieve his great purposes in the world.

Works Cited

Bonk, Jonathan. *Missions and Money.* Maryknoll, NY: Orbis Books, 1991.

Carpenter, Harold R. "Response." Accessed May 3, 2013. *Occasional Bulletin* 9, no. 2 (Spring 1996). http://emsweb.org/images/stories/docs/bulletins/winter_rea-mateurization_2_1996.pdf.

---

41   Ibid., 449.

Corwin, Gary R. "Editorial Response: In Pursuit of Good Communication in Mission." *International Journal of Frontier Missions* 9, no. 4 (October 1992): 117–18.

———. "Just Where Are the Frontiers?" *Evangelical Missions Quarterly* 28, no. 2 (April 1992): 118–23.

———. "Sociology and Missiology: Reflections on Mission Research." In *Missiology and the Social Sciences: Contributions, Cautions and Conclusions,* edited by Edward Rommen and Gary Corwin, 19–29. Evangelical Missiological Series 4. Pasadena: William Carey Library, 1996.

Elliston, Edgar J. "Technology." In *Evangelical Dictionary of World Missions,* edited by A. Scott Moreau, 935. Grand Rapids: Baker Books, 2000.

Escobar, Samuel. "Managerial Missiology." In *Dictionary of Mission Theology: Evangelical Foundations,* edited by John Corrie, 216. Downers Grove, IL: InterVarsity Press, 2007.

Ingleby, Jonathan C. "Colonialism/postcolonialism." In *Dictionary of Mission Theology: Evangelical Foundations,* edited by John Corrie, 62. Downers Grove, IL: InterVarsity Press, 2007.

Johnson, C. Neal, and Steven Rundle. *Business as Mission: A Comprehensive Guide to Theory and Practice.* Downers Grove, IL: InterVarsity Press, 2009.

Layne, Christopher. "The End of the Pax Americana: How Western Decline Became Inevitable." *The Atlantic.* Accessed November 17, 2012. http://www.theatlantic.com/international/print/2012/04/the-end-of-pax-americana-how-western-decline-became-inevitable/256388/.

———, and Benjamin Schwarz. "Twilight of Pax Americana." *Los Angeles Times.* September 29, 2009. Accessed November 17, 2012. http://articles.latimes.com/2009/sep/29/opinion/oe-schwarz29.

Lederer, William J., and Eugene Burdick. *The Ugly American.* New York: Norton, 1958.

McConnell, Douglas. "Holistic Mission." In *Evangelical Dictionary of World Missions,* edited by A. Scott Moreau, 449. Grand Rapids: Baker Books, 2000.

McGavran, Donald A. *Understanding Church Growth.* Grand Rapids: Eerdmans, 1970.

Moll, Rob. "Ted W. Engstrom Dies at 90." *Christianity Today.* July 17, 2006. Accessed March 17, 2012. http://www.christianitytoday.com/ct/2006/julyweb-only/129-13.0.html?start=1.

Moreau, A. Scott. "Epilogue: The Drama of Today's Short-term Missions." In *Engaging the Church: Analyzing the Canvas of Short-term Missions,* edited by Laurie A. Fortunak and A. Scott Moreau, 230. Wheaton, IL: Evangelism and Missions Information Service, 2008.

Ott, Craig, and Stephen J. Strauss. *Encountering Theology of Mission: Biblical Foundations, Historical Developments, and Contemporary Issues.* With Timothy C. Tennent. Grand Rapids: Baker Academic, 2010.

Padilla, C. R. "Holistic Mission." In *Dictionary of Mission Theology: Evangelical Foundations,* edited by John Corrie, 157. Downers Grove, IL: InterVarsity Press, 2007.

Redeemer Presbyterian Church. "Redeemer City to City." Accessed March 21, 2012. http://www.redeemer.com/about_us/church_planting/.

Rowland, Ron. "The Contribution of Technology to Missiology." In *Missiology and the Social Sciences: Contributions, Cautions and Conclusions,* edited by Edward Rommen and Gary Corwin, 84–101. Evangelical Missiological Series 4. Pasadena: William Carey Library, 1996.

Rundle, Steven L., and Tom A. Steffen. *Great Commission Companies: The Emerging Role of Business in Missions.* Downers Grove, IL: InterVarsity Press, 2003.

Russell, Mark L. *The Missional Entrepreneur: Principles and Practices for Business as Mission.* Birmingham, AL: New Hope, 2009.

Saddleback Church. "The PEACE Plan." Accessed March 21, 2012. http://www.saddleback.com/aboutsaddleback/signatureministries/thepeaceplan/.

———. "The PEACE Plan: Why Sign Up?" The PEACE Plan. Accessed May 3, 2013. http://www.thepeaceplan.com/FAQ/why-signup.

Steffen, Tom. Introduction to *Business as Mission: From Impoverished to Empowered,* edited by Tom Steffen and Mike Barnett, 15–16. Evangelical Missiological Series 14. Pasadena: William Carey Library, 2006.

Terry, John Mark. "Indigenous Churches." In *Evangelical Dictionary of World Missions,* edited by A. Scott Moreau, 483. Grand Rapids: Baker Books, 2000.

Wagner, C. Peter. "Church Growth Movement." In *Evangelical Dictionary of World Missions,* edited by A. Scott Moreau, 199. Grand Rapids: Baker Books, 2000.

———. "Homogeneous Unit Principle." In *Evangelical Dictionary of World Missions,* edited by A. Scott Moreau, 455. Grand Rapids: Baker Books, 2000.

Wan, Enoch. "Social Sciences." In *Evangelical Dictionary of World Missions,* edited by A. Scott Moreau, 885. Grand Rapids: Baker Books, 2000.

Whiteman, Darrell L. "Anthropology and Mission: The Incarnational Connection." In *Mission and Culture,* edited by Stephen B. Bevans, 59–98. Maryknoll, NY: Orbis Books, 2012.

Willow Creek Association. "WCA Membership." Accessed March 21, 2012. http://www.willowcreek.com/membership/.

———. "Who We Are." Accessed March 21, 2012. http://www.willowcreek.com/about/.

Winter, Ralph D. "The Re-amateurization of Missions." Accessed May 3, 2013. *Occasional Bulletin* 9, no. 2 (Spring 1996). http://emsweb.org/images/stories/docs/bulletins/winter_reamateurization_2_1996.pdf.

5

A Prolegomena to Contextualized Preaching Concerning the Wrath of God and the Judgment of Man: What Did Roland Allen Know that We Sometimes Forget and at Other Times Never Learn?

DAVID J. HESSELGRAVE

This year we celebrate the centennial of the publication of Roland Allen's classic *Missionary Methods: St. Paul's or Ours?* In chapter 7 of that book Allen measures the missionary preaching of his day and finds it wanting in some key areas.

Fine, but when you stop to think about it, Allen wrote his book decades before the advent of Theological Education Fund, the convening of the Willowbank Consultation, and the appearance of Eugene Nida's dynamic equivalence, to say nothing of Paul Hiebert's critical contextualization. Allen wrote well before the launching of the venerable journal *Practical Anthropology!* How in the world could a missiologist bereft of a knowledge of semiotics, semantic differentials, *Gemeinschaft* and *Gesellschaft* cultures, emic and etic perspectives, and Maslow's Motivational Pyramid, for example, undertake an evaluation of missionary preaching. Furthermore, how can we who live and labor a full one hundred years later and are thus informed expect to learn anything from what he wrote?

The answer is patently obvious. Allen confidently assumes that Paul's "apostolic preaching" is definitive, decisive, and determinative. Paul's preaching is both the rock bottom on which Christian missionary preaching must be anchored and the unerring compass by which it must be guided. Everything else—no matter how scholarly the source, no matter how titillating the substance—is secondary.

My presuppositions here are that (1) Allen is correct in his basic assumption, (2) he is basically accurate in his analysis, and (3) his proposals merit consideration as a prolegomena *to authentic missionary preaching.*

Turning then to chapter 7, "The Substance of Paul's Preaching," in *Missionary Methods,*[1] Allen begins by briefly citing three examples of Paul's preaching as found in the book of Acts: the sermon in the synagogue in Pisidian Antioch (13:16–41), the speech in Lystra (14:15–17), and the speech on Mars Hill in Athens (17:22–31). He then takes note of five incidental references to the substance of Paul's preaching (Acts 16:17; 17:2,3,18; 19:37; 20:21). And that is followed by a brief account of Paul's preaching to the Corinthians as summarized by Paul himself in 1 Corinthians 2:2. However, the "meat" of Allen's understanding of apostolic preaching is subsumed under two rubrics to which Allen devotes the bulk of the chapter: first, a somewhat pedantic review of the distinctives of Paul's preaching and, second, a more hortatory and admonitory application of those distinctives to the preaching of his contemporaries.

What follows represents a modest attempt to summarize what Allen says about "apostolic preaching" (i.e., Pauline missionary preaching), especially as it has to do with preaching the wrath of God and the judgment of mankind—two themes downplayed or even overlooked in contemporary missionary preaching.

Paul's "Synagogue Preaching" and "Heathen Preaching" Characterized and Compared

According to Allen, the New Testament discloses two types of Paul's "apostolic preaching": Paul's "synagogue preaching" to Jews, and Paul's "preaching to 'heathens'" (i.e., to Gentile adherents of other religions). In this section I simply make mention of what he has to say without offering comments.

---

1   Roland Allen, *Missionary Methods: St. Paul's or Ours?*, American edition (1912; repr., Grand Rapids: Eerdmans, 1961), 62–77.

Paul's "Synagogue Preaching" to Jews and Proselytes

Luke's brief account of Paul's sermon in the synagogue in Thessalonica (Acts 17:2,3) is elaborated in 1 Thessalonians and follows the basic pattern of a sermon delivered earlier in the synagogue in Pisidian Antioch. Allen considers this preaching to be typical of Paul's preaching to Jews. It has three primary parts, five elements, and four characteristics.

Three major aspects: (1) Paul rehearses the course of Jewish history. (2) He recounts certain basic truths concerning Christ including his rejection by the Jews. (3) He concludes with an offer of pardon and a stern warning to the unrepentant and unbelieving.

Five "elements": (1) An appeal to the past—a common bond is established on the basis of a common belief system. (2) A statement of facts easily grasped, largely story, and of life-and-death significance. (3) Thoughtful answers to objections raised by Jewish scholars—evidences, testimonies of trustworthy men, agreements with older ideas already accepted by the people. (4) An appeal to spiritual needs—cravings for pardon, peace, and assurance. (5) A grave warning—the rejection of God's message and offer of pardon is indeed perilous.

Four "characteristics": (1) Sympathy with hearers and a recognition of all that is good in them. (2) An open acknowledgment of difficulties and unpalatable truths connected with believing in Christ. (3) Respect for his hearers and an appeal to the highest faculties of mankind. (4) Confidence in the truth of the message and its power to meet man's needs.

Paul's Preaching to Adherents of Other Religions

Overall, Allen gives more attention to Paul's speeches to "heathen" Gentiles than to Paul's preachments to Jews. This is not true with respect to Paul's speeches in Lystra and Athens, however, probably because Allen considers those speeches to have been given under exceptional circumstances and therefore not really typical. Paul's message at Lystra was specifically intended to prove that the apostles were not gods. His discourse on Mars Hill was more philosophical but otherwise quite similar to his speech in Lystra. Both speeches demonstrate Paul's ability to adapt to his audience and the prevailing circumstances, but in Allen's view neither is fully "apostolic," because neither contains much "Gospel" and in apostolic preaching "the supreme subject is 'the Cross, Repentance, and Faith.'"[2]

Allen is of the opinion that, in order to characterize Paul's preaching to Gentiles, we must go to Luke's account of Paul's preaching in Thessalonica (Acts 17:2,3) and, especially, to Paul's own account of his preaching/teaching in that city as summarized in his first letter to the Thessalonians. Because Paul is so careful to remind the Thessalonians concerning what he taught them in a short five-month stay in that city, Allen considers those teachings to be typical of his Gentile preaching generally. In fact, Allen does not hesitate to refer to the sum total of those teachings, not only as "Paul's Gospel" but also as the "full Gospel."

The "supreme subject." (1) The Cross—a stumbling block to Jews and Gentiles alike, the first duty of those who would find salvation was to "embrace the Cross in baptism and, dying to his heathen past, rise into a new life with Christ." (2) Repentance—Paul did not minimize the breach between Christianity and heathenism, the old life and the new life. (3) Faith—Paul so expected his hearers to be moved and so believed his preaching to be "the power of God unto salvation" that these were part and parcel of his gospel presentations.

The "nine elements." The "nine elements" accord perfectly with Paul's preaching in Ephesus as indicated in Acts 20:21 and his letter to the Ephesians. (1) There is one true and living God. (2) Idolatry is sinful and must be forsaken. (3) The wrath of God is ready to be revealed against the heathen for their impurity and against the Jews for rejecting Christ and the gospel. (4) Judgment will come suddenly and unexpectedly. (5) Jesus the Son of God was given over to death, rose from the dead, and is Savior from the wrath of God. (6) The "kingdom of Jesus" is now "set up" and all men invited to enter. (7) Believers expect the Savior to come and receive them. (8) Meanwhile, their life must be pure, useful, and watchful. (9) To that end God has given his Holy Spirit to believers.

The Fundamentals of Paul's "Apostolic Preaching"

Since Allen considers Pauline missionary methodology to be the biblical pattern for Christian missions in general, it is to be expected that he will advance and apply Paul's preaching principles as part of that larger pattern. This he does especially in the latter part of chapter 7—the portion of the chapter that is less rote and more

---

2   Ibid., 67.

expansive. That makes this latter portion more difficult to summarize briefly and objectively. I make the attempt with the caveat that, though the specific points noted are Allen's, the format and style are mine, even though they appear to follow the pattern adopted by Allen in the first part of his chapter.

The Objectives

As is true with respect to Allen's treatment of other aspects of missionary methodology, Allen is very forthright in contrasting the objectives of Paul's apostolic preaching with the preaching objectives of Allen's contemporaries. As Allen understands Paul's objectives, they are reminiscent of those of both early indigenous church theorists as well as Church Growth specialists Donald McGavran and Alan Tippett. All alike contend that, in contrast to some—if not much—modern preaching, Paul's apostolic preaching had at least three very specific objectives in view.

Meaningful decisions. Paul had little or no time for the kind of preaching that did not press for decisions on the part of his hearers. Allen says that Paul "demanded" that his hearers make a choice and act on it.[3] As a matter of fact, if his hearers rejected him and his message, Paul rejected them. He did not stay if they refused to act. Paul concluded that the One who commanded us to go also commanded us to "shake off the dust from our feet."[4]

Total conversion. Whether preaching to Jews or Gentiles, in the synagogues or in the hustings, Paul's objective was to see men and women converted and *soundly* converted. In Allen's words, Paul's desire was for the "total and entire conversion of the inner man," the "absolute doing away of the old and [the] acceptance of the new life."[5]

Church incorporation. For Paul, conversion to Christ was more than getting individuals roundly converted, however. It also involved bringing converts into a proper relationship with each other in the church. Paul's preaching aimed to "gather out of the world the elect of God into the fellowship of His Son."[6]

---

3   Ibid., 74.
4   Ibid., 75.
5   Ibid., 71.
6   Ibid., 70.

The Appeals

Allen finds Paul's preaching to have been both sensitive and demanding. In Paul's approach there is at one and the same time an appreciation and deprecation of the ideas and condition of his hearers—both as to their philosophy and their morals.

The appeal to innate rationality. Unlike the late Carl F. H. Henry, Roland Allen does not think to ground Paul's appeal to heathen rationality in *imago Dei* theology. But he seems comfortable with the idea that all humankind is graced with a kind of innate logicality. He says that Paul made common cause with those confused by polytheism who, nevertheless, seek unity in a world of nature and thought as well as in an intelligent account of the world, its nature and end. Paul did not attack the religion of his hearers except in those respects that their own philosophers did—or would—denounce them.

The appeal to innate morality. Likewise, Allen discovers in Paul's preaching a recognition of moral convictions and ethical sensibilities even among heathen who are downtrodden, hopeless, and oppressed by a sense of sin. Paul appeals to the two highest convictions of men: a sense of individual responsibility and a sense of social communion with their fellows. Allen comments, "In repentance they break with a sinful world; in faith they enter the Church."[7]

The "Substance"

Finally, though Paul's preaching made Christianity appealing, nevertheless "to embrace this new religion was not easy."[8] Paul did not hesitate to preach the whole counsel of God simply because hearers might be disposed to take issue with it.

Preaching Christian doctrine. Paul's preaching was quintessentially doctrinal centered on the person, ministry, and message of Christ but also including the nature and significance of the church. Of much that could be said by way of summary here, it is well to highlight what Allen says about a "full Gospel," "stern doctrine," and a warning of judgment, partly because of the importance Allen attributes to these marks of Paul's preaching and partly because of their pertinence to missionary preaching today.

---

7   Ibid., 77.
8   Ibid., 70.

First, Christ was central to Paul's message—his person and his work but also his word. Christ said that men and women must not only *believe* the gospel, but that they must *repent* and believe the gospel. The alternative is to *perish*. Similarly, Paul not only preached the "Cross" and "Faith"; he also preached "Repentance."[9]

Second, Allen distinguishes between "easy doctrines" such as the love of God and the forgiveness of sins, and what he calls "stern doctrines" such as the wrath of God, the judgment of unbelievers, and the biblical teaching on hell.[10] Allen considers divine judgment and the wrath of God to be intrinsic to the Christian gospel, not ancillary to it and certainly not foreign to it.

Third, Paul did not hesitate to speak of the absolute necessity of true repentance in his effort to win converts. His gospel preaching included a dire warning of the possibility of imminent judgment for anyone who rejected it.

Preaching Christian corporeality. For Allen, participation in the life of the church is more than an objective of missionary preaching, it is an aspect of the apostolic gospel itself. Allen says that it is often taken for granted that Saint Paul's gospel was purely individualistic. But that is not true. Allen insists that, in this respect also and in its very essence, Paul's gospel was calculated to gather believers into a society of which he, Paul—and, of course, by extension Allen himself—are members. Those who repented became one of the brethren, sharing the sacraments. Those who were baptized were admitted to a visible society and liable to attack by its foes. Paul did not shield his converts from the possibility of persecution at the hands of their fellows.

Allen's Critique of the Missionary Preaching of His Generation and Its Applicability Today

Allen's Critique of His Contemporaries

Starting with a critique of the colonialist and paternalistic attitudes of missions in the early twentieth century, *Missionary Methods: St. Paul's or Ours?* is replete with sincere and sometimes scathing criticisms of missionary methods in general. In this essay we are concentrating on Allen's analysis of missionary preaching in the light of the apostolic preaching of the Apostle Paul. If Allen's analysis of Paul's

---

9   Ibid.
10   Ibid., 72.

missionary methods in general—and his preaching method in particular—are essentially valid as I believe they are, then I think it safe to assume that his critique of the missionary preaching methods of his missionary colleagues is essentially valid as well. I do not know it to be a fact, but I strongly suspect that his searching critique of his colleagues contributed significantly to the fact that his book may not have been nearly as well received by his own generation of missionaries as it has been by subsequent generations. Directly and indirectly he accuses his contemporaries of being content with "scattering seeds" rather than pressing for decisions on the one hand, and of having a tendency to want to "Christianize the world" rather than gather believers in the church of Christ on the other. He considers his contemporaries to be misguided when they stay in one place overly long and continue to preach to unrepentant souls. He writes, "We have lost the art of shaking the lap, we have learnt the art of steeling our hearts and shutting up the bowels of compassion against those who cry to us fork the gospel."[11]

As for the three substantive ingredients of Paul's apostolic preaching noted above, Allen's criticism of his contemporaries is particularly pointed. With respect to a "full Gospel," he says that they have neglected to preach repentance. With respect to "stern doctrine," he says, "There is a tendency today to avoid . . . stern doctrine,"[12] adding, "We have lost two prominent elements of Paul's Gospel: the doctrine of judgment at hand, and the doctrine of the wrath of God." This, in turn, leads to a failure to warn those who refuse the gospel of the possibility of imminent judgment and also to the devising of an "easy doctrine of evangelization."[13]

The Applicability of Allen's Critique Today

I would not anticipate many objections when I say that, whether or not Allen's criticism of the missionary preaching of his generation was valid with respect to that generation, it certainly seems valid with respect to ours. That bothers me greatly. But what bothers me even more is that, in reviewing my own preaching and teaching over the years, I discover that I myself have been guilty of avoiding Paul's "stern doctrines" while at the same time encouraging mission teachers, students, and practitioners to emulate the Apostle Paul. If I am a would-be rectifier of the problem, I am also a self-confessed contributor to it.

---

11   Ibid., 57–59.
12   Ibid.
13   Ibid., 72.

At the same time, I am afraid that this neglect is not so much idiosyncratic as it is pandemic. Ask almost any churchgoer including evangelicals how many sermons and references they have heard in the past year on John 3:36 as compared with John 3:16; how many sermons and references on the wrath of God as compared with the love of God; how many mentions of hell as compared with mentions of heaven; how many warnings of judgment as compared with promises of blessing. Lamentably, Allen's criticism at this point is almost unquestionably as true of our generation as it evidently was of his.

That being the case, I would commend to this generation not alone the observations of Roland Allen but also the faith and practice of four notable evangelical preacher-scholars whom I have had the privilege of personally knowing and hearing over the years of my ministry stretching from Allen's time to the present hour.

William Evans on the Cross and God's holiness. William Evans was a Presbyterian, a prolific writer, a professor at Moody Bible Institute in Chicago, and a peerless preacher. He memorized the entire New Testament and was able to quote any reference flawlessly and on a moment's notice. I heard him preach a series of messages at the First Evangelical Church in Chicago in the 1940s and was motivated to buy several of his books in spite of my very meager, limited resources. Evans published one of his early books, *The Great Doctrines of the Bible,* in 1912—the same year that Allen published his *Missionary Methods.* It is from that book that I draw several excerpts illustrative of his position on the matters before us. Evans' position on some of these matters can readily be excerpted from his book on Bible doctrine:

- "The Cross shows how much God loves holiness. The Cross stands for God's holiness even more than His love."[14]
- The righteousness and justice of God are shown in two ways: first in punishing the wicked or retributive justice; second in rewarding the righteous or remunerative justice.[15]
- In Romans 8:7 Paul says that the carnal mind is enmity with God. Reconciliation in its active sense is the removal of that enmity. In its passive sense it may indicate a change of attitude on the part of man toward God.[16]

---

14   William Evans, *The Great Doctrines of the Bible* (Chicago: Moody, 1912), 40.
15   Ibid., 42.
16   Ibid., 72.

- No interpretation holding to the annihilation theory can be maintained by sound exegesis.[17]

Carl F. H. Henry on the pangs of hell and the bliss of heaven. The late Carl F. H. Henry is well known as one of the premier theologians of the twentieth century and champion of Protestant Reformation doctrines. He is also known for advocating a comprehensive worldview inclusive of social and political dimensions. Less known, perhaps, is his profound interest in world mission and evangelism—an interest fueled in part by his wife, Helga, who is the daughter of pioneer Baptist missionaries to Gabon, but also by his dedication to a biblical theology of mission. Two somewhat extended quotations from the works of Henry reflect his commitment to a "full Gospel" in the one case and "stern doctrine" in the other.

> The lifeline of the Protestant Reformation was its rediscovery of the Scriptures—truth that God offers to penitent believers, hopelessly guilty in their strivings to achieve salvation by works, the benefits of Jesus Christ's meditation [sic] on the Cross. God acquits sinners, solely on the ground of a righteousness which He himself provides, a righteousness made known by intelligible Divine revelation and embodied in the life, death and resurrection of Jesus of Nazareth, a righteousness available to sinful men by faith alone.[18]

> There are scholars who consider the eternal punishment of the wicked to be inconsistent with the nature of God. These critics tend to subordinate to divine love all the biblical passages about God's wrath, and ignore the fact that Jesus said even more about the pangs of hell than about the bliss of heaven, and moreover makes their duration coextensive and unending.[19]

Billy Graham on biblical descriptions of hell. In his younger days evangelist Billy Graham spoke more frequently of judgment and even of hell than he has in recent days. By way of example, in one sermon he noted that the concept of hell is not

---

17   Ibid., 260.

18   Carl F. H. Henry, "Justification by Ignorance: A Neo-Protestant Motif?" *Journal of the Evangelical Theological Society* 13, no. 1 (March 1970): 3–14, http://www.etsjets.org/JETS/13-1.

19   Carl F. H. Henry, "God Who Speaks and Shows," Fifteen Theses, Part 3, Book 4, *God, Revelation and Authority* (Waco, TX: Word Books, 1979), 597.

exclusive to the Christian faith. He explained that the ancient Babylonians believed in a "Land of No-Return." The Hebrews wrote about Sheol, or the place of corruption. The Greeks spoke of the "Unseen Land." Classical Buddhism recognizes seven "hot hells." The Hindu *Rig Veda* speaks of the deep abyss reserved for false men and faithless women. Islam recognizes seven hells. He then proceeded to catalogue the Bible's "descriptors of hell"[20]:

- Isaiah 33:11—a place where one's breath is flame.
- Luke 16:2—a place where one begs for a drop of water.
- Luke 16:2—a place where one is tormented with fire.
- Luke 16:23—a place of torment.
- Luke 16:25—a place of memory.
- Luke 16:27—a place where people pray.
- Matthew 8:12—a place of outer darkness.
- Matthew 8:12—a place of weeping.
- Matthew 13:41,42—a furnace of fire.
- Matthew 13:42—a place of wailing.
- Matthew 25:26—a place of everlasting punishment.
- Matthew 25:41—a place prepared for the devil and his angels.
- Psalm 11:16—a horrible tempest.
- Psalm 18:5—a place of sorrows.
- Revelation 14:11—a place of unrest.
- Revelation 16:11—a place of cursing.
- Revelation 20:11,12—a place of filthiness.
- Revelation 20:15—the lake of fire.
- Revelation 21:8—a place where one is tormented with brimstone.

R. C. Sproul on eternal punishment. Founding pastor of St. Mark's Church in Sanford, Florida, R. C. Sproul is uniquely gifted both as a Christian apologist and a Bible expositor. Writing concerning the holiness of God, Sproul notes that the biblical word "holy" has two distinct meanings. The primary meaning is "apartness" or "otherness." It points to the profound difference between God and his creatures. The secondary meaning has to do with his pure and righteous actions. God always

---

20   William Griffin and Ruth Graham Dienert, comp., *The Faithful Christian: An Anthology of Bill Graham* (New York: McCracken, 1994), 183–84.

does what is right; never what is wrong.[21] It is against that backdrop that we can understand Sproul's comments on punishment and hell when he writes:

> Perhaps the most frightening aspect of hell is its eternality. People can endure the greatest agony if they know it will ultimately stop. In hell there is no such hope. The Bible clearly teaches that the punishment is eternal. The same word is used for both eternal life and eternal death. ·

> Punishment implies pain. Mere annihilation, which some have lobbied for, involves no pain. Jonathan Edwards, in preaching on Revelation 6:15–16 said, "Wicked men will hereafter earnestly wish to be turned to nothing and forever cease to be that they may escape the wrath of God."

> Hell, then, is an eternity before the righteous, ever-burning wrath of God, a suffering torment from which there is no escape and no relief. Understanding this is crucial to our drive to appreciate the work of Christ and to preach his gospel.[22]

Conclusion

A consideration of preaching on wrath and judgment almost invariably triggers a recollection of Jonathan Edwards' classic sermon, "Sinners in the Hands of an Angry God." And that, in turn, triggers a rather apathetic silence or, at times, an almost visceral condemnation. The Anglican liberal, David Edwards, for example, suggests that the language of the Lausanne Covenant—"eternal separation from God"—though misguided, is preferable to the traditional phrase "everlasting punishment." The traditional phrase, he goes on to say, "may conjure up the unchristian picture of God as the Eternal Torturer—as in the notorious sermon on 'Sinners in the Hands of an Angry God' preached by Jonathan Edwards in 1741."[23]

We do well to remind ourselves of certain truisms: (1) Jonathan Edwards possessed one of the most brilliant minds America has ever produced; (2) Edwards sacrificed his life to the testing of a vaccine designed to abate the dreaded smallpox

---

21   R. C. Sproul, *Essential Truths of the Christian Faith* (Wheaton: Tyndale House, 1998), 47.
22   Ibid., 286.
23   Ibid., 291–92.

disease; (3) after the passage of over two and one-half centuries, there is a Jonathan Edwards Center at Yale University with satellite centers in Germany, Poland, South Africa, Australia, and the United States (at Trinity Evangelical Divinity School); and (4) concerning Edwards and his preaching, historians can write, "In the 1730s and the early 1740s Edwards' fervid and sometimes brimstony preaching was one of the stimuli to a revival of religion through New England known as 'the Great Awakening' and destined to have its counterparts in other sections of the country as the century advanced."[24]

The United States—indeed the entire Anglo-Saxon world—is in desperate need of another "great awakening." Would the possibility of that happening be enhanced by preaching Allen's "full Gospel," "stern doctrines," and dire warnings? Perhaps, at times, even by preaching that is more akin to Edwards' "fervid and sometimes brimstony preaching"?

Works Cited

Allen, Roland. *Missionary Methods: St. Paul's or Ours?* American edition. Grand Rapids: Ecrdmans, 1961. First published 1912.

Evans, William. *The Great Doctrines of the Bible.* Chicago: Moody, 1912.

Griffin, William, and Ruth Graham Dienert, comp. *The Faithful Christian: An Anthology of Bill Graham.* New York: McCracken, 1994.

Henry, Carl F. H. "God Who Speaks and Shows." Fifteen Theses, Part 3, Book 4. *God, Revelation and Authority.* Waco, TX: Word Books, 1979.

———. "Justification by Ignorance: A Neo-Protestant Motif?" *Journal of the Evangelical Theological Society* 13, no. 1 (March 1970): 3–14. http://www.etsjets.org/JETS/13–1.

"Jonathan Edwards." In *A Treasury of American Literature,* edited by Joe Lee Davis, John T. Frederick, and Frank Luther Mott, 189. New York: Grolier, 1948.

Sproul, R. C. *Essential Truths of the Christian Faith.* Wheaton, IL: Tyndale House, 1998.

---

24   "Jonathan Edwards," in *A Treasury of American Literature,* ed. Joe Lee Davis, John T. Frederick, and Frank Luther Mott (New York: Grolier, 1948), 189.

6

The Rise of Orality in
Modern Missions Practice

ANTHONY CASEY

Introduction

It has been said, "The gospel is being proclaimed now to more people than at any other time in history, yet many of those are not really *hearing* it."[1] Missions and evangelism involve the work of proclaiming the truths about God as revealed through the Scriptures; after all, faith comes by hearing and hearing through the word of Christ. However, the problem is that there are some who are not hearing an understandable and applicable message. The Western approach to missions over the last two hundred years has largely been driven by a literate approach reinforced by Greek philosophical and Enlightenment principles of logic and rationalism. The syllogism came to replace the story in evangelism and many tribes, tongues, and nations have suffered in the wake of what was perceived as the correct way to make disciples of all nations. Many Westerners concluded that God was a God of logic, order, and syllogistic truth, and missionaries ministered in ways that reflected these cultural understandings.

A look to the Scriptures reveals a different picture. Nancy Thomas notes, "God is a storytelling God. Deeper than this, God is the creator of story, and it is in the

---

1   David Claydon, ed., *Making Disciples of Oral Learners* (Lima, NY: Elim, 2005), 3 (italics in original).

context of story that God calls us into mission."[2] God asks sinners to realign their flawed scripts with the scripts of The Story. Modern missions practitioners are beginning to realize that the truths of Scripture can be communicated in a variety of contextualized manners. Even the language used by missions practitioners is changing. Terms like "orality," "Chronological Bible Storying," and "narrative theology" are much more common today in missions journals and books than fifty years ago. This new vocabulary is a result of missionaries encountering what are today described as oral learners. Oral learners largely fall into one of three categories. There are those who cannot read or write, those whose most effective communication and learning format is in accordance with oral formats, and those who prefer to learn and process information by oral rather than written means.[3] Orality is simply the category used to describe issues related to oral learners.

The rise of orality in modern missions practice is a fascinating study. This paper will survey the historical journey of orality in missions praxis. The scope of the paper will primarily cover the modern missions era, from about 1792 onward. It will be shown that missions praxis was driven by Enlightenment principles and that these principles were inadequate to meet the needs encountered in missions among oral peoples.

Historical Approaches to Missions in Oral Contexts

A mind-set commonly found over the past two centuries is that if anything is truly important, it must be in writing, documented, signed, and sealed. According to this mind-set, no merely oral word can carry the kind of legal, scholarly, or administrative authority compared to what a written and published document can.[4] Western missions practitioners historically came from cultures steeped in written history. Graham states that it is difficult to overemphasize the perceived significance of writing. Western social scientists and anthropologists have made written language the major gauge for identifying a civilized culture. Noted authorities in years past have made statements along the lines that purely oral communication is unable to

---

2   Nancy Thomas, "Following the Footprints of God: The Contribution of Narrative to Mission Theology," in *Footprints of God: A Narrative Theology of Mission,* ed. Charles Van Engen, Nancy Thomas, and Robert Gallagher (Monrovia, CA: MARC, 1999), 225.

3   Durk Meijer, "How Shall They Hear?" (presentation at International Orality Network meeting, Plano, TX, February 2008).

4   William A. Graham, *Beyond the Written Word: Oral Aspects of Scripture in the History of Religion* (Cambridge, England: Cambridge University Press, 1987), 9.

provide for progressive cultural development and that only writing can bridge a man from the tribal to the civilized realm.[5]

A great deal of presuppositional bias can be found in the previous statements about the importance of writing. If a written language is indeed the mark of a civilized society, it is no surprise, then, that we find great emphasis historically by Western missionaries on the need for indigenous peoples to learn to read and write. The Age of the Enlightenment has greatly influenced modern missions practice. Beginning in the Middle Ages, the return to the ancient sources, their Greek and Latin languages, and their rational philosophy began influencing the thinking of modern people. Scholars found it difficult to conceive of any other manner of thinking and learning but that of writing and arguing syllogistically. However, not everyone had encountered the Enlightenment.

Missionaries Encounter Oral Peoples

Many peoples of the world were primarily oral. Their cultural heritages were passed down, not in books, but through generations of stories, songs, poems, and proverbs. Theirs were contexts tied to the power of the mind and the ebb and flow of the earth itself. Lunar and solar cycles, monsoon seasons, or animal migrations dictated when things should be done. Education was done by apprenticeship as the younger shadowed the older and learned the skills needed to survive. These primarily oral peoples communicated, passed down historical information, taught, and learned, but their methods were very different than the prevailing Western approach of the nineteenth century.

The missionaries coming to these oral peoples felt one of the first steps for effective evangelism was to build schools so the people could learn to read and write and, therefore, study the Scriptures so as to begin to understand God. Thus, if the villages had any schools, they were usually built by the missionaries. The coming of Western missionaries and colonial rule changed everything in the lives of oral peoples. Those influenced by the Enlightenment said that education was for everyone and was the only way to advance in society. People had to adapt and learn to read, but the changes did not stop there. Oral peoples had to learn a whole new way of life, one not dependent on the seasons, solstices, plowing time, or harvest time. The written calendar introduced days, weeks, months, and years that did not match

---

5   Ibid., 12.

the seasons or agrarian lifestyle. The solar and lunar solstices no longer governed the year; rather, marks on a paper told the people what to do and when to do it.[6] Many Westerners thought that everyone, if properly trained, could become like the Western civilized world. Such drastic change was not so easy, however, and stories like the one below became all too common.

> There was a small tribe, somewhere between Lake Titicaca and La Paz, Bolivia, that was a traditional oral culture. One day in the market, someone gave an elderly grandmother a book and told her it contained many things about salvation and could help her with her illness. The problem: she could not read. Upon return-ing to her community, she sought out someone who could read and they could only tell her that the book was a Bible, a book of the evangelicals.[7]

Preaching and Education Models in Early Missions

Some missionaries were at a loss if they could not use the written word. The two hallmarks of early mission work, preaching and education, became literate affairs. Preaching was often modeled after the style used in Western churches where the sermon was logically argued through syllogisms, propositions, and points until an inevitable conclusion was reached. "Preachers" were men of a certain mold and training, modeled after Western ecclesial structure.[8]

Regarding education, one of the first things many missionaries did was gather materials to build a school so that indigenous peoples could learn to read and write. Rufus Anderson, a man ahead of his time as far as raising up the indigenous

---

6   Paul Hiebert, *Transforming Worldviews: An Anthropological Understanding of How People Change* (Grand Rapids: Baker Academic, 2008), 138–39.

7   Harold R. Thomas, "Conversion Process: James E. Loder in Missiological Perspective," in *Footprints of God: A Narrative Theology of Mission,* ed. Charles Van Engen, Nancy Thomas, and Robert Gallagher (Monrovia, CA: MARC, 1999), 5.

8   See, for example, the letters of Southern Baptist missionary Lottie Moon describing the kind of preaching found in China in the 1880s: Lottie Moon, correspondence with Henry A. Tupper, Lottie Moon Letters, July 17, 1885, http://solomon.3e2a.org/public/ws/lmcorr/www2/lmcorrp/Record?m=20&w=NATIVE%28%27text+ph+is+%27%27preaching%27%27%27%29&upp=0&order=native%28%27corr_date%2FDescend%27%29&r=1; and Lottie Moon, correspondence with Henry A. Tupper, Lottie Moon Letters, October 10, 1878, http://solomon.3e2a.org/public/ws/lmcorr/www2/lmcorrp/Record?upp=0&m=22&w=NATIVE%28%27text+ph+is+%27%27preaching%27%27%27%29&r=1&order=native%28%27corr_date%2FDescend%27%29 /(accessed May 7, 2013). See also Jonathan Edwards, ed., *The Life and Diary of David Brainerd* (repr., Grand Rapids: Baker Book House, 2005), 241; and Ruth Tucker, *From Jerusalem to Irian Jaya* (Grand Rapids: Zondervan, 1983), 92.

church, still succumbed to the antiorality stance of past centuries. He states that without education it is not possible for mission churches to be in any proper way sustained according to the three-self model he developed.[9] Anderson understood a Western form of schooling when he referred to education. Unlearned, illiterate natives are seen as having a

> degraded mental condition of the heathen world, as compared with the field of the apostolic missions. Scarcely a ray of light reaches it from sun, moon, or stars in the intellectual and moral firmament. Mind is vacant, crushed, unthinking, enslaved to animal instincts and passions . . . The common school, therefore, is a necessity among the degraded heathen, to help elevate the converts, and make the village church an effective agency[10]

To Anderson, illiterate pagans had little capacity for knowledge or learning until they came under care of the Western school. He required a shift out of orality in order for a native man to be deemed a successful pastor.

John Nevius followed a similar model where his method of teaching required converts to learn to read, follow traditional Western Bible study methods, and learn to sing Western hymns. Nevius only selected the more advanced church members for his pastoral training classes.[11] The classes are taught to analyze the arguments of such books as Romans. Nevius goes on to explain that only one in twenty Chinese could read and not more than one in a thousand women.[12] Regarding music, Nevius imposed Western hymns and music scales. He notes that "some have learned to read music but have great difficulty with the half tones because the indigenous music scale is vastly different from the Western one."[13] The great oral history, singing, and identity of the Chinese was displaced as the Western model of singing was introduced.

These missionaries were ill equipped to meet the needs of oral-based cultures, largely because the West was so immersed in Enlightenment-driven literacy and logic at that time. Anderson and Nevius, men ahead of their time in calling for the

---

9   Rufus Anderson, *To Advance the Gospel: Selections from the Writings of Rufus Anderson,* ed. R. Pierce Beaver (Grand Rapids: Eerdmans, 1967), 99.

10   Ibid., 99–100.

11   John L. Nevius, *The Planting and Development of Missionary Churches* (Hancock, NH: Monadnock, 2003), 51.

12   Ibid., 52.

13   Ibid.

three-self church unwittingly produced a dependency of a different kind, that of required literacy.

Recognition of the Need for a New Approach to Missions

The Western conclusion is that mission work in the nineteenth and twentieth centuries has been largely successful. After all, have not missionaries translated Scriptures, published books, taught people to read who previously could not, and sent many future indigenous pastors to seminary? Yes, all of these things have been done, but the truth is the "percentage of the [world] population that can be reached with useful knowledge through this kind of communication is still very limited."[14] The majority of the people, specifically the least reached around the world, cannot understand and reproduce a literate approach. Anthropologists and social scientists began studying oral peoples in the mid-twentieth century. The results of these studies revealed that a move from an oral society to a literate society involved a paradigm shift. It is important to recognize that the discovery of literacy as a new paradigm helped missionaries to think more critically about how to approach oral peoples.

Literacy Understood as a New Paradigm

Previously, many people did not understand that moving from orality to literacy was much more involved than simply learning to read. The shift requires an upheaval of society. The printed word disconnects ideas and information from a known source. No longer is the message connected with village leaders who hold real and perceived authority. There is no immediate context for the passing of written information. Writing necessitates interpretation since the speaker is not present to do the task for us. All sorts of problems can now follow. Individualization of ideas arises. Studying and learning can cease to be a communal activity. Again, the Enlightenment has led to many more consequences than first meets the eye.

The end result of a move away from centralized authority can be something like what we see in postmodernism today where a reader response hermeneutic is possible. People feel free to develop meanings isolated from the writer's intent, as

---

14   Herbert Klem, *Oral Communication of the Scriptures: Insights from African Oral Art* (Pasadena: William Carey Library, 1982), 34.

they say no one can really know what the original author meant. Knowledge is now personal and reader dependent. The idea of personal, independent knowledge is a dramatic shift from the way oral societies thought of knowledge before the advent of literacy and writing. These potential consequences must be considered and prepared for if one intends to introduce writing into a society for the first time. Poor consideration of these consequences has resulted in the following problems as missionaries began to realize the implications of a literate society.

Consequences of the Literate Approach

A result of the literate approach is that some native pastors are so conditioned to master Western theology that they have little to offer in the way of a native and original understanding of the Scriptures.[15] Some pastors can only regurgitate what they read in Western textbooks and have trouble transferring their knowledge to the real world when they return to their home villages, if they choose to return after receiving their education. Whatever the training and education, the truth is the vast majority of pastors and their people have simply chosen to remain in the sphere of oral communication. They remain a primarily oral culture but now are caught in the middle between the old way and the new. They have difficulty learning the Bible because the primary teaching method involves written communication.[16] In some cases, people began to believe that the ability to be able to read the Bible was a necessary requirement for salvation.[17] Some mission schools had become so connected with literacy that some oral cultures began rejecting Christianity, not because of the gospel, but because they were rejecting literacy.[18]

Missionaries who require emerging leaders to learn to read and use literacy methods greatly distort social organization and community leadership in many oral-based societies. Recognized leaders in the community are usually older folks who are not the first to learn to read and be discipled. It is often the younger people that learn these skills and are more likely to be put into leadership roles, against the norms of the society. The introduction of literacy, in an attempt to produce capable indigenous leadership, actually disrupts the social structure of the village. Younger, trained people often do not know the oral tradition of the tribe as well

---

15 Stephen Neill, *A History of Christian Missions,* 2nd ed. (London: Penguin Group, 1990), 399.
16 Klem, *Oral Communication,* 35.
17 Ibid., 37.
18 Ibid., 39.

and are ill equipped to lead the people. The decades of literacy training have not produced the hoped-for fruits.

Uncovering the Oral Reality of the Twenty-first Century

Even after two hundred years of literacy-based missions, over 4 billion people, two-thirds of the world's population, are still oral communicators today. In the face of the oral reality, 90 percent of the world's Christian workers still present the gospel using a highly literate communication style.[19] Western theology is still influenced by rationality and often assumes that God is a logical, linear, rational, analytical, and propositional being, and they read their Bibles and teach Scripture accordingly.[20]

Contextualization is a buzzword in missions today, but the orality component is often missing. Lingenfelter defines contextualization as recognizing the need to frame the gospel in language and communication forms appropriate and meaningful to the local cultures.[21] His language aims at orality issues—those of language and communication forms. Communication forms, as seen above, are integral to the structure of many oral cultures. Who gives the message often carries more weight than the actual content of the message. Westerners have realized since about 1950 that many cultures are relational cultures, opposite of the individuality often found in the United States and England. In a primarily oral and relational culture, there is high dependence on one another because all information is stored within the people themselves. Since oral communication is highly relational, a different approach to communicating must be recognized.

Oral communication takes place in specific contexts. Oral communications convey paramessages such as tone, gesture, expression, spatial distance—all things that "speak" as clearly as words do. Proverbs, parables, and sayings do not just supplement logical argument as in a Western sermon, they are the very storehouses that contain knowledge in that society.[22] The oral approach to missions is a totally different paradigm than the old literacy approach. Missionaries, their agencies, and their training institutions are recognizing the failure of a totally literate approach.

---

19   Claydon, *Making Disciples*, 3.
20   Tom Steffen, *Reconnecting God's Story to Ministry: Cross-cultural Storytelling at Home and Abroad* (Waynesboro, GA: Authentic Media, 2005), 1.
21   Sherwood Lingenfelter, *Transforming Culture: A Challenge for Christian Mission* (Grand Rapids: Baker Books, 1992), 15.
22   Hiebert, *Transforming Worldviews*, 116.

A More Fully Oral Contemporary Methodology

A primary step toward an oral methodology must be avoiding the misguided notion that the greatest need is first for literacy for all people.[23] The greatest need is in fact planting contextualized churches that are able to raise up indigenous leadership that can then reproduce themselves in other church plants. Oral cultures are not primitive or incapable of great advances in learning. Orality does not mean the people do not value knowledge. What is knowledge if it is not something that can be applied and transferred to others? The oral paradigm is capable of the task of church planting, evangelism, and discipleship. In fact, there are many advantages in keeping with the society's preference for oral communication.

Advantages of Keeping the Oral Preference in Contemporary Practice

Many oral peoples dance, sing, and share cultural proverbs as they work the fields. These times of oral communication are vital to reinforce the societal worldview and strengthen the cultural identity of the people. Robbing the people of the oral tradition by replacing everything with the written word will begin to drive apart generations within the population.[24] Social structures within oral cultures are already in place, and missionaries are beginning to realize the importance of witnessing to the village leaders before the children. It is vital to at least get the elders' blessing before beginning any kind of work among the village, but it is better still to include the elders in the process themselves. Keeping with the structure of oral societies aids in keeping cohesion between the cultural leadership and the training methods used by missionaries.

Another important point to consider is that many peoples take pride in their ability to recall vast amounts of history from the oral tradition. Several cultures have great "sing-offs" where youths enter manhood through prolonged recitation of the cultural history of the people or by singing great songs that transition them into tribal leadership.[25] Missionaries must realize the importance of such cultural rites of passage and their reliance on the oral tradition. Even if the missionaries wrote down all of the oral tradition, the verbal recitation of it must continue as

---

23   The issue of literacy and its introduction to oral societies will be addressed later in this chapter.
24   Klem, *Oral Communication*, 100.
25   Bruce Olson, *Bruchko* (Lake Mary, FL: Charisma House, 1995), 144–45.

a key cultural element in the tribe. The oral tradition factors into all fibers of the social structure within the culture. Missionaries are taking this tradition into account and far less needless alienation is happening with the coming of the gospel. Many agencies are making contributions to the orality movement, including my own denomination's International Mission Board.

The IMB's Contribution to the Orality Movement[26]

The International Mission Board (IMB) of the Southern Baptist Convention has played a vital role in the development of orality principles in worldwide missions. Many of the discoveries and advancements in missions among oral cultures can be traced back to a select few missionaries who served with the IMB. The movement loosely began in the 1960s when Trevor McIlwain of New Tribes Mission began to see the limitations of the traditional evangelism model among his people in the Philippines. McIlwain developed what was known as Chronological Bible Teaching as a way to teach a biblical worldview to those from animistic backgrounds. The chronological order first taught the people who God was, how the world was created, then who man is, what sin is, what kind of sacrifice is needed to pay for sins, and how Jesus is that ultimate sacrifice. McIlwain's approach was a hybrid of sorts between what is today known as Chronological Bible Storying (CBS) and traditional Bible instruction.

Around the same time, IMB missionary Jim Slack was also working in the Philippines. Slack began to compare notes with McIlwain in hopes to better reach and teach the oral peoples he was working with. Slack was not concerned that his people become literate. He was satisfied to allow them to continue functioning as an oral culture, so he expanded McIlwain's Chronological Bible Teaching and began to solely use scriptural stories to communicate the gospel and disciple believers. Slack and McIlwain worked together to understand as much about oral cultures as they could. Slack was an excellent researcher and took voluminous notes, which later became the basis for much development and teaching on CBS.

Another IMB missionary, J. O. Terry, was head of the media ministry in Asia in the 1960s. Media ministry in other parts of the world focused on producing promotional videos, evangelistic videos, and other visually enhanced tools, but

---

26   Material for this section taken from Hayward Armstrong, interview by author, Louisville, KY, November 22, 2010.

Terry was mainly interested in how he could use media to reach oral learners. He had a fascination with what he learned from Slack's experiments with storying as teaching. Terry began researching storying and contributed his findings to those of Slack and McIlwain.

In the 1980s Jim Slack had moved to Richmond, Virginia, to become the IMB's leading researcher. Here he began reading everything he could about oral peoples and their methods of learning. Slack's research led to the IMB beginning to experiment more heavily with CBS among its missionaries in oral cultures. Slack met another man, Grant Lovejoy, a professor of preaching at Southwestern Baptist Theological Seminary, in 1995. Lovejoy's specialty was in narrative preaching, and he began working with Slack and Terry as their theological consultant with CBS. Lovejoy helped to develop storying as a means for leadership training and became involved with several oral seminary projects in Africa.

CBS became a movement within the IMB in the mid to late 1990s as Slack, Terry, and Lovejoy began training IMB personnel more extensively in orality and CBS. Hayward Armstrong had just returned from two decades of missionary work in South America, much of it working in leadership training of primary oral peoples. Jim Slack brought all of his CBS research to Armstrong and asked if he might condense it into a training manual for IMB personnel. The result was a published CBS training manual[27] and several CBS training courses done through the International Centre for Excellence in Leadership at the IMB training center in Richmond.

Avery Willis, a name often associated with CBS, was actually more responsible for promotion than content. Willis was an IMB missionary in Indonesia in the 1970s. He left the field to produce the *MasterLife* discipleship series, for which he is best known. Willis heard about the success of CBS in Asia and asked Slack and others to produce a written and recorded set of the stories they used on the field. *Following Jesus: Making Disciples of Oral Learners* is the fruit of their collective labor. The audio set contains hundreds of Bible stories told by Slack, Lovejoy, Terry, and Mark Snowden.

Willis was at the Lausanne Forum for World Evangelization in 2004 and met with several leaders of major missions agencies. Willis shared what he knew of the IMB's use of CBS with leaders from Campus Crusade, Wycliffe Bible Translators, and Youth With A Mission. The One Story partnership developed with all four

---

27   Hayward Armstrong, *Tell the Story: A Primer on Chronological Bible Storying* (Rockville, VA: International Centre for Excellence in Leadership, 2003).

agencies working together to plant reproducible churches among oral peoples. Willis was the catalyst for much of that partnership, though he contributed little actually having to do with CBS itself.

Today the IMB vigorously promotes the use of CBS among its missionaries. Storying and orality are taught to new missionaries at the Field Personnel Orientation in Richmond. Once on the field, the missionaries receive further training in context from their field supervisors and through regional training conferences. In addition, several classes on CBS are made available to the missionaries through the training center whenever they have time to take them. The IMB was at the forefront of the present orality movement, contributing many resources, both financially and experientially. Many agencies have taken the IMB's lead and are promoting CBS and more contextualized approaches to oral peoples. The next section will examine several practical ways one might use to minister among an oral people.

Practical Ways to Minister in an Oral Culture

The progression of learning more about oral cultures coupled with advances in missions strategy has resulted in a conglomeration of orality-based methodologies. Many of these methods are hybrids or adaptations of previous literate approaches. It is difficult, if not impossible, for someone steeped in literacy to fully understand and function in an oral culture. That being said, great strides can be made. Below are some practical ways one can begin to minister in an oral culture.

Utilize Narrative Theology over Systematic Theology

Western missionaries are familiar with systematic theology textbooks. These books seek to take a topic, gather all relevant Scripture relating to that topic, and provide a logical explanation of the topic. The problem with this approach for oral learners is that the theology is divorced from its biblical context. Systematic theology tends to be abstract and philosophical rather than concrete and immediately applicable. One must connect a series of abstract thoughts in order to come to an application of the material. A better approach for oral learners is theology tied to story or narrative.

Narrative theology is described as "discourse about God in the setting of a story. It combines form (narrative) with content (theology) in a creative way that seeks to understand God and God's dealings with [people]… in terms of stories."[28] The theology is in the story rather than abstracted from the story. Much of Scripture is already in narrative format. God calls man to himself and reveals his salvation plan through narrative. The stories of the Creation, the Fall, Cain and Abel, Noah, Abraham and Isaac, the Exodus, Hosea, and on to the recorded stories about Jesus show that much of what is understood about God is understood through story. These stories are a powerful and useful tool for evangelism and discipleship among oral peoples, as the next section will show.

Utilize Chronological Bible Storying

Proper Bible storying involves much more than simply picking a story from the Scriptures and telling it to someone. The first step is to research the worldview of the target people.[29] Missiologist Paul Hiebert defines worldview as the "fundamental cognitive, affective, and evaluative presuppositions a group of people make about the nature of things, and which they use to order their lives."[30] Worldviews seek to explain such things as: if there is a God, where humans come from, what causes sickness, how to cure sickness, what is food, who gets the food, what happens when people die, and what the afterlife is like. Understanding the target culture's worldview helps the missionary know what the people believe about foundational things in life. Worldviews are made up of stories. The worldview stories are the contact point that CBS works with so well. The key is to begin replacing the culture's faulty worldview stories with the truth about God and man from biblical stories.

Most CBS story sets begin with a story describing the world before it was created. Next, God is introduced as the creator and so on. There will always be certain foundational stories used in every culture, but many of the stories will be selected because of their relevance to particular issues the missionary discovers through worldview research. If drunkenness is a problem, the story of Lot and his two daughters may be told. Many cultures worship idols of various sorts. There are many stories from Isaiah concerning idol worship and God's judgment of it. Over time the biblical stories will construct a new worldview that is shaped by the Scripture.

---

28   Nancy Thomas, *Footprints of God*, 226.
29   *Armstrong, Tell the Story*, 33.
30   Hiebert, *Transforming Worldviews*, 15.

Stories should be told chronologically so that the people first receive a biblical picture of God, man, sin, sacrifice, and the hoped-for Savior so that when the gospel is shared, Jesus and his sacrifice make sense in light of the stories that have come before. Each story should be short and without added commentary so that the people will be able to remember the story and keep it as close to biblical accuracy as possible. Each story session should include a time of thorough examination, with the missionary asking someone to retell the story to check for accuracy.[31] Application questions can be asked and general questions answered. The missionary must be careful to not begin with an oral-based story but then follow up with logical and linear questions. The goal is for each person in attendance to be able to understand, remember, and reproduce the story so that, eventually, an oral Bible of sorts is developed in the memories of the people.

CBS is useful for evangelistic purposes and also for discipleship purposes. For evangelism, CBS typically includes a "creation to cross" story set of a dozen to up to one hundred or more biblical stories. Again, these stories lay the foundation for the gospel, replace the faulty worldview of the target people, and provide an oral Bible for people who do not or cannot read. CBS works well with the stories that are already present in Scripture such as Abraham's call or David's sin with Bathsheba. Storying can work with more didactic passages of Scripture, but the Scripture must be significantly altered to fit a story format. The next section will examine a method useful for teaching the more didactic and logical portions of Scripture, especially the New Testament.

Utilize Orality-based Doctrinal Instruction

CBS can provide oral peoples with hundreds of biblical stories and set much theology in a concrete context. But what is one to do with issues like the Trinity or other doctrinal issues that do not easily fit into story form? What if Mormons or Jehovah's Witnesses come along and teach about the Trinity in a subtly different way than what is orthodox? How does one teach through a primarily didactic book of the Bible like James? Such complex issues can be best handled by what is described as patterned drilling. This drilling can be done as a stand-alone exercise or it can be combined with CBS for a more focused time on specific verses and doctrinal issues.[32] The

---

31   David Sills, *Reaching and Teaching: A Call to Great Commission Obedience* (Chicago: Moody, 2010), 185.

32   Daniel Sheard, *An Orality Primer for Missionaries* (self-published, 2007), 37.

drills can be repetitions of exact scriptural phrases or short rhythmic statements about a doctrine. The repetition of words aids the oral learner to capture the concept and the key verses at once. The greatest difficulty will be for the teacher himself, as patterned repetition is uncomfortable and monotonous for literate people.[33]

Closely associated with patterned drilling is the idea to place theology and doctrinal issues in the context of a song or poem. Herbert Klem translated the entire book of Hebrews into a style of Yoruba song that could be sung. Klem then performed an experiment by teaching the book to those who could read by normal literate methods. Klem found that those who studied Hebrews only using songs learned as much as those who studied it using books.[34] Many cultures have specific song styles that are suited for spiritual truths, so the missionary would be wise to discover them and their uses and utilize them for teaching Scripture, especially doctrines that do not fit the storying model well. The orality-based doctrinal instruction method is ideal for discipleship and leadership training so that indigenous believers might be able to soundly defend their faith against incoming heretics. The discipleship method itself must also be contextualized into an orality-based format, as the next section will examine.

Utilize Apprenticing-style Discipleship

Nationals need to be the primary trainers of their own people for effective church planting. The problem is, many missionaries who train first-generation national believers attempt to do discipleship in a Western, institutionalized manner that is not transferable to the new believer's own people. There is a disconnect between the trained nationals and the local church.[35] This move towards institutionalized training is a recent occurrence. Hundreds of years ago, if one were training to become a blacksmith, one would not receive the training in a classroom setting. An experienced blacksmith would take the trainee under his care and show him the ropes. The apprentice model is still the method many oral cultures are using today to teach younger generations how to hunt, fish, weave, and do business. Missionary Tom Julien suggests that missionaries would be wise to teach nationals the

---

33   Ibid., 42.
34   David Hesselgrave, *Communicating Christ Cross-culturally: An Introduction to Missionary Communication*, 2nd ed. (Grand Rapids: Zondervan, 1991), 539.
35   Darrell L. Whiteman, "Integral Training Today for Cross-cultural Mission," *Missiology* 36, no. 1 (January 2008): 8.

fundamentals of the faith and ministry in a similar style. Julien describes a series of "seed truths" that are best taught in a personal mentoring approach.[36] This shadowing learning style provides not only teaching but also encouragement and character development, all in the familiar relational context oral cultures prefer. The final component of this section seeks to deal with whether to move towards literacy or allow the target people to remain a solely oral culture.

Consider Whether Oral Cultures Should Remain Oral

It only seems natural that it be beneficial to teach all peoples to read and write. The missionaries have the power to do a great service for the locals. If the people can read and write, they can get better educations, better jobs, and create better conditions for their communities. The people will be able to have a voice in government and protect themselves from exploitation. These advantages to literacy sound wonderful. The reality is, however, that the move to literacy does not always go smoothly and is not as beneficial as one might initially think. Many Westerners would never think to consider that oral peoples would not want to become literate.[37] There are two issues in favor of allowing oral peoples to remain oral—lack of effectiveness and loss of indigenous leadership structures.

Herbert Klem reports that after more than one hundred years of intensive literacy training in Africa, the number of people who can or will read to gain information is very small. In many areas illiteracy is as high as 95 percent.[38] As stated earlier in this chapter, oral peoples have everything they need to function well in society. Literacy is not always needed and in many cases goes completely against the grain of all they have ever known. Oral peoples have the ability to retain their entire cultural heritage in the form of songs, stories, and poetry. They have no need to write it down. Forcing literacy on such people, as helpful and necessary as it may seem, is not always productive.

The second case against introduced literacy is the potential for loss of indigenous leadership. This topic has already been explored earlier in this chapter. In summary, most oral cultures rely on village elders to be the gatekeepers of all cultural knowledge, rules, and heritage. When literacy is introduced, the elders are often not the

---

36   Tom Julien, "Training Leaders by Planting Seed Truths," *Evangelical Missions Quarterly* 44, no. 3 (October 2008): 509.

37   Sills, *Reaching and Teaching*, 181.

38   Klem, *Oral Communication*, xvii.

first to respond; the younger members of the culture are. If literate approaches to discipleship and leadership training are used, only those who can read can become leaders. If only younger people can read and they are placed in leadership positions in the church, the whole societal leadership structure is turned on its head. Societal upheaval is not conducive to a contextualized and reproducing church.

So should oral peoples be allowed to remain oral? Does an oral Bible suffice indefinitely? Some would say yes. The author's opinion is that the first generation of believers should be allowed to remain fully oral. Leadership training must be in an oral format, even if some of the leaders can read. Literacy should not be seen as a requirement for any believer or church function. Orality should be the primary method for all instruction. Once the first band of indigenous leadership is set up, if there is a desire among the people, literacy can begin to be taught. Still, it should not be used to supplant the oral structure and teaching methods. At some point, preferably earlier rather than later, missionaries and believers should begin work together on a written translation of the Scriptures. A written copy will help ensure the oral tradition remains faithful to the Word of God over time. Even though a written Scripture is produced, oral teaching and training should still be the primary method.

David Hesselgrave suggests there is a place for literacy in an oral culture. He says the best method is to combine at least one indigenous instructional approach, CBS for example, with some literacy approach, written Scripture memorization cards for example. An oral and literate approach can be valid and helpful when used together wisely.[39] Hesselgrave's idea has merit as long as local leaders are not *required* to be literate in order to be discipled or lead the church. In summary, literacy is not the magical solution for fixing problems or helping the church grow in oral cultures. In fact, its introduction has the potential to cause more harm than good. Westerners need to have full faith that oral peoples already have everything they need to be effective church planters and leaders. It is the Westerner who needs to grow and expand his horizon to benefit from the oral world.

Conclusion

Seventy percent of the world's population prefers an oral approach to learning. Modern missions has historically failed to recognize the unique needs of oral learners, largely because, until recently, most missionaries were Westerners driven

---

39   Hesselgrave, *Communicating Christ*, 540.

by Enlightenment principles of education and literacy. The historical approach to missions reached many people with the gospel, but it failed to reach them where they were as oral peoples. Sociological and anthropological field research began revealing the shortcomings of the literate approach to missions that had existed for nearly two hundred years. New research enabled a new approach to missions as Jim Slack and others pioneered the way for more fully oral methodologies like Chronological Bible Storying. Today many new approaches to missions among oral peoples exist. Westerners are beginning to realize their arrogance in equating literacy with the ability to achieve and advance in society. More and more indigenous believers are being equipped to reach their own people with methods that are already familiar to them.

The discipline of orality is still a relatively new field, however. There is much to be learned. In the next generation or two we will be able to measure more carefully the results of introducing literacy to oral cultures, of allowing oral cultures to remain oral, and to shed more light on whether it is necessary to have a written translation of the Scriptures in every language. Many of these insights will come from the indigenous believers in oral cultures themselves. People have been hearing the gospel for generations, but it is time more of them are allowed to *hear* it in a way that they can understand, remember, and reproduce. Orality is one of the major issues in current missions practice. We must let history be our teacher, learning from the rise of orality in modern missions practice, and move forward to the ultimate oral reality—that of people from every tribe, tongue, and nation confessing that Jesus Christ is Lord of all.

Works Cited

Anderson, Rufus. *To Advance the Gospel: Selections from the Writings of Rufus Anderson.* Edited by R. Pierce Beaver. Grand Rapids: Eerdmans, 1967.

Armstrong, Hayward. Interview by author. Louisville, KY. November 22, 2010.

———. *Tell the Story: A Primer on Chronological Bible Storying.* Rockville, VA: International Centre for Excellence in Leadership, 2003.

Brainerd, David. *The Life and Diary of David Brainerd.* Edited by Jonathan Edwards. Reprint, Grand Rapids: Baker Books, 2005.

Claydon, David, ed. *Making Disciples of Oral Learners.* Lima, NY: Elim, 2005.

Graham, William A. *Beyond the Written Word: Oral Aspects of Scripture in the History of Religion.* Cambridge, England: Cambridge University Press, 1987.

Hesselgrave, David. *Communicating Christ Cross-culturally: An Introduction to Missionary Communication.* 2nd ed. Grand Rapids: Zondervan, 1991.

Hiebert, Paul. *Transforming Worldviews: An Anthropological Understanding of How People Change.* Grand Rapids: Baker Academic, 2008.

Julien, Tom. "Training Leaders by Planting Seed Truths." *Evangelical Missions Quarterly* 44, no. 3. (October 2008): 508–11.

Klem, Herbert. *Oral Communication of the Scriptures: Insights from African Oral Art.* Pasadena: William Carey Library, 1982.

Lingenfelter, Sherwood. *Transforming Culture: A Challenge for Christian Mission.* Grand Rapids: Baker Books, 1992.

Meijer, Durk. "How Shall They Hear?" Presentation at International Orality Network meeting. Plano, TX. February 2008.

Moon, Lottie. Correspondence with Henry A. Tupper. Lottie Moon Letters. October 10, 1878. Accessed November 18, 2010. http://solomon.3e2a.org/public/ws/lmcorr/www2/lmcorrp/Record?upp=0&m=22&w=NATIVE%28%27text+ph+is+%27%27preaching%27%27%27%29&r=1&order=native%28%27corr_date%2FDescend%27%29.

————. Correspondence with Henry A. Tupper. July 17, 1885. Accessed November 18, 2010. http://solomon.3e2a.org/public/ws/lmcorr/www2/lmcorrp/Record?m=20&w=NATIVE%28%27text+ph+is+%27%27preaching%27%27%27%29&upp=0&order=native%28%27corr_date%2FDescend%27%29&r=1.

Neill, Stephen. *A History of Christian Missions.* 2nd ed. London: Penguin Group, 1990.

Nevius, John L. *The Planting and Development of Missionary Churches.* Hancock, NH: Monadnock, 2003.

Olson, Bruce. *Bruchko.* Lake Mary, FL: Charisma House, 1995.

Sheard, Daniel. *An Orality Primer for Missionaries.* Self-published, 2007.Sills, David. *Reaching and Teaching: A Call to Great Commission Obedience.* Chicago: Moody, 2010.

Steffen, Tom. *Reconnecting God's Story to Ministry: Cross-cultural Storytelling at Home and Abroad.* Waynesboro, GA: Authentic Media, 2005.

Thomas, Harold R. "Conversion Process: James E. Loder in Missiological Perspective." In *Footprints of God: A Narrative Theology of Mission,* edited by Charles Van Engen, Nancy Thomas, and Robert Gallagher, 5–18. Monrovia, CA: MARC, 1999.

Thomas, Nancy. "Following the Footprints of God: The Contribution of Narrative to Mission Theology." In *Footprints of God: A Narrative Theology of Mission,* edited by Charles Van Engen, Nancy Thomas, and Robert Gallagher, 225–35. Monrovia, CA: MARC, 1999.

Tucker, Ruth. *From Jerusalem to Irian Jaya.* Grand Rapids: Zondervan, 1983.

Whiteman, Darrell L. "Integral Training Today for Cross-cultural Mission." *Missiology* 36, no. 1 (January 2008): 5–16.

7

Missionaries in Our Own Backyard: The Canadian Context

JOEL THIESSEN

Introduction

The Christian community around the world, particularly in evangelical settings, continues to grapple with effective missionary methods that are scripturally and theologically sound, yet sensitive to changing world realities. My goal is to draw on sociological theory and empirical research to help us think about being missionaries in our own Canadian backyard; to think about how we might recalibrate our approach to "making disciples" in the Canadian context where values of multiculturalism, diversity, pluralism, and tolerance have facilitated a seismic shift in the Canadian religious landscape over the past fifty years.

In any Introduction to Sociology course, students learn that one of the benefits of the sociological perspective is it helps us to assess "common sense" ideas that are not always true. In a previous speaking engagement with a group of missiologists, I was asked to address the relationship between immigration from non-Western countries, multiculturalism, and Christianity in Canada. Before, during, and after that presentation, I repeatedly confronted several assumptions in academic, church, and public settings surrounding the state of religion in Canada due to the de-Europeanization of immigration patterns. These assumptions range from (1) religious diversity is the new Canadian reality, to (2) Christianity is eroding in the face of changing immigration patterns from the Southern and Eastern regions of the world, to (3) Canadian congregations are increasingly multiracial. In turn, each assumption is explicitly or implicitly accompanied by a series of implications for fulfilling the Great Commission in Canada—above all, that immigrants could be a likely source of missionary efforts in Canada in the twenty-first century. In some respects these assertions are "common sense" to many, yet recent demographic information and in-depth studies reveal that these three assumptions are partially true, but not to the degree that some assume. Remaining faithful to foundational sociological principles to distill fact from fiction, I will devote the first part of this paper to delineate how and why immigration is not the key variable to consider for missionary efforts in Canada.

If immigration is not as important a variable to consider for missionary efforts in Canada, then how should we think of Canada as a mission field, what variable(s) ought we to pay attention to, and what does it mean to be a missionary in Canada today? Without denying the value of "sending" missionaries from Canada to other countries or of directing missionary efforts within Canadian borders toward immigrants, I will argue that missionary efforts should mainly focus on the large percentage of the Canadian population who either attends church once a year (43 percent), who never attend religious services (23 percent), or who claim to have "no religion" (16 percent—the fastest growing "religious" group in Canada, especially among immigrants). In the not-too-distant future, immigrants may lead such an initiative to reach this segment of the Canadian population.[1] In turn I offer several practical considerations for missionary activity in Canada that integrates sociological theory and empirical data with Scripture and theology.

Immigration and Christianity in Canada

With 250,000 immigrants coming to Canada each year, increasingly from non-Western countries, the face of religion, and Christianity specifically, in Canada has changed. But what does that change entail? Many in the general public and in church settings typically adopt one of the following three interpretations. First, Canada is

---

1   Reginald Bibby, *Beyond the Gods and Back: Religion's Demise and Rise and Why It Matters* (Lethbridge, Canada: Project Canada Books, 2011), 46–47.

becoming religiously diverse as people bring their non-Christian religions with them to Canada. Second, Canada is growing evermore secular as non-Christians immigrate to Canada. Third, Christian congregations are becoming multicultural, and multiracial to be precise, institutions like many other Canadian social institutions. Yet which if any of these understandings are correct, and how might this discussion contribute to our approach to missionary methods in Canada?

Beginning with the first interpretation, there is some truth to the notion that religious diversity is the new Canadian norm, given the changing immigration flow into Canada from non-European nations. 2001 Canadian census data reveals that 6 percent of the Canadian population identifies with a non-Christian religious tradition,[2] and estimates suggest that by 2031 this figure could climb to 13–15 percent.[3] When combined, just over 30 percent of immigrants to Canada in the 1990s identified with a non-Christian religious tradition, led by 15 percent of all immigrants identifying as Muslim.[4] Without denying members' realities in these religious traditions, the fact remains that most Canadians do not identify with a non-Christian religious tradition, and over two-thirds of immigrants identify with something other than a non-Christian religion. I am not dismissing the fact of religious diversity in Canada or the separate and relevant question about how Christians might respond to religious diversity and non-Christian religious groups, but religious diversity is not as widespread in Canada as many assume.

With respect to the second assumption that immigration facilitates a post-Christian and secular Canadian society, there are two points to consider. On one hand, fewer immigrants identify themselves as Christian today than fifty years ago, but Christianity, particularly in Roman Catholic and evangelical Protestant settings, remains the leading religious identifier among immigrants today.[5] During the 1990s, Statistics Canada data shows that 23 percent of immigrants identify as Ro-

---

2   Statistics Canada, *2001 Census: Analysis Series; Religions in Canada* (Ottawa: Statistics Canada, 2003), http://www12.statcan.ca/english/census01/products/analytic/companion/rel/pdf/96F0030XIE2001015.pdf (accessed March 3, 2010), 18.

3   Éric Caron Malenfant, André Lebel, and Laurent Martel, *Projections of the Diversity of the Canadian Population: 2006–2031* (Ottawa: Statistics Canada, 2010), http://www.statcan.gc.ca/pub/91–551-x/91–551-x2010001-eng.pdf (accessed November 29, 2011), 25.

4   Statistics Canada, *2001 Census*, 19.

5   See, for example, Peter Beyer, "From Far and Wide: Canadian Religious and Cultural Diversity in Global/Local Context," in *Religion and Diversity in Canada*, ed. Lori Beaman and Peter Beyer (Boston: Brill, 2008), 9–39; Bibby, *Beyond the Gods*; Kurt Bowen, *Christians in a Secular World: The Canadian Experience* (Montreal: McGill-Queen's University Press, 2004), 55–59; Paul Bramadat and David Seljak, eds., *Christianity and Ethnicity in Canada* (Toronto: University of Toronto Press, 2008); and Philip Jenkins, *The Next Christendom: The Coming of Global Christianity* (New York: Oxford, 2002).

man Catholic and 11 percent identify as Protestant.[6] Mining the data further, 14 percent of all Roman Catholics in Canada today were born outside of Canada, and over 61 percent of those immigrants came to Canada since 1971. Researchers agree that Roman Catholic identification and involvement across Canada would likely be much lower without immigration from the global South and East.[7] Among Canadian evangelicals, over 17 percent are foreign-born, and nearly 71 percent of those immigrants came to Canada since 1971.[8] In fact, evangelical numerical growth is not attributable to conversion as much as it is to immigration, particularly among the Chinese community in Toronto and Vancouver.[9] Taken together, some may suggest that Christianity in Canada is reaping the rewards of its foreign mission movement during the eighteenth and nineteenth centuries. As Bramadat and Seljak remind us, "To meet a first- or second-generation Canadian of African descent who is in fact a third-, fourth-, or twenty-fifth-generation Christian, reminds us of the global reach of Christianity."[10]

On the other hand, following Christians, the second largest individual "religious" group among immigrants are those who have no religion (21 percent of immigrants). This is partially attributable to increased immigration from eastern Asia where it is uncommon to distinguish between Chinese culture, for example, and Chinese religion. Since there is no option for "Chinese religion" on the Canadian census, many default to selecting "no religion," even though they may participate in a variety of religious practices.[11] More research is needed surrounding the relationship between immigration and the "no religion" category, which would prove worthwhile to the larger conversation about the growing "no religion" faction in Canada.

In terms of the third belief that Christian congregations are evermore multiracial in Canada, empirical data suggests otherwise. By definition, multiracial congregations are those where no single racial group makes up more than 80 percent of a congregation and where the different groups interact with each other as opposed

---

6   Statistics Canada, *2001 Census*, 19.
7   See, for example, Bibby, *Beyond the Gods*; 30–31 and Bramadat and Seljak, *Christianity and Ethnicity*.
8   Bramadat and Seljak, *Christianity and Ethnicity*, 440.
9   Bruce Guenther, "Ethnicity and Evangelical Protestants in Canada," in Bramadat and Seljak, *Christianity and Ethnicity*, 378–83.
10   Bramadat and Seljak, *Christianity and Ethnicity*, 5.
11   Beyer, "From Far and Wide," 27–28; and David Chuenyan Lai, Jordan Paper, and Li Chuang Paper, "The Chinese in Canada: Their Unrecognized Religion," in *Religion and Ethnicity in Canada*, ed. Paul Bramadat and David Seljak (Toronto: Pearson, 2005), 89–110.

to separating ministries into racial or ethnic silos.[12] As Emerson points out, "Sunday morning is the most segregated hour of the week."[13] Estimates in the United States suggest that approximately 7–8 percent of all American congregations are multiracial, and this seems to be true in Canada as well.[14] Sociologically, this is not surprising given the "homogeneity principle": individuals tend to attend congregations with people who are like themselves ethnically or economically; people tend to feel more comfortable worshiping with people whom they believe may have a similar perspective on the world.[15]

Though it goes beyond my fundamental objective to explore Canada as a mission field, some missiological practitioners may find a deeper sociological explanation and understanding of monoracial and multiracial congregations useful for practical ministry purposes, and thus I will devote a bit of attention to this subject here.

The overarching presence of monoracial congregations among Christian immigrants can largely be explained by what sociologists call "institutional completeness" whereby most, if not all, of their psychological, social, and spiritual needs are fulfilled through their local congregation and/or ethnic group.[16] For instance, their social networks are concentrated with those they know in their church, and practical needs such as language skills, finding a job, or prayer are met through fellow congregants. In other words, their religious community is their cultural and social community. In contrast to many other Canadian Christians, immigrants rely on institutional completeness to provide them with stability in life via a strong Christian ethnic subculture in the face of significant personal transition and upheaval and possible prejudice and discrimination upon immigrating to Canada.

As beneficial as institutional completeness is for many immigrant Christian communities, it is not without its drawbacks. Nowhere are difficulties more pronounced than between first- and second-generation immigrants in areas of language

---

12   Michael O. Emerson, *People of the Dream: Multiracial Congregations in the United States*, with Rodney Woo (Princeton, NJ: Princeton University Press, 2006), 42; and George Yancey, *One Body, One Spirit: Principles of Successful Multiracial Churches* (Downers Grove, IL: InterVarsity Press, 2003), 15.

13   Emerson, *People of the Dream*, 5.

14   Bramadat and Seljak, *Christianity and Ethnicity*.

15   For an excellent summary of this, see Michael O. Emerson, William A. Mirola, and Susanne C. Monahan, *Religion Matters: What Sociology Teaches Us about Religion in Our World* (Boston: Allyn & Bacon, 2010).

16   Bramadat and Seljak, *Christianity and Ethnicity*; Raymond Breton, "Institutional Completeness of Ethnic Communities and the Personal Relations of Immigrants," *American Journal of Sociology* 70 (1964): 194; and Helen Rose Ebaugh and Janet Saltzman Chafetz, eds., *Religion and the New Immigrants: Continuities and Adaptations in Immigrant Congregations* (Walnut Creek, CA: AltaMira, 2000).

and values.[17] Beginning with language, first-generation immigrants tend to prefer religious services that are offered in their native tongue, because it provides them with an added sense of familiarity during their transition into Canada. Their children prefer English services, largely to become more like their peers at school and in their neighborhoods. The result is that second-generation immigrants feel alienated when English is not used, while their parents feel equally alienated when English is used. Some congregations respond to this dilemma by offering multiple services, some in English and some in the native tongue, while others target generation-specific services that suit their language and worship style preferences.

In addition to language, first-generation immigrants are frequently concerned that their children will stray from their conservative religious roots, particularly in areas of drugs, alcohol, sex, marriage, and violence. Strict rules, tight regulations, and the pursuit of institutional completeness are some of the ways that parents adapt in response. As parents seek to instill conservative values in their offspring, children are fearful that they will be estranged from the surrounding culture if they are insulated in their ethnic and religious enclave, a sentiment that is magnified if they believe that their religion is boring and irrelevant to their everyday experiences. Youth groups and camps are some of the programs that some denominations offer young people to help them process identity questions that are shared among some of their peers in a new cultural and religious setting.

In addition to generational tensions, Christian immigrants stand apart from Canadian-born Christians, including evangelicals, in their staunch conservative approach to Christianity and their higher levels of religiosity[18]—partially attributable to the conservative cultures that they migrate from, but also a product of conservative evangelical missionary efforts in other parts of the world. There are some suggestions that we may witness tensions between immigrant and Canadian-born Christians in the future due to different conceptions of Christianity and of the public role that Christianity ought to play in society. Such tensions are potentially magnified in Canada, which is far less conservative than the United States or the nations where immigrants migrate from, where "good" Canadians (including Christians) tend to avoid being too exclusive or intolerant of those who believe or behave differently than themselves.

---

17   Bramadat and Seljak, *Christianity and Ethnicity*, 87–89; and Ebaugh and Chafetz, *New Immigrants*, 105–30.

18   Bowen, *Christians*, 55–59; and Bramadat and Seljak, *Christianity and Ethnicity*.

Monoracial congregations are the norm in Canada, but multiracial congregations do exist and commonly arise in a couple settings. Outside of the obvious fact that they are typically located in urban centers, especially "global" cities such as Toronto or Vancouver, multiracial congregations are normally found in a parish environment. For example, it is not uncommon for a Catholic congregation to have members from Cambodia, Congo, Haiti, Latin America, Latvia, Lithuania, Italy, Portugal, Spain, and Vietnam. Of course, one of the notable shifts in church attendance patterns in the modern world is the willingness to drive beyond one's immediate community to attend a church that suits their religious tastes and preferences. If denominational leaders desire their congregations to be multiracial, one strategy might include encouraging members to attend churches in their geographic neighborhood (presuming that people live in multiracial neighborhoods).[19] Not only would this endorsement possibly appeal to individuals' practical concerns surrounding the time involved to attend church, but also to an array of other theological beliefs such as worshiping and ministering in one's own community, to reaching multiracial communities, to promoting racial reconciliation, to demonstrating racial unity as a witness—themes stressed throughout the New Testament especially.[20]

Possibly out of the aforementioned theological motivations, multiracial congregations also surface when groups intentionally construct a global self-narrative or identity of themselves (e.g., Roman Catholics or Pentecostals). Emerson stresses that intentionality toward building a multiracial congregation requires effective leaders and a willing congregation, which typically arises among those who are personally involved in or have past experiences in meaningful interracial relationships.[21] Yancey goes further to emphasize intentionality around a lively and diverse worship style, leadership from different racial groups, leaders with effective interpersonal skills,[22] and locating churches in multiracial neighborhoods.[23] In other words, multiracial congregations do not develop by accident. However, a multiracial congregation is not an end in itself; it is a means to a larger end surrounding a group's entire theological orientation to the Christian message. As Marti highlights, multiracial

---

19   Research shows that church leaders tend to claim that their congregation is not multiracial because their church neighborhoods are not multiracial, when in fact they are quite multiracial. See Emerson, *People of the Dream*, 42–46.

20   Yancey, *One Body*, 41–50.

21   Emerson, *People of the Dream*. See also Dan Sheffield, "Can Multicultural Social Theory Help Us in Leading Multicultural Faith Communities?," in *Reflecting God's Glory Together: Diversity in Evangelical Mission*, ed. Scott Moreau and Beth Snodderly (Pasadena: William Carey Library, 2011).

22   See Emerson, *People of the Dream*, 131–57.

23   Yancey, *One Body*. 41–42, 56–59, 128–137.

congregations are generally successful not because they emphasize race, but because they deemphasize race for the sake of a larger common bond rooted in following Jesus; sharing rites of baptism, membership, and the Lord's Supper; and developing Christlike attitudes and behaviours.[24] I defer to missiologists to sort out the theological and practical implications of these descriptive findings, but it is clear that with continued immigration into Canada, churches will need to grapple with the emerging realities.

To summarize, religious diversity is a reality in Canada; however, not to the extent that many assume. Immigration is not about the de-Christianization of Canadian society per se, but the de-Europeanization of Canadian Christianity. Further, monoracial rather than multiracial congregations are common in multicultural Canada. Together these findings crystallize our understanding of three assumptions outlined earlier regarding the impact of immigration on Christianity in Canada. Without question, immigration is an important aspect of Canadian and congregational life. However, while focused attention on Christian and non-Christian immigrants can and should be part of the church's mission in Canada, I am not convinced that immigration is the key variable for thinking about Canada as a mission field.

Recalibrating Our View of Canada as a Mission Field: Practical Considerations

Another demographic reality ought to be considered to potentially recalibrate the Christian community's perspective on being missionaries in our own Canadian backyard: fewer Canadian adults and teens identify with a religious group, believe in God or a supernatural being, or attend religious services regularly.[25] In terms of its growing secularity, Canada falls between higher levels of secularity throughout Europe and stronger levels of religiosity in the United States.[26] Explanations for the move away from Christianity in Canada (and much of the Western world) are

---

24   Gerardo Marti, *A Mosaic of Believers: Diversity and Innovation in a Multiethnic Church* (Bloomington: Indiana University Press, 2005), 155–79.

25   Reginald Bibby, Sarah Russell, and Ron Rolheiser, *The Emerging Millennials: How Canada's Newest Generation Is Responding to Change and Choice* (Lethbridge, Canada: Project Canada Books, 2009), 176; and Bibby, *Beyond the Gods*, 51.

26   See Peter Berger, Grace Davie, and Effie Fokas, *Religious America, Secular Europe? A Theme and Variations* (Burlington, VT: Ashgate, 2008); and David Lyon and Marguerite Van Die, eds., *Rethinking Church, State, and Modernity: Canada between Europe and America* (Toronto: University of Toronto Press, 2000).

numerous, and space does not permit me to go into detail here, though I will highlight a few dominant explanations. First, individual religious belief and practice are less likely to exist in plural and diverse societies, because no single sacred canopy dominates social life.[27] Where religious, social, or cultural pluralism are evident, no religious belief system is privileged in society, and all worldviews, religious or otherwise, must compete for people's allegiances. Pluralism, therefore, reduces the social stigma once attached to being irreligious, and in the Canadian circumstance, one might argue that social stigma is reserved for those who are deeply religious.

In societies where pluralism exists, it is common for people to turn away from religion when a religious group exerts too much public influence or when religious groups are perceived in a negative light by outsiders. The resurgence of evangelical Christianity in the United States as well as fundamentalism and religious conservatism in other regions of the world contributed to some turning away from religion.[28] Kinnaman and Lyons demonstrate that many people view Christians to be hypocritical, antihomosexual, sheltered within a Christian subculture, too political, too judgmental, and motivated to make friends with non-Christians only to convert them, findings verified elsewhere too.[29] In other words, exclusive religious beliefs and actions turn many away from religion in plural and diverse societies.

According to Berger and Bruce, individualism and choice are natural consequences to pluralism of any kind.[30] One way, among others, that this is manifested today is in religious socialization between parents and children. In contrast to fifty years ago when few children received the option of whether or not to attend church, today teens are given the choice of whether to attend church with their parents, which often results in teens not attending and, in some cases, parents also ceasing

---

27   Peter Berger, *The Sacred Canopy: Elements of a Sociological Theory of Religion* (Garden City: Doubleday, 1967); and Steve Bruce, *God Is Dead: Secularization in the West* (Malden, MA: Blackwell, 2002).

28   See Michael Hout and Claude S. Fischer, "Why More Americans Have No Religious Preference: Politics and Generations," *American Sociological Review* 67, no. 2 (April 2002): 168; Phil Zuckerman, *Faith No More: Why People Reject Religion* (New York: Oxford University Press, 2012); and David Niose, *NonBeliever Nation: The Rise of Secular Americans* (New York: Palgrave Macmillan, 2012).

29   David Kinnaman and Gabe Lyons, *UnChristian: What a New Generation Really Thinks about Christianity . . . And Why It Matters* (Grand Rapids: Baker Books, 2007). See also Robert Putnam and David Campbell, *American Grace: How Religion Divides and Unites Us* (New York: Simon & Schuster, 2010): 499–501; and Joel Thiessen, "Churches Are Not Necessarily the Problem: Lessons Learned from Christmas and Easter Affiliates," *Church and Faith Trends* 3, no. 3 (December 2010): 1–24.

30   Berger, *The Sacred Canopy*; Bruce, *God is Dead*.

their church attendance patterns.[31] It is unsurprising, then, that each generation in Canada appears less religious than the previous one.

In light of the discussion to this point, I want to bring together sociological theory, empirical evidence, Scripture, and theological reflections to inform five considerations for missionary methods in Canada. First, missionary activity will not occur without church leaders and lay members depending on and being attentive to the Holy Spirit's leading. As Christians slow down and listen to and obey the Spirit of God, they might pray for missionaries to arise, for the missionary efforts themselves, and for nonbelievers to come to salvation.[32] Christians may invest their money in missionary efforts, or be attentive to God's voice in everyday conversations with non-Christians, or share and model the light and life of Christ in a dead and broken world. Furthermore, as the Holy Spirit grips people's lives, they may become less ashamed and timid to share the gospel message in Canada where Christians are more likely to be "nice" than to offend those around them with a highly exclusive and potentially "offensive" message (e.g., John 14:6). In fact, this is one of the starkest differences between evangelicals in Canada and the United States, a finding reinforced in my interview research with both those who attend religious services weekly and those who attend mainly for religious holidays or rites of passage: Canadians are far more timid than Americans to openly share their faith with others.[33] Together, the question for missiological practitioners is how those in the Christian community can be encouraged to slow down their frenetic lives and adopt a posture that is constantly sensitive to the Holy Spirit's leading to participate in missionary efforts in Canada, and in turn, to respond in obedience regardless of the dominant cultural values that may conflict with Christ's calling on his disciples. Only after this occurs can we take seriously the remaining practical reflections on being missionaries in Canada.

Second, Christian individuals and congregations need to work to change the negative perceptions that many irregular or nonattenders have towards the Christian community and that are barriers to hearing or receiving the gospel. According to Wil-

---

31   See David Voas, "Explaining Change over Time in Religious Involvement," in *Religion and Youth*, ed. Sylvia Colins-Mayo and Pink Dandelion (Aldershot, England: Ashgate, 2010), 25–32; Bibby, *Beyond the Gods*, 13; and Thiessen, "Churches.," 4–5.

32   John Dickson, *The Best Kept Secret of Christian Mission: Promoting the Gospel with More than Our Lips* (Grand Rapids: Zondervan, 2010).

33   See Sam Reimer, *Evangelicals and the Continental Divide: The Conservative Protestant Subculture in Canada and the United States* (Kingston, Canada: McGill-Queen's University Press, 2003), 132–42; and Thiessen, "Churches."

liam I. Thomas, "Situations that are defined as real are real in their consequences,"[34] and many Canadians have very negative perceptions of the Christian community. These perceptions are informed by a range of personal experiences and observations that include financial and sexual scandals, the strong and offensive presence of the Christian right in the United States (that some fear characterizes the Canadian evangelical community), and the belief that Christians are judgmental and hypocritical. It is of little benefit for the Christian community to question the validity of such assertions, for as Thomas reminds us, these perceptions are people's reality. The question becomes, how might the Christian community change Canadian perceptions of Christianity?

One approach, in response to widespread perceptions that Christians are too inward looking, is for churches to centre their group identity in ministry initiatives that look beyond the walls of their congregation. Gibbons builds on sociological research on "third culture," a common phrase for missionary kids whose identities and experiences span geographical borders, to discuss how a sound understanding and conversation between two cultures can lead to a distinct third culture.[35] The challenge for Christians is to converse within the Christian culture as well as the larger Canadian culture, and then develop a bridge between the two. Practically speaking, how can Christians do this? How can Christians be known for what they stand for rather than against? Approaching Canada as a mission field entails that the Christian community humbly seeks to build bridges with non-Christians, to eagerly respect and listen to diverse viewpoints and perspectives, even if disagreement ensues. For instance, Canadians, Christian or otherwise, are generally bound by a shared concern for the welfare of others, popularly known as "social justice" and Gibbons argues that this is a logical point of intersection between the church and the "world."[36] How are Christian groups helping the less fortunate in society or partnering with those outside their congregation to help the less fortunate? Are mechanics within a church offering free oil changes to single mothers in the community? What are religious groups doing for the nearly 80 percent of two-parent working families in Canada? Are they offering activities for kids and families, particularly for those children who come home from school to an empty house for a couple of hours

---

34   William I. Thomas, *On Social Organization and Social Personality* (Chicago: University of Chicago Press, 1966), 301.

35   Dave Gibbons, *The Monkey and the Fish: Liquid Leadership for a Third-culture Church* (Grand Rapids: Zondervan, 2009).

36   Ibid.

before their parents return home from work? How are churches responding to the individual needs associated with an ageing Canadian population? Are they shovelling snow, doing yard work, or simply befriending seniors in their neighbourhood? Would communities notice if churches were no longer in their community? If we talk about reaching immigrant populations, research studies continuously reveal successes around congregations that host ethnic-specific events which enable fellow members of one's ethnic community to share in a common language, food, music, and culture—this can be a gateway for people to join a Christian community or for a monoracial congregation to evolve into a multiracial one. Simply stated, real, personal, and sustained Christian ministry that more intentionally focuses on those beyond the walls of one's congregation may not only change people's negative social perceptions towards Christians, but may also be instrumental in forging new relationships with non-Christians for the purposes of evangelism. Building bridges surrounding "social justice" and other things that Christians stand "for" on behalf of the marginalized can open a doorway where many simply view Christianity through a negative light. Changing perceptions and participating in social justice initiatives may not necessarily lead to "making disciples," but making disciples is far more difficult in the Canadian context when these things are not present.

Third, countless sociological studies show that one of the leading reasons that someone joins a religious group is because they were invited by someone in that group.[37] Conversely, one of the leading reasons for people leaving a religious group is because of a negative experience that they had with another in their religious group.[38] In contrast to assertions made by some pastors or the leading sociologist of religion in Canada, Reginald Bibby,[39] people in general do not attend church or stop attending church altogether because of the "supply" of religion (e.g., seeker-sensitive services, livelier music, relevant preaching, better programming), though "supply" is helpful to keep those already at a church there or to attract those from other congregations.[40] Instead, personal relationships are a critical method for

---

37   See, for example, Rodney Stark, *The Rise of Christianity* (Princeton, NJ: Princeton University Press, 1996); Rodney Stark and William Sims Bainbridge, *The Future of Religion: Secularization, Revival, and Cult Formation* (Berkeley: University of California Press, 1985); and Rodney Stark and Roger Finke, *Acts of Faith: Explaining the Human Side of Religion* (Berkeley: University of California Press, 2000).

38   Alan Jamieson, *A Churchless Faith: Faith Journeys beyond the Churches* (London: Society for Promoting Christian Knowledge, 2002); and Thiessen, "Churches."

39   Reginald Bibby, *Restless Gods: The Renaissance of Religion in Canada* (Toronto: Stoddart, 2002); and Reginald Bibby, *Restless Churches: How Canada's Churches Can Contribute to the Emerging Religious Renaissance* (Ottawa: Wood Lake Books, 2004).

40   See Dickson, *Best Kept Secret*; and Thiessen, "Churches."

effective missionary work, and if evangelicals in particular wish to truly live out the distinctive beliefs of their group (i.e., to proclaim the good news), they will be intentional to build relationships with non-Christians. Theologically speaking, I am not sure that one can call themself an evangelical and not be intentional about this. This begs the question: what are churches or individuals doing to forge relationships with non-Christians? Are church leaders providing space in their congregants' volunteer schedules so that they can invest time in building and maintaining meaningful relationships outside their congregation? Are Christians decluttering their lives to make way for relationship building with non-Christians? Giving greater primacy to building relationships with non-Christians may not only grow the local congregation, but it will also give Christians an opportunity to change people's perceptions about Christianity, one person at a time. Namely, as individuals model love, compassion, grace, and mercy, they can begin, in and through the work of the Holy Spirit, to melt away people's negative perceptions of Christianity. This is particularly important as Christians journey alongside other Canadians through their highs and lows, committing themselves to long-term relationships, a desire for many Canadians.

In saying all of this, it is important to recognize that people are more likely to convert if they are not currently attached to a religious group. In other words, with the growing prevalence of Canadians with "no religion" and fewer parents socializing their children into a religious faith,[41] the time could be ripe for Canadians to convert to Christianity. At the same time, those who believe that members of non-Christian religious groups are possible candidates for conversion to Christianity, academic studies on religious conversion suggest that this is extremely rare.

If we combine the first three points, I agree with Ravi Zacharias who in his foreword to John Dickson's book says, "I have little doubt that the single greatest obstacle to the impact of the gospel has not been its inability to provide answers but the failure on our part to live it out."[42] Being a missionary in Canada today requires that the Christian community faithfully seeks the heart of God and relies on the Holy Spirit regularly, attempts to change people's perceptions of Christianity by looking outward in their ministry activities, and intentionally builds relationships with non-Christians. In all of this, Christians must live lives full of Christ's light,

---

41   Another recommendation for churches is to work with parents on how to jointly and effectively socialize children with the Christian message so that this task is not solely left to parents or the church but both.

42   Dickson, *Best Kept Secret*, 15.

grace, mercy, and compassion, willing to dialogue and walk alongside others with an attitude of love, humility, and respect.

Fourth, Philip Jenkins argues that the centre of Christianity is now in the global South and East and that it should not surprise people if there is a reversal in the missionary flow up to the North and the West.[43] Recent immigration trends in Canada relative to Christianity seem to support Jenkins' argument. Given the fairly strong conservative nature to many Christian immigrants' faith and the declining levels of Christian belief and practice in Canada as a whole, it is not unreasonable to possibly expect that immigrants to Canada may lead the evangelism charge in the not-too-distant future (and this is already happening in some areas). Canadian-born Christians may want to take note of and learn from this evangelistic zeal and even participate alongside immigrant Christians in missionary efforts locally rather than (or in addition to) abroad—the spiritual needs are great in Canada and the religious trends bear this out. The earlier discussion of monoracial and multiracial congregations may provide some sound starting points for those serious about taking tangible steps in this direction.

Finally, Roland Allen wisely raises the following question: at what point does one "wipe the dust off their feet" when preaching to an unreceptive crowd (e.g., Matt 10:14; Acts 13:51)?[44] As much as I believe in the power of the Christian message to change people's hearts and minds and the various aforementioned strategies for mission in Canada, we should not be naive about the reality in Canada today. Canada is an increasingly secular society at the societal and individual level, and more and more Canadians are areligious or antireligious or they adopt a highly relativistic posture towards religion. While those who claim to have "no religion" are, sociologically speaking, the most likely to convert to a religious group because they are not formally tied to a set of religious beliefs and practices, sociologists are also discovering that these are well-informed and thoughtful nonreligious individuals; this is not a default category. It would be wise for Christians to be attentive to the Spirit of God to know when to wipe the dust off their feet. This does not mean that one abandons personal relationships or continual prayer if the other does not appear open to converting; however, it does mean that one carefully and strategically considers their "return for investment" when serving as a missionary in Canada. Roland Allen concludes the following, which I agree with:

---

43   Philip Jenkins, *The Next Christendom*.
44   Roland Allen, *Missionary Methods: St. Paul's or Ours?* (Chicago: Moody Press, 1912), 99–101.

St. Paul did not establish himself in a place and go on preaching for years to men who refused to act on his teaching . . . the refusal to teach those who refused to act on the teaching, was a vital part of the Pauline presentation of the Gospel . . . we should refuse to give intellectual teaching to a pupil if he refused to give us his attention: we might equally refuse to give religious teaching to a pupil who refused to give us religious attention.[45]

Conclusion

By way of conclusion, when thinking about being missionaries in our own backyard in Canada, sociological theory and evidence should lead us to conclude that the recent surge in non-Western immigrants is not likely to be the main source of missionary focus. Although partially true, assertions that immigration leads to increased religious diversity, growing secularity, and multiracial congregations are not as accurate or precise as many assume. Rather, Canadian discussions surrounding missionary activity in the world ought to consider Canada as a mission field due to the growing prevalence of Canadians who do not identify with a religious group, believe in God or a supernatural being, or attend religious services with any degree of regularity. Toward this end, a continual dependence upon the Holy Spirit, an attentiveness and response to negative perceptions surrounding Christianity, a resurgence in building meaningful relationships with non-Christians, learning from and partnering with Christian immigrants in missionary endeavours, and knowing when to "wipe the dust off our feet" may be effective missionary methods in Canada in the twenty-first century—practical considerations that fuse sociological theory and method with scriptural and theological truths.

Works Cited

Allen, Roland. *Missionary Methods: St. Paul's or Ours?* Chicago: Moody, 1912.

Berger, Peter L. *The Sacred Canopy: Elements of a Sociological Theory of Religion.* Garden City: Doubleday, 1967.

———, Grace Davie, and Effie Fokas. *Religious America, Secular Europe? A Theme and Variation.* Burlington, VT: Ashgate, 2008.

---

45   Ibid., 99–100.

Beyer, Peter. "From Far and Wide: Canadian Religious and Cultural Diversity in Global/Local Context." In *Religion and Diversity in Canada,* edited by Lori Beaman and Peter Beyer, 9–39. Boston: Brill, 2008.

Bibby, Reginald. *Beyond the Gods and Back: Religion's Demise and Rise and Why It Matters.* Lethbridge, Canada: Project Canada Books, 2011.

———. *Restless Churches: How Canada's Churches Can Contribute to the Emerging Religious Renaissance.* Ottawa: Wood Lake Books, 2004.

———. *Restless Gods: The Renaissance of Religion in Canada.* Toronto: Stoddart, 2002.

———, Sarah Russell, and Ron Rolheiser. *The Emerging Millennials: How Canada's Newest Generation Is Responding to Change and Choice.* Lethbridge, Canada: Project Canada Books, 2009.

Bowen, Kurt. *Christians in a Secular World: The Canadian Experience.* Montreal: McGill-Queen's University Press, 2004.

Bramadat, Paul, and David Seljak, eds. *Christianity and Ethnicity in Canada.* Toronto: University of Toronto Press, 2008.

Breton, Raymond. "Institutional Completeness of Ethnic Communities and the Personal Relations of Immigrants." *American Journal of Sociology* 70 (1964): 193–205.

Bruce, Steve. *God Is Dead: Secularization in the West.* Malden, MA: Blackwell, 2002.

Dickson, John. *The Best Kept Secret of Christian Mission: Promoting the Gospel with More than Our Lips.* Grand Rapids: Zondervan, 2010.

Ebaugh, Helen Rose, and Janet Saltzman Chafetz, eds. *Religion and the New Immigrants: Continuities and Adaptations in Immigrant Congregations.* Walnut Creek, CA: AltaMira, 2000.

Emerson, Michael O. *People of the Dream: Multiracial Congregations in the United States.* With Rodney M. Woo. Princeton, NJ: Princeton University Press, 2006.

———, William A. Mirola, and Susanne C. Monahan. *Religion Matters: What Sociology Teaches Us about Religion in Our World.* Boston: Allyn & Bacon, 2010.

Gibbons, Dave. *The Monkey and the Fish: Liquid Leadership for a Third-culture Church.* Grand Rapids: Zondervan, 2009.

Guenther, Bruce. "Ethnicity and Evangelical Protestants in Canada." In *Christianity and Ethnicity in Canada,* edited by Paul Bramadat and David Seljak, 365–410. Toronto: University of Toronto Press, 2008.

Hout, Michael, and Claude S. Fischer. "Why More Americans Have No Religious Preference: Politics and Generations." *American Sociological Review* 67, no. 2 (April 2002): 165–90.

Jamieson, Alan. *A Churchless Faith: Faith Journeys beyond the Churches.* London: Society for Promoting Christian Knowledge, 2002.

Jenkins, Philip. *The Next Christendom: The Coming of Global Christianity.* New York: Oxford, 2002.

Kinnaman, David, and Gabe Lyons. *UnChristian: What a New Generation Really Thinks about Christianity . . . And Why It Matters.* Grand Rapids: Baker Books, 2007.

Lai, David Chuenyan, Jordan Paper, and Li Chuang Paper. "The Chinese in Canada: Their Unrecognized Religion." In *Religion and Ethnicity in Canada,* edited by Paul Bramadat and David Seljak, 89–110. Toronto: Pearson, 2005.

Lyon, David, and Marguerite Van Die, eds. *Rethinking Church, State, and Modernity: Canada between Europe and America.* Toronto: University of Toronto Press, 2000.

Malenfant, Éric Caron, André Lebel, and Laurent Martel. *Projections of the Diversity of the Canadian Population: 2006 to 2031.* Ottawa: Statistics Canada, 2010. Accessed November 29, 2011. http://www.statcan.gc.ca/pub/91–551-x/91–551-x2010001-eng.pdf.

Marti, Gerardo. *A Mosaic of Believers: Diversity and Innovation in a Multiethnic Church.* Bloomington: Indiana University Press, 2005.

Niose, David. *NonBeliever Nation: The Rise of Secular Americans.* New York: Palgrave Macmillan, 2012.

Putnam, Robert, and David Campbell. *American Grace: How Religion Divides and Unites Us.* New York: Simon & Schuster, 2010.

Reimer, Sam. *Evangelicals and the Continental Divide: The Conservative Protestant Subculture in Canada and the United States.* Kingston, Canada: McGill-Queen's University Press, 2003.

Sheffield, Dan. "Can Multicultural Social Theory Help Us in Leading Multicultural Faith Communities?" In *Reflecting God's Glory Together: Diversity in Evangelical Mission,* edited by Scott Moreau and Beth Snodderly, 3–20. Pasadena: William Carey Library, 2011.

Stark, Rodney. *The Rise of Christianity.* Princeton, NJ: Princeton University Press, 1996.

————, and William Sims Bainbridge. *The Future of Religion: Secularization, Revival, and Cult Formation.* Berkeley: University of California Press, 1985.

————, and Roger Finke. *Acts of Faith: Explaining the Human Side of Religion.* Berkeley: University of California Press, 2000.

Statistics Canada. *2001 Census: Analysis Series; Religions in Canada.* Ottawa: Statistics Canada, 2003. Accessed March 3, 2010. http://www12.statcan.ca/english/census01/products/analytic/companion/rel/pdf/96F0030XIE2001015.pdf.

Thiessen, Joel. "Churches Are Not Necessarily the Problem: Lessons Learned from Christmas and Easter Affiliates." *Church and Faith Trends* 3, no. 3 (December 2010): 1–24.

Thomas, William I. *On Social Organization and Social Personality.* Chicago: University of Chicago Press, 1966.

Valpy, Michael, and Joe Friesen. "Canada Marching from Religion to Secularization." *The Globe and Mail.* December 10, 2010. Accessed December 16, 2010. http://www.theglobeandmail.com/news/national/canada-marching-from-religion-to-secularization/article1833451/page1/.

Voas, David. "Explaining Change over Time in Religious Involvement." In *Religion and Youth,* edited by Sylvia Collins-Mayo and Pink Dandelion, 25–32. Aldershot, England: Ashgate, 2010.

Yancey, George. *One Body, One Spirit: Principles of Successful Multiracial Churches.* Downers Grove, IL: InterVarsity Press, 2003.

Zuckerman, Phil. *Faith No More: Why People Reject Religion.* New York: Oxford University Press, 2012.

8

Islands of the Gods: Productive and Unproductive Missionary Methods in Animistic Societies—Roland Allen's Examination of Saint Paul's Use of Miracles

ROBERT H. BENNETT

Animism continues to permeate every sector of society in one form or another, even within the Western world. Spiritualism is making a comeback. Fortune-tellers, mediums, and gurus have experienced an upswing in their popularity, and Christians are engaging in syncretism without even recognizing their departure from the orthodox faith. Solomon of old had warned us, "What has been is what will be, and what has been done is what will be done, and there is nothing new under the sun" (Eccl 1:9 ESV). Taking this philosophy to heart, this essay returns to the writings of Roland Allen and examines the doctrines of charity and salvation within the context of miracles and the missionary activities found in both Haiti and Madagascar.

Both Haiti and Madagascar remain to this time heavily influenced by animism and show considerable difficulty with syncretism. The inhabitants of these islands place an emphasis on spirits and ancestors. In each case, African Traditional Religion (ATR) is the basis of religious thought among the inhabitants. Missionary work among these islands continues to experience trouble as it wrestles with a difference of worldviews.

One finds two different reactions among missionaries confronted with animism. On the one hand, they simply ignore the holistic/animistic worldview of the people and ignore any thoughts of a spiritual world. On the other hand, they believe wholesale in the spiritual worldview of the people and turn it into a form of Christian animism.[1] These extremes are problematic and eventually tend to promote syncretism rather than eliminate the problems of animism.

Disregarding the worldview of the people forces a trench between people and the missionaries. They simply cannot understand one another. However, the difficulty of accepting the animistic worldview wholesale should be obvious. Jesus Christ is the only intermediary between the Father and us. To believe that subrealms of spirits or ancestors are required to obtain help from God is anything but Christian. Moreover, it prevents the person from escaping the ever-tightening chains of sacrifice and service, which animism demands of its adherents. As a result, many people associate with evil spirits, who disguise themselves as familiar ancestors, previous kingly figures, and helpful deities. Saint Paul warns, "Satan disguises himself as an angel of light. So it is no wonder if his servants, also, disguise themselves as servants of righteousness" (2 Cor 11:14,15 ESV). While denial of the spiritual world leads to syncretism, acceptance of the spiritual world on its own terms leads to despair and bondage. Therefore, it is necessary to avoid both of these two extremes. Roland Allen can be of some assistance in this regard, as he reminds his readers of how Saint Paul handled the animistic society of his time.

In his book *Missionary Methods: St. Paul's or Ours?* Allen provides a section on "Miracles." However, this section may well be titled, "St. Paul's Methods in Animistic Societies." Allen writes, "St. Paul's use of miracles may provide an interesting light upon some principles of contrast value which should guide us in the practice of many forms of missionary enterprise common today."[2] In this section, Allen provides three warnings that he finds in Saint Paul's methods. First, the miracles of Paul should not be overexaggerated. Next, the miracles of Paul were not intended to encourage people to follow him. Finally, miracles did not help Paul in preaching. Allen has provided valuable warnings to us as we engage this issue. However, just as Allen gave us three warnings, he also provides three positive thoughts about Paul's miracle usage. Allen notes that while Paul's use of miracles was not to persuade people

---

1   Pierre Gilbert, "Further Reflections on Paul Hiebert's 'The Flaw of the Excluded Middle,'" *Direction* 36, no. 2 (Fall 2007): 210.

2   Roland Allen, *Missionary Methods: St. Paul's or Ours?* (1912; repr., Grand Rapids: Eerdmans, 1983), 41.

to follow him, they did attract hearers. They demonstrated the power of Jesus, of whom Paul preached. Paul's miracles became illustrations of two new doctrines: the doctrine of charity and the doctrine of salvation. These two doctrines will provide a portal of investigation into the missionary methods found in Madagascar and Haiti. While animism continues to permeate the Christian church through syncretism, an analysis of missionary methods employed on the islands of Madagascar and Haiti shows some effective and ineffective methods that missionaries have engaged over the years. They also provide insight into how Christianity in the Western world might deal with the problems of animism and syncretism found within the church.

The Doctrine of Charity

Allen reminds us that charity is something new to religious systems. He finds its origin in Christianity, specifically the work of Saint Paul. Charity, Allen writes, opened the eyes of the people "to see in every case of trouble and disease, not a loathsome thing to be avoided, but an opportunity for the revelation of grace and loving-kindness."[3] The modern church has embraced the doctrine of charity. It is continually the focus of efforts of short-term mission activities, which include medical missions, clinics, orphanages, building projects, food programs, clean water programs, and the like. Sometimes these activities are useful, and sometimes they come with unintended consequences. We are learning that many times these activities are best if left under the direction of mission partners, rather than directly through Western institutions or short-term mission trips. This debate continues, and I have no intention of dealing with it in this essay. However, Allen's focus finds charity in the local congregation as a starting point. Local people better understand the needs of others. Unintended problems still occur but, due to their locality, local congregations can accommodate more readily to problems when they arise.

The charity demonstrated in Haiti is well known, especially following the earthquake of 2010. However, the charity employed through missionary methods in Madagascar remains invisible to most of the world. This could be due to the remoteness of the island or simply the lack of exposure Madagascar receives, but as we shall demonstrate, Christian charity is one of the driving forces behind mission work on the island. Within the Malagasy church, the *toby* system best demonstrates Christian charity.

---

3   Ibid., 45.

The *toby*, a Malagasy word that means "camp," is a place of healing where doctors, nurses, pastors, laity, and the family members of the afflicted work together to provide charity to the sick. A shaman named Rainisoalambo established the first *toby* in 1894 in Soatanana, Madagascar. This movement has now spread outside the island to places like Paris and Toronto.

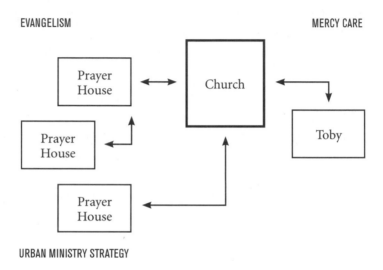

The *toby* system provides one aspect of the overall mission strategy found in Madagascar. We will examine the prayer houses when we return to the second doctrine, namely the doctrine of salvation. For now we continue to explore the *toby* system.

Medical care is extremely difficult to obtain for the poor; this is especially true for the inhabitants of Madagascar. Few hospitals exist on the island, and even fewer people can afford treatment in their facilities. The *toby* system is a way of providing charity to the poor. The sick—either physically, mentally, or spiritually—enter into the *toby* under the care of the church. The accommodation provided takes the form of narrow rooms joined one after another. The rooms are modest in size and furnishings. They may only contain a foam mattress on the floor and a small table with a candlestick. Family members of the residents provide for physical needs such as bathing, feeding, laundry, etc. The *toby* provides some food if necessary. Medications, doctors, and pastors for spiritual care are all funded by the local congregations.

The aspect of spiritual care provided by the *toby* sets it apart from many Western institutions. Charity means more than just physical care. Charity brings release and freedom to the oppressed, whether the oppression comes from men, disease, or demons. Allen understood Paul's charity in regards to exorcism. He writes:

> St. Paul healed the sick and cast out devils because he was grieved at the bitter bondage of the oppressed or because he welcomed with the insight of sympathy the first signs of a faith which could respond to the power of the Lord. In this respect his miracles were the first steps in the path by which the early Church became renowned amongst the heathen for its organized charity, its support of widows and orphans, its tender care for the sick, the infirm and disabled, its gentle consideration for slaves, its constant help afforded to prisoners and those afflicted by great calamities.[4]

Therefore charity is closely attached to the doctrine of salvation and liberation. For charity to be beneficial, it requires an understanding of the problem faced by the people. The sick are in bondage and are in need of release. Release comes through the doctrine of justification or, as Allen calls it, the "doctrine of salvation."

The Doctrine of Salvation

Through his work as a missionary to China, Allen had seen and experienced many things unknown to his Western worldview. One of those was no doubt exorcism. Allen suggests that the church must continue to deal with the necessity of exorcism. Allen writes, "Into a world burdened with sin and misery and death Saint Paul came in the Spirit of Jesus who went about doing good and healing all that were oppressed of the devil."[5] Many missionaries doubted such statements in the nineteenth and twentieth centuries. Theological education had moved past the acceptance of such fantastic stories. Today theological education has turned its attention toward psychology and mental illness. For many, Allen's treatment of the demonic may be questionable, especially the power he attached to exorcism and its importance in the early church. In his book he agrees with Harnack about the necessity of exorcism for the church, writing:

---

4   Ibid., 46.
5   Ibid., 47.

> There can be no doubt that this power of working marvels, this striking demonstration of the authority of Jesus over evil spirits, was in the early Church considered to be a most valuable weapon with which to confute opponents and convince the hesitating. 'It was exorcisers,' says professor Harnack, 'that the Christians went out into the great world, and exorcism formed one very powerful method of their mission propaganda.'[6]

In stating this, Allen recognized and even lamented that such things had been lost to the church. "One day we shall perhaps recover the early faith in miracles,"[7] he writes. One hundred years after the writing of his book, theological institutions may be finally hearing Allen's lament. Postmodernism, with its many theological problems, is still opening the minds of theologians and missionaries to the possibility of such phenomena. Missionaries like Allen, Hiebert, and Nevius[8] have tried to remind us that demons continue to exist and that the church must continue to bring release to the oppressed, both physically and spiritually. This occurs through the doctrine of salvation. For many the doctrine of salvation remains within an eschatological framework that focuses on the end of time and the resurrection. While the *eschaton* brings the fulfillment of the doctrine of salvation, to lose sight of its temporal benefits is a travesty. Missiologist David Bosch writes, "The church can be a credible sacrament of salvation for the world only when it displays to humanity a glimmer of God's imminent reign—a kingdom of reconciliation, peace, and new life. In the here and now that reign comes whenever Christ overcomes the power of the devil."[9] Likewise, Roland Allen reminds his readers of the temporal release that comes in the gift of salvation. Satan and his demons lose their hold upon the individual, as the yoke of sacrifice and veneration are replaced by the peace of God in Christ Jesus.

Missionaries serving in the field continue to observe the freeing affect of the gospel in the lives of their converts. Allen and many other missionaries of which we are familiar continue to educate modern missionaries. Jesus is Savior, but a Savior from what? What is the work of Jesus? The Apostle John is clear on this point, "The reason the Son of God appeared was to destroy the works of the devil" (1 John 3:8

---

6   Ibid.
7   Ibid., 48.
8   John Livingston Nevius, *Demon Possession* (Grand Rapids: Kregel, 1985).
9   David Jacobus Bosch, *Transforming Mission: Paradigm Shifts in Theology of Mission* (Maryknoll, NY: Orbis Books, 1991), 377.

ESV). These works include the oppression placed upon those who serve the devil. Allen writes, "The heathen appealed to miracles, to oracles, to portents, as proof of the existence of gods; Christians appealed to exorcism as proof of the divinity of Christ and His superior authority over all heathen gods and demons."[10] Times have changed since Allen wrote these words. Missionaries have begun to understand the concept of spiritual warfare due to the number of missionary accounts and books written on the subject over the years. Nevertheless, Allen should receive at least some of the credit for bringing the issue of spiritual warfare out into the open.[11] The doctrine of salvation requires an understanding of the doctrine of the fall into sin and its relationship to Satan and his demons. How does Christianity on the islands of Haiti and Madagascar address the problem of spiritual warfare? We will answer this question by analyzing the situation in Madagascar and Haiti as it compares to Allen's view of the doctrine of salvation and its relationship to spiritual warfare

The Doctrine of Salvation and Spiritual Warfare in Haiti

Missionaries in Haiti are well aware of the influence of Satan in the lives of the people. The inhabitants of Haiti continue to face oppression. Their oppression began as they were carried to the island as slaves under French colonialism, and continues through their slavery to voodooism. The Haitian church understands the situation on the ground and at times finds itself engaged in spiritual warfare, which includes exorcism. However, exorcism in Haiti seems to be more reactionary than it is to the Christian church of Madagascar. Generally exorcism in Haiti is carried out when someone comes forward showing signs of possession. These signs may occur during the preaching or at other times during the Sunday service. Rarely do the pastors interact with voodoo priests. The problem seems to be that pastors have at times had an unnatural fear of the voodoo priests, thereby avoiding all involvement with them.

On a recent trip to Haiti I convinced one of the pastors to come with me and explore voodooism in his village. He was extremely nervous. However, because he was a friend, he agreed. As a result, he contacted one of the local voodoo priests and asked if I might question him and some of the other priests. When the priest agreed,

---

10   Allen, *Missionary Methods*, 47.
11   Bosch, *Transforming Mission*, 40.

we spent the next few days traveling to the local voodoo temples and interviewing the priests. The Haitian pastor was amazed how easy it was to interact with these priests. They answered our questions, showed us the rituals, and welcomed us into their holy places. Following numerous conversations it became apparent that the priests, while they were oppressors of their people, were also under considerable oppression from the gods they served. At one location, one of the voodoo priests decided he was going to have some fun with us and asked us how he could be saved. The Haitian pastor was unsure of how to respond. Thereby he asked me to give an answer. I responded that I could do nothing to help him but that Jesus could do all things. Jesus' death and resurrection bring salvation to those who believe. After hearing these words, he sat down next to his altar and silently placed his head in his hands. Understandably, the Haitian pastor had always seen the voodoo priest as an adversary, but on that day the pastor saw only a man shackled with extraordinary oppression and in need of salvation.

The church is called to engage the world, not to react to it. Allen understood this well. He describes Saint Paul as an engaging missionary. Saint Paul was not seeking miracles or to demonstrate spiritual power. Nevertheless, such miracles resulted from Paul's preaching. Similarly, such things continue to occur today in many places in the world where Jesus' name is proclaimed in the midst of satanic worship. It is necessary for missionaries to understand this and be prepared to respond when needed. However, it is appropriate at this point to remember the warnings that Allen placed before us. The focus of Saint Paul's miracles was not to persuade people to follow him. However, his miracles attracted hearers and demonstrated the power of Jesus, of whom Paul preached. Christopher Wright, in his book *The Mission of God,* also provides some useful thoughts in this matter as he reminds his readers, "The battle and the victory belong to God . . . The conflict with the gods is a conflict waged by God for us, not a conflict waged by us for God."[12] Paul did not seek out such conflict, neither should the church. However, the Haitian church has learned to deal with the reality of spiritual warfare. We can learn much from them in this regard. In the Malagasy church, to which we now turn, we see spiritual warfare institutionalized within the church.

---

12   Christopher J. H. Wright, *The Mission of God: Unlocking the Bible's Grand Narrative* (Downers Grove, IL: InterVarsity Academic, 2006), 178.

The Doctrine of Salvation and Spiritual Warfare in Madagascar

Spiritual warfare and the rite of exorcism are essential methods of evangelism within the Christian church of Madagascar. We have already made some mention of this in the Christian charity demonstrated through the *toby* system. Malagasy Christians understand the deep-seated beliefs of the world of spirits and ancestors common among people. One of the primary locations of spiritual warfare in Madagascar takes place in the prayer houses represented on the previous diagram.

Prayer houses incorporate street evangelism where members of the church meet daily in locations found in the heavily traveled areas of the city. These prayer houses are lay-led places of prayer held before and after work. As the people walk on the street, they hear the singing of hymns and prayers resonating out into the street. Oftentimes people with no religious background or relationship to the church enter the prayer houses out of curiosity. Frequently, those who enter the prayer houses for the first time enter under tremendous oppression from the spiritual forces that they serve. As we have mentioned, these are lay-led events, but what we have not mentioned is that all of the laity in the church are trained as exorcists. It should be noted that Protestant denominations established the prayer houses, the largest denomination being the Lutheran Church of Madagascar; however, the Reformed churches also operate under a similar model. One Malagasy missiologist describes his understanding of spiritual warfare:

> Exorcism carries a central message of salvation. It therefore, puts the Christian at the forefront of a daily battle over against Satan and his kingdom. Consequently, exorcism cultivates in the life of the Christian a life of continuing relationship with Jesus Christ who is the only guarantee leading to victory. Therefore, through the exorcism, the church is always a fighting church at the forefront of the battle and at the same time a church in mission. Forgiveness of sin, liberation from the devil and his kingdom, healing from incomprehensible diseases and escaping from death is no more mere paroles and empty words just to comfort someone in difficult times and posture. They become historically real and in the flesh in the life of the person through exorcism. These fleshly historical happenings boost and propel

> evangelism in an incredible way towards the heavens and give joy
> to the angels. That is the dynamism in the strength of the growth
> of the Malagasy Church.[13]

From these remarks, it is clear that for the Malagasy church exorcism is an invaluable tool connected with conversion and necessary for a growing church that is engaging the syncretism of the culture and leading people out of bondage and into the light of the gospel. Moreover, they have much to teach us about engaging our own culture.

Conclusion

Allen still has much to teach the missionary community. Animism has not retreated from our time, but continues to influence Christians around the globe. There may have been a time when Allen was thought to be too extreme in his acceptance of Paul's use of miracles, and some critics are sure to likewise fault this essay. However, many will agree that Allen and his understanding of Paul's use of miracles provides a good balance between the overstatements of some who exaggerate the power of miracles over against others who reject that miracles continue to occur. Wherever and whenever the powerful word of Jesus is proclaimed, spiritual warfare will remain. Let us thank Allen for his reminders and continue to rediscover his book, for it faithfully represents the methods of Saint Paul and continues to have much to teach the church.[14]

---

13   Joseph Randrianasolo, email message to author, June 22 2010.
14   Gerald H. Anderson, "Roland Allen," in *Biographical Dictionary of Christian Missions* (New York: Macmillan Reference USA, 1998), 12.

Works Cited

Allen, Roland. *Missionary Methods: St. Paul's or Ours?* Grand Rapids: Eerdmans, 1983. First published 1912.

Anderson, Gerald H. "Roland Allen." In *Biographical Dictionary of Christian Missions.* New York: Macmillan Reference USA, 1998.

Bosch, David Jacobus. *Transforming Mission: Paradigm Shifts in Theology of Mission.* Maryknoll, NY: Orbis Books, 1991.

Gilbert, Pierre. "Further Reflections on Paul Hiebert's 'The Flaw of the Excluded Middle,'" *Direction* 36, no. 2 (Fall 2007): 206–18.

Nevius, John Livingston. *Demon Possession.* Grand Rapids: Kregel, 1985.

Wright, Christopher J. H. *The Mission of God: Unlocking the Bible's Grand Narrative.* Downers Grove, IL: InterVarsity Academic, 2006.

9

Leaders Reproducing Churches:
Research from Japan

JOHN W. MEHN

Introduction

The words of Roland Allen again were haunting me, like they had each month, as I departed to minister in a Japanese church 150 miles away. I was sent to this "pastorless" church so I could preach monthly the Word and officiate over Communion for the twenty-five people attending this church. Throughout my two-hour trips by bus, local train, and eventually the bullet train, I could hear Roland Allen admonishing me, "Why is it necessary for you to travel so far and spend all this time and money when someone locally could be raised up for this ministry? Paul would have prepared some local elders to serve this function, since his presence would not be required for the church to be the church."

Our mission and our partnering Japanese denomination mutually agreed that this church needed to be sent temporary assistance until they were able to secure a pastor. I felt honored to serve Communion monthly over a period of years. The reality of the situation was that without an ordained, seminary-trained, full-time pastor this local church believed it could not fulfill its biblical functions and operate independently. From my experience with many church groups in Japan, this is not a problem unique to my denomination, and some situations may be much worse.

Roland Allen's challenging questions were always haunting my mind. Because he viewed the Eucharist as one vital element for a local church,[1] he would question why it is necessary to wait until you have a full-time, graduate-trained, ordained leader to celebrate Communion. For him, simply training and credentialing some lay pastors would allow more Christians to have the blessing of sharing the Lord's Supper together.

During this period of assisting this church, I was also conducting field research into characteristics of leaders reproducing churches in Japan. I discovered that there were churches in Japan that were not only healthy and flourishing but were also multiplying leadership internally and for church expansion into new areas. On these long trips I would often muse about the contrasts between the churches that were constantly spinning out new leaders and the profound lack of qualified leadership that was forcing me to make these trips.

As I believe Roland Allen also would observe, I would identify a complexity of several problems hindering the natural growth and reproduction of healthy churches in Japan. Allen deeply loved Christ's church and would oppose any limitation that people would place on the natural or spontaneous growth and expansion of the church. He would challenge us to think that the reason the church was not growing as God intended is that we have forgotten the scriptural principles for church formation and expansion.

The Reality of Japan

After 150 years of Protestant missions, Japan remains relatively unreached with the gospel. Even the accelerated mission activity following World War II did not substantially improve the situation.[2] At the beginning of the twenty-first century, Japan is an extremely spiritually needy country, evidenced by the modest Christian presence in number of believers and churches. In a country of over 126 million people, there are less than 280,000 Christians in worship gatherings on any given Sunday. With less than eight thousand churches nationally, this means there is on average

---

1   J. D. Payne, *Roland Allen: Pioneer of Spontaneous Expansion* (Lexington, KY: CreateSpace, 2012), 60.
2   David J. Hesselgrave, *Paradigms in Conflict: 10 Key Questions in Christian Missions Today* (Grand Rapids: Kregel, 2005), 138.

only one church for about every sixteen thousand people. The conclusion is there is less than one-half of 1 percent (0.43 percent) who are part of a church in Japan.[3]

Viewing the nation of Japan as a whole stirred Ralph Winter to write, "There has never been a time when I have not considered Japan's hundreds of peoples mainly unreached peoples. Why? Because there is not yet a sufficiently Japanese church movement."[4] This is due to the inadequate number of churches, their small size (thirty-five average), and the present decline in the rate of church growth. The small struggling Japanese church[5] seems by itself incapable of completing the task of evangelizing every person in Japan without outside assistance. The Joshua Project considers the Japanese people group as the world's second largest unreached population.[6]

One reason for the lack of rapid church growth in Japan has often been identified as the existing church. According to Braun, "The slow growth of the Church in Japan is due not only to the disinclination of the Japanese to become Christian, but to the cumbersome and faulty way in which the Church goes about its task."[7] Dale has accurately described the source of the problem as both (1) the Japanese culture and (2) the existing church, which lacks engagement and contextualization with the culture.[8]

Many authors have identified problems with the Japanese church. First, a clergycentric ministry has been acknowledged. Many have observed that "a totally pastor-centered"[9] and lone autocratic managerial style remains common in Japan.[10] This autocratic leadership pattern, prone to a lack of delegation, hinders the growth and reproduction of churches. This is not unlike the observation Roland

---

3   Church Information Service, "The Protestant Church in Japan in 2011," *Church Information Service News* 74 (2011): 4–5.

4   Ralph D. Winter, "Three Types of Ministry," *Evangelical Missions Quarterly* 33, no. 4 (October 1997), 421.

5   Kenneth J. Dale, *Coping with Culture: The Current Struggle of the Japanese Church*, Lutheran Booklets 3 (Tokyo: Lutheran Booklet Press, 1996); K. Lavern Snider, *It's Happening in Japan Today: The Story of 8 Growing Churches* (Osaka, Japan: Japan Free Methodist Mission, 1980); and K. Lavern Snider, *Ten More Growing Churches in Japan Today* (Osaka, Japan: Japan Free Methodist Mission, 1985).

6   Joshua Project, "Unreached Listings: 100 Largest Unreached Peoples," http://www.joshuaproject.net/unreached.php?listing=1&sf=population&so=asc (accessed October 5, 2012).

7   Neil Braun, *Laity Mobilized: Reflections on Church Growth in Japan and Other Lands* (Grand Rapids: Eerdmans, 1971), 19.

8   Dale, *Coping with Culture.*

9   Stanley R. Dyer, "Japan's Group Consciousness as It Relates to Evangelism" (DMiss major project, Trinity Evangelical Divinity School, 1982), 87.

10   Hideo Ohashi, *Kyokai Seicho Dokuhon* [*Church Growth by the Book*] (Tokyo: Inochi no Kotobasha [Word of Life Press], 2007), 95–97, 142–143; cf. Mark R. Mullins, *Christianity Made in Japan: A Study of Indigenous Movements* (Honolulu: University of Hawai'i Press, 1998), 180.

Allen had concerning the role of missionaries where "the leader is confirmed in the habit of gathering all authority into his own hands, and of despising the powers of his people, until he makes their inactivity an excuse for denying their capacity."[11]

Second, the church is often viewed organizationally, statically, and institutionally. This cue taken from Japanese society and a product of Confucianism-influenced social relationships prevents dynamic growth. Third, resulting from the first two points, the primary role of the leader is frequently a maintainer of order and structure. The leader is expected to protect the flock and the organization, certainly not send members out on their own ministry.

Roland Allen's Emphases

Roland Allen gleaned from the apostles' methods many emphases that are in sharp contrast to today's reality of the Japanese church.[12] First, the primary role of the leader is facilitating and catalyzing ministry to take place in the lives of other leaders, including the rapid expansion of churches. Allen affirmed that someone would be labeled a radical today if they considered implementing the methods of the apostolic church, because we no longer believe those results possible. As he explained, there is an astonishing contrast between the rapid and stable establishment of new churches by Paul and the view of modern missions insisting on long preparation of new believers and churches before they can be released in expansive ministry.[13]

Second, lay elders are to be selected and developed to share in church leadership.[14] These leaders were given authority to minister the sacraments[15] and also to ordain others for leadership.[16] Allen prefers that these "voluntary clergy" are not paid from the outside but paid by the local church itself or are possibly bivocational.[17]

Third, churches were founded in every sense indigenous. The local church could stand on its own without outside support, and the believers, dependent on the Holy Spirit, could conduct with authority all church matters.[18] These concepts

---

11   Roland Allen, *Missionary Methods: St. Paul's or Ours?*, American ed. (1912; repr., Grand Rapids: Eerdmans, 1962), 81.

12   Ibid., 147, cf. 107.

13   Ibid., 3–4.

14   Ibid., 160, cf. 89.

15   Hubert J. B. Allen, *Roland Allen: Pioneer, Priest, and Prophet* (Grand Rapids: Eerdmans, 1995), 174.

16   Allen, *Missionary Methods*, 100–103.

17   Payne, *Roland Allen*, 89–101.

18   Allen, *Missionary Methods*, vii.

correspond with the three-self formula (self-propagating, self-governing, and self-supporting) of Henry Venn and Rufus Anderson.[19]

Fourth, leaders catalyzing others for ministry, mobilizing and sharing leadership with lay people, and emphasizing the full authority of the independent local church, infused with the power of the Holy Spirit, would lead to "spontaneous expansion." Paul expected the churches he planted to reproduce and saturate their regions with the gospel.[20] This *spontaneous expansion* briefly sums up all of Roland Allen's missiology.[21]

Research into Leaders of Reproducing Churches

In the midst of downward trends in the growth of the church in Japan, there are a number of churches that have been birthing new churches on a regular basis and reproducing themselves in the Japanese culture. Due to their rate of reproduction, some consider these promising churches as possible small-scale church multiplication movements. Though some of the theological perspectives of these Japanese leaders (lay people planting churches, for example) may be perceived as radical in Japan, these churches demonstrate the application of indigenous principles advocated by Roland Allen. Applying what Allen would call "the method of St Paul,"[22] these Japanese churches are growing spontaneously in a traditionally hard mission field. This is extremely encouraging and gives many laborers in the difficult ministry context of Japan hope for the future.

Field Research Methodology

The research began with gathering information on reproducing churches throughout Japan from the databases of Church Information Service Japan, the *Christian Shimbun*, together with relational contacts of key leaders in Japan. The first objective was to pinpoint churches in Japan that had reproduced themselves at least three

---

19   Craig Ott and Stephen J. Strauss, *Encountering Theology of Mission: Biblical Foundations, Historical Developments, and Contemporary Issues* (Grand Rapids: Baker Academic, 2010), 115–6; cf. Tom Steffen, *The Facilitator Era: Beyond Pioneer Church Planting* (Eugene, OR: Wipf & Stock, 2011), 19.

20   Allen, *Missionary Methods*, 12–13.

21   Payne, *Roland Allen*, 113.

22   Allen, *Missionary Methods*, 82, cf. 147.

times in a twenty-year period. Approximately sixty potential churches with Japanese leadership were identified.[23]

Of those churches, forty-four were asked to complete a questionnaire to determine basic information on church reproduction. Of the thirteen churches that completed the questionnaire and were willing to participate in the research, leaders of six churches, which planted a total of sixty-two churches in less than twenty years, were selected for face-to-face, in-depth, semistructured interviews.

The aim of this phase of research was to determine a representative cross-section of churches to eliminate other factors from influencing the results for leadership characteristics. The six churches reside in different regions of Japan, are from four different denominations and two independent churches, are of various age spans (from 1950s to 2005), have different sizes (average worship attendance 40 to 250), and have diverse styles of ministry. They represent various church models, as two are cell churches, two are churches with small groups, and two would be considered standard models.

Six primary leaders and eight secondary leaders were interviewed about personality, giftedness, leadership development, theological perspective, role, style, priorities, behavior, and practice of church reproduction. Data collected from transcriptions and notes of interviews were subjected to qualitative data analysis using summary memos and computer-aided, qualitative data-analysis software.

Field Research Results

Research analysis found six preliminary characteristics of leaders reproducing churches: (1) envisioning the church as a dynamic sending community, (2) receiving ministry vision from God, (3) exercising risk-taking faith, (4) developing lay people for ministry, (5) leading relationally through encouragement, and (6) implementing aggressively through practical ministry. These six characteristics seem closely interrelated and all function in concert, so they should not be considered independently.

---

23   John W. Mehn, "Characteristics of Leaders Reproducing Churches in Japan" (DMin major project, Trinity International University, 2010), 71–89. The following quotations of Japanese church leaders are taken from this research project.

Envision the Church as a Dynamic Sending Community

As it was not a goal of the research, the most unexpected aspect was the leaders' "view of the church" (*kyokaikan*). Leaders envision the church as a spiritual, organic, dynamic sending community that spontaneously grows and reproduces. In their comprehension of the church, the people of God, unbound by cultural Christianity, are missionally sending others out in transformational ministry.

These leaders insist that reproduction is God's primary strategy for the local church and central to the Scriptures. This kingdom understanding of the reproducing church is grounded in biblical theology as one leader affirmed:

> Church multiplication is like a mission base for the Kingdom of God. It is like a center or a core. It is where the church will grow abundantly as His Kingdom. I think that the mission of the gospel or church multiplication is to increase the number of churches that are the gospel (or mission) centers, the front line bases of the Kingdom, and the footholds in the world.[24]

These reproducing leaders envision the church as a dynamic, relational community that grows naturally and reproduces itself by sending community members into like-minded mission. Many of these leaders had a transformed view of the church. For them, (1) the church is more than a building or organization; (2) the church is viewed more relationally; (3) the church is more outwardly or missionally oriented; (4) a church should grow more than simply its size; (5) church reproduction "is nothing special . . . It is normal, it is standard and average"[25]; and (6) the church must move away from cultural Christianity. Their applied theological view of the church is a relational community, a dynamic living organism, a reproducing church, and a sending mission.

Receive Ministry Vision from God

These leaders, through their personal ministry calling and their habits of listening to God with sensitivity (*binkan*) and reflecting on Scripture, received God's vision for their ministry, which is faithfully linked to God's vision for global mission. One

---

24   Primary Leader 1 (PL1).
25   PL2.

leader encourages, "Listen to God through worship, prayer and fasting, he will lead you with guidance, then obey him without question and overcome anything in the way of obedience."[26]

All of these leaders have reproducing churches which grew out of a vision given to them from God. For some of these leaders, listening to God meant giving up the goal of a large church in order to become a reproducing church. These leaders had a clear understanding of God's plan for their church to reproduce as revealed in the Scriptures and an unwavering obedience to that vision God had given them.

Exercise Risk-taking Faith

Reproducing leaders exercise faith that overcomes obstacles and even their own weaknesses. Their faith battles discouragement and potential failure, and leads in risky directions. The vision for God's church requires great faith.

These leaders risked much by giving up key leaders, money, and gifted people to reproduce churches. Risk-taking faith is a characteristic that Roland Allen saw in the methodology of the Apostle Paul: "It is characteristic of St. Paul that he had such faith in Christ and in the Holy Spirit indwelling in the Church that he did not shrink from risks."[27] These leaders expect obstacles in reproduction but also expect to overcome them. They challenge potential failure by a confidence in obeying God, as shared by one leader:

> Just do it [church reproduction]. You may succeed or you may not. It does not matter. But if you do not do it, you do not even fail. If you do it and fail, it is a great resource. There is no greater resource than failure . . . As we fail over and over again, we reflect. There is no guarantee that church planting will succeed . . . We make a lot of mistakes while we plant churches.[28]

Develop Lay People for Ministry

The church, as a dynamic sending community, is constantly developing and mobilizing people. All six primary leaders confirmed the importance of developing and

---

26   PL3.
27   Allen, *Missionary Methods*, 91.
28   PL4.

mobilizing lay people by sharing ownership of the reproduction vision, preparing people for practical ministry, and entrusting responsibility to them.

All of these reproducing leaders mobilize lay people as their best practical answer to fulfill the Great Commission. In Japan, since practically there never will be enough professional pastors and missionaries, laity must be mobilized. However, in most Japanese churches there is a wide clergy-laity gap. Theologically these leaders consider lay people as God's chosen people (1 Pet 2:9,10). As one pastor affirmed, the clergy-laity gap does not have to exist: "Ordinarily the essential principle is that we are mutually equal on the same basis as the Lord's people under God's authority. Equally, the pastor and the believers are the Lord's people . . . The pastor is not the only leader in the church; it also extends to the lay people."[29] Mobilizing lay people profoundly affects the relationships, authority, and structure of their church.

The leaders' sharing joint ownership for church reproduction produces some who feel called to this ministry. These leaders spend much time preparing people in practical training as one shared: "Evaluate those who have received the burden to plant churches from God. Evaluate their desire if it truly comes from the Lord. Then have the people around them also think about [their suitability] . . . Then if it is okay, we will send them out."[30]

To give members freedom and trust them to work interdependently takes remarkable risk-taking faith by the primary leaders. From the beginning, enjoying an open relationship of trust (*shinrai suru*) between the leaders and the believer is crucial in freely entrusted ministry.[31] One leader clarified, "Even though they do ministries freely, they thoroughly talk it through with the [directors] and ministries are handed over based on trust (*shinrai kankei*)."[32]

Lay people are mobilized by sharing and nurturing ownership of a church reproduction vision. Those with vision are selected based on their calling, giftedness, and experience in practical ministry. They are then prepared through practical hands-on training and eventually entrusted with ministry. "Disciples are born, raised up, and sent out in this great work. They are sent out to many places including the workplace," asserted one leader.[33] One leader cautioned about leadership for new churches:

---

29 PL1.
30 PL4.
31 Secondary Leader 7 (SL7).
32 PL6.
33 PL4.

> If a person wants to multiply churches (as the leader of the church),
> he needs to actually do it and also develop people. [He needs] to
> develop people who can be responsible for church planting. I think
> this is the key for everything. If the person does not think about
> planting churches, he will put the people he developed under him
> and make them his subordinates. Then church planting does not
> happen. It is important to develop people for the sake of church
> planting and send them out. Unless we keep developing people,
> church multiplication will not occur.[34]

Though it was not a focus of this research, there were two common methods of church reproduction revealed. First, people felt called by God to plant a church in their major city or geographical region. Second, members are transferred or relocated for schooling or employment in geographical locations farther from the mother church. In both cases the church prepared, resourced, and encouraged these workers in their church planting ministry.

Lead Relationally through Encouragement

These church-reproducing leaders choose a leadership style that is predominantly relational and is focused on encouragement. Their authority in these relationships allows them to release others into ministry, which generates less organizational and a more relational structuring of the church. Overall, their priority is people, and they are extraordinarily patient with those they lead.

These leaders' chosen role is not a pastoral role but more as a coach, equipper, mentor, and encourager. They lead principally by means of their relational authority and exert appropriate relational and spiritual authority to maximize personnel resources. A study of growing churches in Japan found leadership that exercised spiritual authority to empower and entrust ministry to others was the most effective.[35] Leaders exercise authority through relationships, so are more like spiritual fathers than bosses.

Their preferred leadership style through patience provides freedom to release others into ministry. While Japanese society continues to have vertical organiza-

---

34   Ibid.
35   OC International Japan, *Establishing the Church in Japan for the Twenty-first Century: A Study of 18 Growing Japanese Churches* (Kiyose City, Japan: OC International Japan, 1993), 14.

tion and relationships, these leaders through relational leadership have lowered the vertical leadership pyramid, making it less hierarchical, thus making it both flatter and wider.

This leadership avoids control and stifling of ministry, as one leader cautioned: "Do not control . . . Give encouragement and give blessing [to them] . . . Never control the person who does the new ministry. Give him 'full independence' and encourage him."[36] Rather than controlling people, releasing people for ministry actually develops more production capacity for church reproduction. Entire movements, not solely individuals, can be restricted: "If you control (*shihai*), it will die, the fire of church planting will be lost and the multiplication will be stopped."[37]

Implement Aggressively through Practical Ministry

These church-reproducing leaders decisively lead their ministry teams. They are concerned for real-world fulfillment and obedience to the Great Commission. These leaders implement ministry aggressively, achieve ministry objectives practically and realistically, and lead the church into new directions.

Their role as a leader is to see the church expand and reproduce as a living, growing organism. Due to the nature of the church being dynamic and alive, they believe you cannot control or manage the church. Detailed planning prevents the leader "go[ing] with [the] flow,"[38] so their planning and strategy is practical, based on vision, can overcome obstacles, following simple leadership structure and decision making.

In order to be obedient to the Scriptures, these courageous leaders, through risk-taking faith (see above), overcome obstacles and hindrances to reproduction. They see themselves as practical and realistic, utilizing the tools of flexibility and creativity to birth new churches, as stated by one leader: "Just do it and find out. I do not believe that if you do this that this will happen. We do not know until you do it. I am a realist."[39] They are not afraid of experimenting with new approaches to overcome hindrances to church reproduction in faith.

---

36   PL4.
37   Ibid.
38   PL2.
39   Ibid.

These leaders believe in the church taking aggressive new directions rather than defending or protecting (*mamori*) what already exists.[40] These leaders do not believe stability to be the true nature of the church and ministry, as one asserted, "The church is always wanting stability but it cannot reproduce without instability."[41] Moreover, leaders must do what is necessary to lead a church in new directions.[42] As they are aggressive leaders, their direction is not security or stability, as that would undercut risk.[43]

Field Research Summary

The six characteristics outlined above are closely interrelated. One of these characteristics, though exemplary, would not necessarily indicate a reproducing leader. These characteristics: envisioning the church as a dynamic sending community, receiving ministry vision from God, exercising risk-taking faith, developing lay people for ministry, leading relationally through encouragement, and implementing aggressively through practical ministry are more like an interactive cluster where they all work in concert.

In some sense, the result of this research seems more about their vision, faith, and view of the church than other aspects of their leadership. Their vision, faith, and theology appear predominant and affect leadership behavior. In order to fulfill their vision for their image of the church, they feel compelled to practically train people and send them out. This practical application seems to define their ministry role, style, and behavior. The final step of sending others would probably not happen without this change in foundational leadership. To view it another way, their practical leadership of reproducing churches derives from their applied theology of the church. A change in leadership role or behavior without the corresponding foundational changes of the view of the church (*kyokaikan*) will surely not result in the same ministry effects.

Some may argue that the key characteristic is the major function of developing lay people for church reproduction. These leadership characteristics should be viewed as a whole cluster rather than individually. However, that function cannot be accomplished without the vital foundation of vision, faith, and view of the church.

---

40   SL5.
41   SL3.
42   PL5.
43   PL6.

Missiological and Theological Implications

The real possibility of reproducing churches in a difficult mission field generates tremendous hope. The effectiveness of these churches parallels what Roland Allen would anticipate from following the principles of the apostolic method. These churches all demonstrate that broadening the number of pastoral leaders beyond the pastor-centered model and narrowing the large clergy-laity gap through empowering other leaders is effective in Japan. These leadership changes in turn demand a corresponding change in the normal application of the church as primarily an organization in which stability must be maintained.

Allen had a deep concern for ecclesiology and confronted the commonly held ecclesiological stance of his day.[44] From the results of this field research, it seems reasonable that Japanese leaders equally need to be challenged in their ecclesiology. Specific issues to discuss are (1) what defines a local church, and (2) issues related to church leadership.

First, what constitutes a local church?[45] Allen insisted that we had forgotten the basic principles of a simple church that the Apostle Paul followed.[46] In defining the local church, care must be taken as to what must be included and what is optional. Garrison warns against hindering the natural reproduction of indigenous churches.[47] Allen's view of the church was minimalistic but not reductionistic.[48] Churches and leaders "must understand that the process of developing a biblical ecclesiology begins with allowing the Scriptures to speak for themselves . . . to understand what is the *irreducible ecclesiological minimum,* or the basic essence of the church, for the church to be the church."[49] Such a statement suggests that a church definition must be based on what is biblically essential for the church instead of what is only desired or traditional.

Second, in regards to the theology of leadership, there are two vital issues: first, who qualifies as a church leader and, second, what is the primary role of pastoral leadership?[50] An irreducible, minimum definition of a pastoral leader would

---

44   Payne, *Roland Allen*, 37–46.
45   Cf. Mehn, "Leaders Reproducing Churches," 131–34.
46   Payne, *Roland Allen*, 43–44.
47   David V. Garrison, *Church Planting Movements* (Richmond, VA: Office of Overseas Operations, International Mission Board of Southern Baptist Convention, 1999).
48   I am thankful to Ed Stetzer for this useful terminology.
49   J. D. Payne, *Discovering Church Planting: An Introduction to the Whats, Whys, and Hows of Global Church Planting* (Colorado Springs: Paternoster, 2009), 32.
50   Cf. Mehn, "Leaders Reproducing Churches," 134–47.

reflect on a traditional view of a church leader, but would include bivocational and nonformally trained leaders. What qualifications are essential, and what are often understood as necessary but are extrabiblical?

Over thirty-five years ago Braun described the traditional Protestant church leader in Japan as the "pattern of one-paid-pastor-per-church, a professional clergy of one type with high educational qualifications."[51] An overview of the church scene in Japan today would appear very similar. Many writers on the church in Japan have appealed for a movement away from a clergy-centered church which encourages passivity by lay people to a member-oriented church that would empower lay people.[52] Several see the need for the church to mobilize the laity in church planting.[53]

As stated above, Roland Allen would advocate shared leadership among clergy and laity, with "voluntary clergy" who do not have formal education or other high level qualifications.[54] Allen, who believed in the "pestilent distinction between clergy and laity,"[55] was a campaigner for simple biblical qualifications and not professionalism. Murray, echoing Allen and others, calls for a "rejection of clericalism."[56] He believes, for the church to move forward, an elitist approach to ministry must be discarded; however, he does not advocate an abdication of leadership. In the removal of elitism, "the underlying issue is the empowerment of church members and release of ministry from the grip of a special class."[57] Lay pastors, qualified and affirmed by their congregations, may have received nontraditional training, work bivocationally, and possibly be part of a multiple pastoral staff. Pastoral leaders need to wrestle with these issues and develop a renewing comprehension of the true essence of spiritual leadership.

Many years ago, Braun proposed a system for Japan of fully ordained ministers (*Seikyoushi*), pastor-teachers (*Bokkai-Kyoushi*), preparatory ministers (*Hokyoushi*), elders, and other workers all involved in church reproduction.[58] For each level of

---

51   Braun, *Laity Mobilized*, 118.

52   Dale, *Coping with Culture*, 15; Mullins, *Christianity Made in Japan*, 180; and Thomas J. Hastings and Mark R. Mullins, "The Congregational Leadership Crisis Facing the Japanese Church," *International Bulletin of Missionary Research* 30, no. 1 (January 2006), 20–22.

53   Braun, *Laity Mobilized*; and Dafinn Solheim, "Church Planting in Japan since 1945," In *Church Planting Patterns in Japan*, ed. Carl C. Beck (Amagi Sanso, Japan: The Twenty-seventh Hayama Men's Missionary Seminar, 1986), 16.

54   Allen, *Missionary Methods*, 104.

55   Hubert J. B. Allen, *Roland Allen*, 125.

56   Stuart Murray, *Church Planting: Laying Foundations*, North American ed. (Scottdale, PA: Herald, 2001), 219–24.

57   Ibid., 223.

58   Braun, *Laity Mobilized*, 124–6.

leadership, there were commensurate levels of training and credentialing paralleling the level of spiritual responsibility. Braun and Murray agree, "The issue church leaders must wrestle with is: How do you propose to free the Church to provide pastoral care and the Sacraments for people, in whatever numbers, whenever and wherever they can be persuaded to acknowledge Jesus Christ as Savior and Lord?"[59] This issue is the same today but perhaps more urgent. Roland Allen had a vision for how lay leadership could be done for twentieth-century Anglicans, why cannot we in the twenty-first century see similar possibilities?

As Paul encourages, "Whoever aspires to be an overseer desires a noble task" (1 Tim 3:1), so more Japanese believers should be encouraged to investigate the pastoral ministry, and this desire should be encouraged, discovered, and affirmed in all leaders who are qualified for pastoral ministry. Various forms of leadership, whether or not seminary trained or full time, should be utilized and developed through appropriate formal or informal support and training.[60]

The mobilization of lay pastoral leadership would provide practical solutions to many vexing leadership problems in Japan. First, one reason for the declining numbers of the church is aging pastors retiring, leaving a leadership void. There is a distinct lack of seminarians to fill currently open positions and also replace soon-to-retire pastors. Second, the development of lay leadership can solve the problems of churches without pastors (*muboku*) or shared pastorates (*kenboku*). Third, raising up lay leaders from the harvest for the harvest would be vital in church planting strategies to reverse the declining growth rate in the number of churches in Japan. Fourth, lay people could provide the manpower for the many geographical regions within Japan where there are no churches today (twenty-four cities and 545 towns and villages are without a church and over 140 areas are underchurched).[61]

The second leadership issue is the primary role of pastoral leadership. As shared above, Roland Allen was a champion of leaders in a catalyzing role and preparing God's people for ministry (Eph 4:11). Leadership style and the lack of lay mobilization are recurring themes in research on the church in Japan.[62] Both Japanese

---

59   Ibid., 126.

60   Mehn, "Leaders Reproducing Churches," 27–28; cf. Eckhard J. Schnabel, *Paul the Missionary: Realities, Strategies and Methods* (Downers Grove, IL: IVP Academic, 2008), 389.

61   Church Information Service, "Protestant Church in Japan," 4–5.

62   Braun, *Laity Mobilized*; OC International Japan, *Establishing the Church*; Richard Bruce Pease, "Japanese Leadership Styles: A Study in Contextualizing Leadership Theory for Church Growth in Japan" (ThM thesis, Fuller Theological Seminary, 1989); and Michael John Sherrill, "Church Vitality in Japan" (PhD diss., Fuller Theological Seminary, 2002).

leaders and those outside Japan repeatedly mention these as a reason for the lack of growth in the church over the past decades. As exemplified by these reproducing leaders, what is needed is not just lay leadership development, but also the coinciding change in role of the leadership to empower lay ministry.[63] Garrison summarized worldwide research and strategic understanding related to church planting movements and found several universal elements to all these multiplication movements, including using local and lay leadership and multiplying lay leaders through on-the-job training.[64]

As seen in these reproducing leaders, a simple definition of the church and the mobilization and empowerment of lay people resonates with what Roland Allen saw in the Scripture and describes as "spontaneous expansion."

> I mean the expansion which follows the unexhorted and unorganized activity of individual members of the Church explaining to others the Gospel which they have found for themselves; I mean the expansion which follows the irresistible attraction of the Christian Church for men who see its ordered life, and are drawn to it by desire to discover the secret of a life which they instinctively desire to share; I mean also the expansion of the Church by the addition of new Churches.[65]

Conclusion

Leaders who have aggressive plans for church expansion at the expense of building a stable structure and organizational formation are generally viewed as mavericks among church leaders in Japan. The Apostle Paul is certainly revered by all Japanese church leaders for his theology and contributions to the Scripture. However, his entrepreneurial methods in establishing churches are not widely emulated.

These leaders of reproducing Japanese churches prove that the application of biblical principles advocated by Roland Allen actually do cause the spontaneous expansion of the indigenous church. This gives great hope for the church, as these reproducing Japanese churches are figuratively everywhere. Like Roland Allen we

---

63   Mehn, "Leaders Reproducing Churches," 137–40.

64   Garrison, *Church Planting Movements*.

65   Roland Allen, *The Spontaneous Expansion of the Church and the Causes Which Hinder It*, North American ed. (1927; repr., Grand Rapids: Eerdmans, 1962), 7.

must all return to scriptural authority for how we conduct missionary and church work in the twenty-first century.

May Roland Allen's words continue to haunt us and challenge us as we apply our missionary methods!

Works Cited

Allen, Hubert J. B. *Roland Allen: Pioneer, Priest, and Prophet.* Grand Rapids: Eerdmans, 1995.

Allen, Roland. *Missionary Methods: St. Paul's or Ours?,* American ed. Grand Rapids: Eerdmans, 1962. First published 1912.

———. *The Spontaneous Expansion of the Church and the Causes Which Hinder It.* North American ed. Grand Rapids: Eerdmans, 1962. First published 1927.

Braun, Neil. *Laity Mobilized: Reflections on Church Growth in Japan and Other Lands.* Grand Rapids: Eerdmans, 1971.

Church Information Service. "The Protestant Church in Japan in 2011." *Church Information Service News* 74 (2011): 4–5.

Dale, Kenneth J. *Coping with Culture: The Current Struggle of the Japanese Church.* Lutheran Booklets 3. Tokyo: Lutheran Booklet Press, 1996.

Dyer, Stanley R. "Japan's Group Consciousness as It Relates to Evangelism." DMiss major project, Trinity Evangelical Divinity School, 1982.

Garrison, David V. *Church Planting Movements.* Richmond, VA: Office of Overseas Operations, International Mission Board of Southern Baptist Convention, 1999.

Hastings, Thomas J., and Mark R. Mullins, "The Congregational Leadership Crisis Facing the Japanese Church." *International Bulletin of Missionary Research* 30, no. 1 (January 2006): 18–23.

Hesselgrave, David J. *Paradigms in Conflict: 10 Key Questions in Christian Missions Today.* Grand Rapids: Kregel, 2005.

Joshua Project. "Unreached Listings: 100 Largest Unreached Peoples." Accessed October 5, 2012. http://www.joshuaproject.net/unreached.php?listing=1& sf=population&so=asc.

Mehn, John W. "Characteristics of Leaders Reproducing Churches in Japan." DMin major project, Trinity International University, 2010.

Mullins, Mark R. *Christianity Made in Japan: A Study of Indigenous Movements.* Honolulu: University of Hawaii Press, 1998.

Murray, Stuart. *Church Planting: Laying Foundations,* North American ed. Scottdale, PA: Herald, 2001.

OC International Japan. *Establishing the Church in Japan for the Twenty-first Century: A Study of 18 Growing Japanese Churches.* Kiyose City, Japan: OC International Japan, 1993.

Ohashi, Hideo. *Kyokai Seicho Dokuhon* [*Church Growth by the Book*]. Tokyo: Inochi no Kotobasha [Word of Life Press], 2007.

Ott, Craig, and Stephen J. Strauss. *Encountering Theology of Mission: Biblical Foundations, Historical Developments, and Contemporary Issues.* Grand Rapids: Baker Academic, 2010.

Payne, J. D. *Discovering Church Planting: An Introduction to the Whats, Whys, and Hows of Global Church Planting.* Colorado Springs: Paternoster, 2009.

———. *Roland Allen: Pioneer of Spontaneous Expansion.* Lexington, KY: CreateSpace, 2012.

Pease, Richard Bruce. "Japanese Leadership Styles: A Study in Contextualizing Leadership Theory for Church Growth in Japan." ThM thesis, Fuller Theological Seminary, 1989.

Schnabel, Eckhard J. *Paul the Missionary: Realities, Strategies and Methods.* Downers Grove, IL: IVP Academic, 2008.

Sherrill, Michael John. "Church Vitality in Japan." PhD diss., Fuller Theological Seminary, 2002.

Snider, K. Lavern. *It's Happening in Japan Today: The Story of 8 Growing Churches.* Osaka, Japan: Japan Free Methodist Mission, 1980.

———. *Ten More Growing Churches in Japan Today.* Osaka, Japan: Japan Free Methodist Mission, 1985.

Solheim, Dafinn. "Church Planting in Japan since 1945." In *Church Planting Patterns in Japan,* edited by Carl C. Beck, 7–19. Amagi Sanso, Japan: Twenty-seventh Hayama Men's Missionary Seminar, 1986.

Steffen, Tom, *The Facilitator Era: Beyond Pioneer Church Planting.* Eugene, OR: Wipf & Stock, 2011.

Winter, Ralph D. "Three Types of Ministry." *Evangelical Missions Quarterly* 33, no. 4 (October 1997): 420–22.

10

Paul's or Theirs?—A Case Analysis of Missionary Methods among Muslims of the Philippines

MARK S. WILLIAMS

In the process of introducing the Muslims of the Philippines, it is always interesting to relay the story of Ferdinand Magellan and the first circumnavigation of the globe. The reader might pause and wonder: what is the relationship between the two? First of all, while it is true that Magellan was a Portuguese captain commissioned to lead a Spanish expedition that happened to complete the first circumnavigation, it is sometimes forgotten that Magellan himself did not finish that voyage. Instead, he was killed in battle on Mactan Island (now part of central Philippines) by Lapu-Lapu, "a native Muslim on Mactan and a representative of the Sultan of Sulu."[1] The sultan was a Muslim ruler whose domain was linked by intermarriage and trade to the vast Islamic sultanates of what is now Indonesia before its invasion by Dutch explorers.[2]

---

1   Richard J. Gordon, "An Act to Declare April 27 of Every Year as a Special Non-working Holiday throughout the Country to Commemorate the Victory of Lapu-Lapu and His Men over the Spaniards Led by Fernando Magallanes in the Historic Battle of Mactan on April 27, 1521, to Be Known as Lapu-Lapu Day or *Adlaw ni Lapu-Lapu*," Fourteenth Congress of the Republic of the Philippines—First Regular Session, Senate S. No. 2162, Senate of the Philippines (Manila: Government of the Republic of the Philippines, 2008), http://www.senate.gov.ph/lis/bill_res.aspx?congress=14&q=SBN-2162 (accessed December 3, 2011).

2   Jonathan Fuller, *Cross Currents: The Story of the Muslim and Christian Encounter in the Philippines* (Manila: OMF Literature, 2005), ch. 5.

When the Philippines became a Spanish colonial possession in the second half of the sixteenth century, the Filipino Muslim perception of Christianity as embodied by Spanish Roman Catholicism would resemble the Islamic animosity towards those that instigated the Crusades nearly five hundred years earlier.

> When the Spanish began to colonize the northern and central Philippine islands from 1565 onward, they came into direct conflict with the . . . Muslim people of the south. The Spaniards identified the Islamized natives with their traditional enemies, the Moors of North Africa, and thus called them Moros . . . Attempts to conquer and subjugate these Muslims led to the prolonged, although intermittent, hostilities known as the Moro Wars, which spanned more than 300 years of Philippine history. In the notorious tradition of divide and conquer, the Spanish manned their armies for these wars with Christian converts from the northern islands. This was to have profound and lasting consequences, for it led to a bitter enmity between Christian and Muslim Filipinos, even though these peoples probably shared a similar cultural heritage in pre-Islamic, pre-Christian times.[3]

By the dawn of the twentieth century, Spain lost the Philippines as a colony to the United States in the aftermath of the Spanish-American War. This provided the opportunity for American missionaries of all varieties, but especially mainline Protestant denominations, to join American colonial administrators in the task "to develop, to civilize, [and] to educate" all the peoples of the Philippines, including the Muslims.[4] More often than not, these American missionaries collaborated with the colonial administrators in order to ensure that Filipino Muslims would welcome "integration" into a cohesive, national Philippine state.[5] When the United States

---

3   James C. Stewart, "Maguindanao," in *Muslim Peoples: A World Ethnographic Survey*, 2nd ed., ed. Richard V. Weekes (Westport, CT: Greenwood, 1984), 464.

4   Peter G. Gowing, "Muslim-American Relations in the Philippines, 1899–1920," in *The Muslim Filipinos: Their History, Society and Contemporary Problems*, ed. Peter G. Gowing and Robert D. McAmis (Manila: Solidaridad, 1974), 33.

5   Thomas M. McKenna, *Muslim Rulers and Rebels: Everyday Politics and Armed Separatism in the Southern Philippines* (Berkeley: University of California Press, 1998), 104, 106. "Muslims were not to be excepted from direct colonial rule; close American supervision was required in order for Philippine Muslims to achieve a level of 'civilization' sufficient to allow their integration with their Christian counterparts in an eventual Philippine republic . . . The sole purpose of propelling Philippine Muslims along a path of development parallel to that of Christian Filipinos [was] to prepare their eventual integration into an inevitable postcolonial Philippine nation."

granted this island-nation its independence in 1946, the Philippines was known then (as it is now) to be the only Christian nation in Asia, based mainly upon the fact that 85 percent of Filipinos surveyed consider themselves to be *Katoliko*—that is, Roman Catholic. Penetration of the gospel and the hopeful establishment of churches among Filipino Muslims, however, has been paltry at best.

The immediate discussion evokes a pointed question raised by a seminal book on missionary methods first published one hundred years ago: "Was the moral, social and religious condition of the Provinces so unlike anything known in modern times as to render comparison between St. Paul's work and ours futile?"[6] This question then serves to guide the following analysis.

The Utility of the C1–C6 Spectrum

While there are many ways to conduct an analysis of case studies, we employ here the gauge of the C1–C6 Spectrum, which has been in vogue now for nearly fifteen years.[7] If the reader wonders why this format has been favored over other choices, the best answer is that this Spectrum came about directly from observing different manifestations of "church" in Muslim contexts.[8] Much has been written on this Spectrum since its advent; therefore, even a short literature review is beyond our scope here. Rather, in this chapter the Spectrum defines the categorizations (C1, C2, etc.) in the subsequent case studies.

---

6   Roland Allen, *Missionary Methods: St. Paul's or Ours?*, American ed. (1912; repr., Grand Rapids: Eerdmans, 1962), 1.

7   The C1–C6 Spectrum was first introduced in two seminal articles: Phil Parshall, "Danger! New Directions in Contextualization," *Evangelical Missions Quarterly* 34, no. 4 (October 1998): 404–6, 409–10; and John Travis, "The C1 to C6 Spectrum: A Practical Tool for Defining Six Types of 'Christ-centered Communities' ('C') Found in the Muslim Context," *Evangelical Missions Quarterly* 34, no. 4 (October 1998): 407–8. Other select articles in the *Evangelical Missions Quarterly* (1996–2007), the *International Journal of Frontier Missions* (2000–2007), and recent volumes of the online *St. Francis Magazine* (2009–11) continue the discussion for the interested reader.

8   John Travis, personal communication to the author, November 29, 2011.

The C1–C6 Spectrum[9]

	C1	C2	C3	C4	C5	C6
Christ-centered community description:	A church foreign to the Muslim community in both culture and language	C1 in form but speaking the language used by Muslims, though their religious terminology is distinctively non-Muslim	C2 using non-Islamic cultural elements (e.g., dress, music, diet, arts)	C3 with some biblically acceptable Islamic practices	C4 with a "Muslim follower of Jesus" self-identity	Secret believers, may or may not be active members in the religious life of the Muslim community
Self-Identity:	"Christian"	"Christian"	"Christian"	"Follower of Isa [Jesus]"	"Muslim follower of Jesus"	Privately: "Christian," or "Follower of Isa" or "Muslim follower of Jesus"
Muslim Perception:	Christian	Christian	Christian	A kind of Christian	A strange kind of Muslim	Muslim

9   Joshua Massey, "God's Amazing Diversity in Drawing Muslims to Christ," *International Journal of Frontier Missions* 17, no. 5 (Spring 2000): 5–14, 7.

One more point of clarification: because of the widespread assumption that "church" means "a building for public and especially Christian worship,"[10] Travis termed the six C categories in the Spectrum as variants of "Christ-centered communities" (indicated above). This was done intentionally to distinguish between an apparent popular understanding of "church," and how the Spectrum encourages a return to a more biblical understanding of *ekklesia*.[11]

The Reason for Using Historical and Fictitious Composite Case Studies

There are some places in the world where it is against the law to preach the gospel. While that is true for some Islamic nations of the world, it is not true in the Philippines. Whereas a detailed history of the impact of Spanish and American colonialism upon Muslims of the Philippines might prove helpful, it is beyond our scope here. What such a historical account would show is that Filipino Muslims are now minorities in their own homeland: the designs for "integration" mentioned above succeeded to the extent that there are now more non-Muslim Filipinos in the former sultanate ancestral domain of the southern Philippines than there are Muslims. This is the main reason why jihadist movements and rebel fronts were battling the Armed Forces of the Philippines[12] until a tentative agreement was penned in the fourth quarter of 2012. Therefore, at the risk of oversimplification, Filipino Muslims by and large are defined by their stand against perceived Christian influences in the Philippines, whether espoused by expatriate Westerners or Roman Catholic Filipinos.

It will not come as a surprise, then, to realize that Christian mission work among Muslims of the Philippines is perceived negatively, since the end result is that the Muslim becomes a "Christian." It would therefore be irresponsible of me to document with transparency the efforts of expatriate and national missionaries to Filipino Muslims which might place them in unintended danger. The use of the

---

10   *Merriam-Webster Online*, s.v. "church," accessed April 30, 2013, http://www.merriam-webster.com/dictionary/church.

11   Allen, *Missionary Methods*, 127: "The churches did not make up the Church, but the Church established the churches."

12   One of the best recent studies on the complexity of this situation is Astrid S. Tuminez, "This Land Is Our Land: Moro Ancestral Domain and Its Implications for Peace and Development in the Southern Philippines," *SAIS Review* 27, no. 2, (Summer–Fall 2007): 77–91, http://muse.jhu.edu/journals/sais/summary/v027/27.2tuminez.html (acessed December 18, 2008).

case-study method here, however, offsets this potential through the use of pseudo-nyms and geographic generalization.[13]

The cases that follow, therefore, are short narratives describing the characteristics of select missionary methods used among Filipino Muslims. These cases are presented below in C-number category designation, and are either fictitious constructs or historical composites of persons, places, and events. Indeed, some of the names and places have been changed to protect identities.

C1 Missionary Methods among Filipino Muslims

Roman Catholic Methods

Missionaries of the Society of Jesus—the Jesuits—from Spain accompanied the armada that landed in Manila Bay in the late sixteenth century. After a ninety-year period where Jesuits were expelled from the Philippines (1768–1859), the spread of the Roman Catholic faith on Mindanao in the southern Philippines did become the sole responsibility of the Jesuits from mid-nineteenth century on through to the present. The Jesuit legacy in the Philippines is similar to that in Latin America: establish a mission compound where the Catholic church building would be the epicenter from which influence over dogma (and commerce) affecting society would radiate outwards. Despite great successes on the northern island of Luzon, and even more in some of the central islands of the Visayas, it was only towards the end of the nineteenth century that Jesuits were erecting such mission compounds on Mindanao, especially in those areas under previous control by Muslims.

When Spaniards finally wrested control of the river delta at Cotabato from the ruling Muslim sultanate there, Jesuits settled and built the compound at Tamuntaka, hispanized as "Tamontaca." The place was the ancestral domain for a non-Muslim people group, the Teduray, as well as some Muslims that lived there. Both Muslim and non-Muslim members of the indigenous populations were enticed to come live at the Tamontaca mission in exchange for their allegiance and conversion to Roman Catholicism. One such noteworthy Muslim, with the name of Ignacio Ortuoste, was actually captured as a young child during a skirmish between Spanish and Muslim

---

13   While many case-study formats exist, those presented here resemble the shorter cases of Marvin K. Mayers, *Christianity Confronts Culture: A Strategy for Crosscultural Evangelism*, revised and enlarged ed. (Grand Rapids: Zondervan, 1987), 313–88.

warriors. Brought to the mission compound, he was baptized in the Catholic faith, given a Spanish Christian name (Ignacio Ortuoste), and educated by the Jesuits.[14]

The preceding case is characteristic of the method that Jesuits used all over the Philippines: (1) separate them from their birth community, (2) extract them culturally (especially by giving them Christian names), and (3) convert them to the practices and traditions of the Catholic Church. Because Roman Catholics are "a church foreign to the [indigenous] Muslim community in both culture and language,"[15] this attests to the C1 category designation. Not much has changed in the nearly one hundred years since the time of Ignacio Ortuoste; the policy of extraction has been the primary methodology in Catholic conversion in this region during this period.

Protestant Methods

The American victory over the Spanish at the turn of the twentieth century brought the opportunity for American Protestant missions to expand into the Philippines. With regard to the southern Philippines, agreements were reached by various Protestant groups that the Episcopal Church and the Christian and Missionary Alliance (CMA) would have primary jurisdiction on Mindanao. Since 1902, the CMA concentrated on mission work in the predominantly Muslim areas of the Sulu archipelago, Zamboanga, and Cotabato. Somewhat similar to the Catholics was the CMA method of attracting Muslim youth with the promises of the gospel, housing and educating them as needed, and requiring that they renounce Islam and become Christians of the CMA denomination. Whereas most Protestants could not compete against the centrifuge of Roman Catholic influence in the township centers, it is interesting that in the center of downtown Cotabato City there is a large CMA church compound—and not a Roman Catholic cathedral.

Muslims who become CMA Christians do not have to change their Arabic-sounding names to more hispanized names, but they do have to affirm and subscribe to a CMA catechism of biblical and doctrinal belief. Rev. Akmad Ibrahim[16] was a Muslim youth growing up with Catholic and Protestant classmates at the public high

---

14   This historical narrative is reconstructed from Philippine Jesuits, "Jesuits in the Philippines," http://www.phjesuits.org/who-we-are/jesuits-in-the-philippines (accessed December 25, 2011); Nicholas P. Cushner, "The Abandonment of Tamontaka Reduction (1898–1899)," *Philippine Studies* 12, no. 2 (Manila: Ateneo de Manila University, 1964): 288–95; McKenna, *Muslim Rulers*, 97; and Peter Scheurers, *The Rio Grande Mission: Jesuit Missionary Letters from Mindanao* (Manila: University of the Philippines Center for Integrative and Development Studies, 1990).

15   Massey, "God's Amazing Diversity," 7.

16   This name is a pseudonym, but the narrative is a historical composite reconstruction.

school in the immediate years of post–World War II Cotabato. Befriending some CMA Christians, they encouraged Ibrahim to come to church with them, which he did. By the time he was ready to enter college, Ibrahim had been baptized as a CMA Christian and encouraged to attend Ebenezer College in Zamboanga. After graduating from Ebenezer, Ibrahim enrolled at Alliance Biblical Seminary in Manila to become a CMA pastor. The Reverend Akmad Ibrahim is a Muslim background believer (MBB) and CMA pastor for many decades since.

This case highlighting the methods of CMA in the southern Philippines is similar to the Jesuit counterpart above: there was separation and extraction once Ibrahim decided to become a CMA Christian. But the retention of his original Arabic Muslim name is a notably different feature. Still, CMA institutions and practices manifest a "foreign" church as perceived by neighboring Muslim inhabitants; hence, it produces a C1 result.

C2 Missionary Methods among Filipino Muslims

Roman Catholic Methods

Fast-forwarding from the turn of the twentieth century to the last fifty years (post–Vatican II), Roman Catholics everywhere—including the Philippines—have been using vernacular expressions for God (and for Jesus, etc.) instead of insisting on Latin terms only.[17] Ironically, this is problematic in the southern Philippines where Muslim use of Allah or the Catholic rendering of Diyos for God incites disdain for the other. To lessen this derision, Filipino Catholics involved in dialogue with Muslims have little trouble substituting Allah for Diyos, especially if it will win the Catholics audience with the latter. Some justify the use of the Arabic name for God on the basis that Arab Christians hundreds of years before Muhammad used Allah to refer to Yahweh (God). The concern for the cultural baggage attached to Diyos (God, as brought by the imperial *conquistadores* of Spain) has others equally worried about the baggage attached to Allah (God, for all Muslims). In its use within the

---

17   Jose M. de Mesa, "Doing Theology as Inculturation in the Asian Context," in *New Directions in Mission and Evangelization 3*, ed. James A. Scherer and Stephen B. Bevans (Maryknoll, NY: Orbis Books, 1999), 118: "The Church, in Vatican II, once again reiterated her commitment to re-root the Good News within specific socio-cultural contexts just as Jesus enfleshed himself within the Jewish culture. It expressly stated that 'theological investigation must necessarily be stirred up in each major socio-cultural area' (A.G. 22) if cultural rootedness of the Gospel and of the Church is to be achieved."

conciliar circles of Philippine Catholic-Muslim dialogue, then, the jury is still out regarding the efficacy and merit of this limited contextualization of terminology.

This composite case account shows willingness on the part of these Catholics-in-dialogue to relinquish the constricting reins of complete C1 extraction and establish a common point of reference. This willingness is manifest in names terminology only, however. Because when it comes to deeper Christian theological explanations for what the atonement of Christ has actually done for the believer, terms such as "propitiation," "absolution," and even "the Trinity," do not exist in the Islamic religious lexicon. Therefore, as indicated in the chart above, this characterizes a C2 category designation.

Mennonite Methods

The emergence of Mennonite peace initiatives between Christians and Muslims on Mindanao has been impressive. Emanating from the exuberant leadership of a Filipino-Canadian Mennonite, Rev. Daniel Pantoja, "Peacebuilders Community" is a grassroots movement in bringing Filipino Muslims and Christians together to discuss, apologize, and repent for the bitter attitudes each has had for the other. Starting by making relationships with *ustadz* (religious teachers) and other Islamic leaders, Pantoja has catalyzed a network of goodwill[18] that has led to the creation of a retail store on the main boulevard leading into Davao City called "Coffee for Peace"—a veritable business-as-mission approach to reconciliation. A missionary colleague has recently corroborated that Rev. Pantoja has made arrangements to use volcanic soil-rich lands belonging to John Perrine (of Unifrutti-Chiquita planta-tions) in Bukidnon Province, Central Mindanao, to be a permanent place to grow coffee for this ministry enterprise.[19] While there is use of names terminology to show respect to Muslim partners, Rev. Pantoja does not invoke any other forms of contextualization in his novel approach.

This case is based upon true events of Pantoja's organization in Davao City and other places on Mindanao. They are a matter of public record and formal press releases. Pantoja's method digresses from the Roman Catholic conciliar approach as it is less about "talk" (dialogue) and more about "walk" (relationship building

---

18   PeacebuildersCommunity.org, "Update: April–June 2006; A Christian-Muslim Peacebuilding Partnership Begins! A Joint PBC and CIAPDI News Release," http://peacebuilderscommunity.org/archives/updates/2006.2q.html (accessed August 26, 2007).

19   Andy Tillman, personal communication to the author, October 12, 2011.

and business activity), but it is similarly rooted in the experimental limit of using Arabic names terminology. While some would maintain that Pantoja's approach espouses passive evangelism only, it fits within the evangelism pattern of the Mennonite tradition.

C3 Missionary Methods among Filipino Muslims

Moving further up the C categories on the Spectrum, there might be certain Protestant denominations equally steeped in tradition that begin to get nervous, as the upward move leaves the comfort zone of more accepted Western worship expressions. Others who find older methods wanting entertain the idea of experimenting with newer ones that might appear to be "out of the box," while keeping the tether of biblical guidance as a restraint.

In one such experiment, after a few years of evangelism and Bible studies, Korean Baptist missionaries founded the Isa Al Masih[20] Baptist Church, with services on Sundays (in accordance with traditional Christian observance). The worshipers leave their footwear at the door before entering a large room that functions as the sanctuary (and fellowship hall after services are over). The people sit on floor mats (no pews in this church building) where the men tend to be in front, more separated from the women (akin to Muslim style). Worship songs are contemporary praise songs (not from the Baptist hymnal), accompanied by an electric keyboard, electric bass guitar and drum set, but there is also a set of Muslim brass gongs (played xylophone-style), with some other indigenous percussion instruments. After lively worship, where the worshipers are free to move in the Spirit and lifting hands up in worship, the lead minister preaches from the Bible. As a Filipino MBB, this minister can choose to preach either in the local Muslim language, in Tagalog, or in English.

This case is mostly factual, with few fictitious composite elements; however, the geographic location is not specified directly, out of concern for the security of those worshiping there to this day. Consulting the C-number chart again, it is evident that this mixture of traditional-church and indigenous elements, including the use of translated praise songs, categorizes this fellowship as C3. The result is an apparent compromise between certain traditional elements that appealed to the Korean missionaries and other incorporated indigenous practices to make the Muslim seekers and converts feel more comfortable. Perhaps these Korean missionaries took a lesson

---

20   Isa Al Masih is the Arabic name for "Jesus the Messiah."

from the pages of Allen's seminal book: "In order that Christianity might be fairly represented to the Greeks, it was necessary for St. Paul to emphasize the truth that Christianity was not a sect of Judaism."[21] Make the following substitutions—(1) "Muslims" for "Greeks," (2) "the Korean missionaries" for "St. Paul," and (3) "faith for non-Muslims only" for "sect of Judaism"—and the point here is made.

C4 Missionary Methods among Filipino Muslims

The C Spectrum categories were first introduced in a seminal article by Phil Parshall in 1998 (as mentioned in footnote 8). This is significant because Parshall "certainly became the vanguard of C4 in the late 70s [since he] . . . took the necessary time and actually wrote a book to build his case for C4, *New Paths in Muslim Evangelism* (Baker Books, 1980)."[22] After success in Bangladesh drew too much attention to his novel methodology,[23] Parshall and his wife relocated to the Philippines in the early 1980s where their daughter was in boarding school at Faith Academy.

Optimistic that these principles were translatable to other Islamic contexts, Parshall convinced the Philippine branches of OMF and SEND to join forces with SIM with the goal of reaching Muslims of the Philippines through similar C4 methods. Since this approach was very incarnational, in less than ten years by the mid-1990s Filipino evangelical Christians were also challenged to experiment with ways to contextualize the gospel and witness to Filipino Muslims in a manner that would not be threatening to the latter's values and culture. The following, therefore, is a broad composite of select Filipino and expatriate missionary C4 experiments among Muslims of the Philippines.

Urban centers on Mindanao resemble small townships in their development and infrastructure (with the exception of Davao City in the east and Cotabato City in the west). In Alhambra,[24] Muslims have been living side by side with non-

---

21   Allen, *Missionary Methods*, 21.

22   Joshua Massey, "His Ways Are Not Our Ways," *Evangelical Missions Quarterly* 35, no. 2 (April 1999), 188–97 (italics in original).

23   Frank M. C. Pardue, "The Philippines' Last Frontier" (DMin. diss., Columbia International University, 2001), 105; "*Bangladesh*: In 1975, after years of very little fruit in his ministry, Parshall began in a new direction. He emphasized contextualization: living close to the level of the people, dressing in native dress, using Allah as the name for God, fasting especially during Ramadan, and using contextualized worship. Evangelism emphasized Old Testament stories that were found in the Qur'an, as well as discussion on issues of sin, atonement, and end times. A room was rented in villages where they could serve tea and dialogue. Ministry targeted male heads of families. Baptism was done in groups, not individually. The result was that between 5,000 and 35,000 came to know Christ" (italics in original).

24   In this composite case, the name used for this city—Alhambra—is a pseudonym. Alhambra is a

Muslims since the strong national integration thrust of the early twentieth century. Most Muslims are farmers or fishermen, with some being merchants in the wet and dry markets of the town center of Alhambra. With friendship evangelism as a goal, missionaries enter Alhambra by getting permission to live in-community with Muslim neighbors. Learning the vernacular language and local Muslim culture is of primary importance in order to gauge the felt needs of the Muslim community by which to expand the incarnational approach.

After many years of positive community presence and witness, Alhambra residents and officials have allowed various expatriate and Filipino missionaries to assist in medical needs, in farming techniques and animal husbandry, and in educational needs for school-age Muslim children. In the context of building community trust, some missionaries have been able to incorporate biblical stories and values that resonate with the Qur'an, and this has sometimes led to interest in Scripture study (in which the Qur'an can serve as a bridge to presenting biblical truth), as well as a subsequent desire for corporate worship. In these worship gatherings, footwear is left outside, and

> instead of ablutions, they emphasize "cleanliness of the heart." It begins with a greeting, the "washing of hearts," singing, sharing requests and thanksgiving, a children's presentation, and the message. In this C-4 approach, Muslim background believers are offered a functional substitute for the community they have left.[25]

This case seems to present an unrealistic, idyllic situation. Certainly, the charge of "rice Christianity" could be leveled against these who have apparently benefited from the missionaries' efforts to address their felt needs. However, the communities represented by this composite are real and, recently, some of them experienced the terror and destruction of the December 2011 flash floods in Northern Mindanao. The aforementioned seminal book posits, "Who is to decide whether the candidate is honest in his confession of repentance and faith?"[26] Actually, every two years these MBBs are given the chance to reflect this honesty when they come and attend the BCER somewhere on Mindanao.[27]

---

fortress-citadel in southern Spain and, though mistaken at times to be a Spanish term, the name is Arabic in origin.

25   Pardue, "The Philippines' Last Frontier," 131–32.

26   Allen, *Missionary Methods*, 97.

27   Pardue, "The Philippines's Last Frontier," 97: "The Biennial Conference on Ethnic Religion

C5 Missionary Methods among Filipino Muslims

Again we reference Parshall. In the last paragraph of his seminal 1998 article, he states, "[Due to] the Islamic charge of deception . . . I am convinced that C5 missionaries are on very shaky theological and missiological ground."[28] There is more to unpack in that statement than space here allows. Two things can and must be said, however, for clarity purposes: (1) there are C5 missionaries, and (2) there are C5 believers. Enough has been written on the former[29] to present *prima facie* evidence on "the Islamic charge of deception," which, of course, is unfortunate.

In regard to experience in the Filipino Muslim context, there is a true case (with pseudonyms in place) in which a Filipino MBB subscribes to the C5 / Insider Movement methodology.[30]

> Khalid is a Muslim [background] believer. He grew up in traditional Muslim culture in southern Philippines. He upholds the teachings of Islam and worships according to the Islamic faith. He adheres to the claim that Muhammad is a prophet of *Allah*. At the same time, he bases his salvation on the teachings of *Isa al Masih*. He finds support and evidence for this salvation from within the *Injil* [New Testament Gospels] and the *Qur'an* . . .

(BCER) started in 1985, in an effort to help people in Muslim ministry . . . The BCER is a workers' consultation of individuals, church leaders, mission leaders, field and support mission workers . . . The BCER continues to grow . . . and the mixture of attendees has shifted from mainly foreigners years ago, to primarily a Filipino audience." In the October 2009 BCER, this included nearly two dozen Filipino MBBs.

28   Parshall, "Danger!," 410.

29   Select articles include Gary Corwin, "A Humble Appeal to C5 / Insider Movement Muslim Ministry Advocates to Consider Ten Questions," *International Journal of Frontier Missions* 24, no. 1 (Spring 2007): 5–21; Timothy C. Tennent, "Followers of Jesus (Isa) in Islamic Mosques: A Closer Examination of C-5 'High-spectrum' Contextualization," *International Journal of Frontier Missions* 23, no. 3 (Fall 2006): 101–15; J. Dudley Woodberry, "To the Muslim I Became a Muslim?" *International Journal of Frontier Missions* 24, no. 1 (2007): 23–28; and Scott Woods, "A Biblical Look at C5 Muslim Evangelism," *Evangelical Missions Quarterly* 39, no. 2 (2003): 188–95.

30   Proponents for Insider Movements (IM) argue that IM and C5 are not one and the same: Kevin Higgins, "Acts 15 and Insider Movements among Muslims: Questions, Process, and Conclusions," *International Journal of Frontier Missions* 24, no. 1 (Spring 2007): 29–40, 37; and Rebecca Lewis, "A Note about the C-scale," *International Journal of Frontier Missions* 24, no. 2 (Summer 2007): 76. Others disagree—namely, Gary Corwin and Ralph Winter, "Reviewing the September–October *Mission Frontiers*," *Mission Frontiers* (January–February 2006): 17–20: "Regarding what the term 'insider movement' conveys . . . my own acquaintance with the term comes primarily from the sphere of discussions of Islamic contextualization. In that context it is used pretty much as a synonym for C5 contextualization."

This agenda is in relation to the paradigm of the insider movement (or IM) to which these believers have committed themselves. The conditions of this paradigm are the same as those which Khalid has practiced in his own life. These believers have chosen to remain Muslims and worship the One Supreme God named *Allah* according to Islamic religious tradition. They read the *Qur'an,* the *Injil* and the rest of the Bible. They have entrusted their salvation to *Isa al Masih,* strive to obey his commands and strive to live according to his teachings. They serve their fellow Muslims because this is the calling of *Allah* in their lives. In serving their fellow Muslims, they want to bring the presence of God's Kingdom among them, which is what *Isa al Masih* taught his disciples to do. As a whole, these groups of Muslims have remained legally and socio-religiously within their local Muslim communities while coming to an understanding of faith in *Isa al Masih.*[31]

In such a case as this, the C5 missionary has sought to impart less of himself or herself so that the C5 believer realizes that it is acceptable to retain the cultural and socioreligious identity of a Muslim (as per the C5-missionary interpretation of 1 Corinthians 7:20).[32] What has been little voiced until now is the separatist nature of C5 believers who adopt the Insider Movement paradigm. Recently published are the following C5 sentiments:

> "Most of us [in this C5 ministry] do not want anything to do with [traditional] Christian religion. We want *Isa Almasih* [Jesus Christ] . . . but not Christianity."

> "[As a C5 MBB] I have reconverted to being a Muslim. I even like the Jesus more of the Qur'an than of the New Testament."[33]

At this, there is a proclamation in that missionary methods book that "spiritual unity is unity, means unity, and is expressed in terms of unity. Outward opposition

---

31   Emo Yango, "Towards a Hermeneutic of Affirmation for Local Theologizing in Closed Access Communities" (DMiss diss., Asian Graduate School of Theology, 2009), 127–28, 131–32. ch. 4.

32   "Each person should remain in the situation they were in when God called them." Issues of exegesis (or eisegesis) surrounding this verse are expounded on more fully in Tennent, "Followers of Jesus," 107; and Woods, "A Biblical Look," 190.

33   Mark S. Williams, "Revisiting the C1–C6 Spectrum in Muslim Contextualization," *Missiology* 39, no. 3 (July 2011): 345. (italics in original).

is a certain sign that spiritual unity does not exist."[34] Corollary, then, is the question: "Whither *koinonia?*" Where indeed is the unity of the body of Christ (as represented by the church) between C1, C2, C3, and C4 believers, and those of the C5 approach?

C6 Missionary Methods among Filipino Muslims

As noted above on the chart, C6 represents the phenomenon of secret believers. Given the Islamic precept that apostates from Islam can be killed even by their own family members, the situation of secret believers of Jesus in Islam is more widespread than has been recorded. In the Philippines, accounts by some MBBs attest to the fear that generates this phenomenon; hence, the C6 status of secret believers. Any assurances that an expatriate or Filipino missionary might make to a secret believer to "come away" and "come out" of hiding becomes tantamount to an indirect form of extractionism. Encouraging their solitary stance as a secret believer, however, is akin to the metaphor of a branch not grafted properly into the vine. How then shall this solitary one grow and even survive under such conditions?

With this background in mind, the current protocol for secret believers anywhere in the Muslim world has been to "remain within the mosque, not uniting with a visible church," which then begs the question: "Can a Hindu or a Muslim or a postmodern American disillusioned with the institutional church come to Jesus Christ, accept him as Lord and Savior, and not unite with the visible church?"[35] On this point, the aforementioned book is unambiguous regarding Paul's methods:

> We have seen that St. Paul did not set out on his missionary journeys as a solitary prophet, the teacher of a solitary individualistic religion. He was sent forth as the messenger of a Church, to bring men into fellowship with that body. His converts were not simply united one to another by bonds of convenience arising from the fact that they lived in the same place, believed the same doctrine, and thought it would be a mutual assistance to form a society. They were members one of another in virtue of their baptism. Each was united to every other Christian everywhere, by the closest of spiritual ties, communion in the one Spirit.[36]

---

34   Allen, *Missionary Methods*, 128.
35   Timothy C. Tennent, "The Challenge of Churchless Christianity: An Evangelical Assessment," *International Bulletin of Missionary Research* 29, no. 4 (October 2005): 171.
36   Allen, *Missionary Methods*, 126.

The previous concern for *koinonia* presents itself once again and uncovers challenging aspects of the higher-end C categories—in the southern Philippines and other parts of the Muslim world.

Concluding Remarks

One hundred years after its initial publication, Allen's seminal book was referenced in this chapter for the examination of select Christian missionary methods in reaching Muslims of the Philippines. Recall that book's evocative, pointed question: Are the "moral," "social," or "religious conditions" sufficiently different in the southern Philippines from first-century Asia Minor to question the motives behind some of the methods used?

First of all, Allen would say that Paul was not one to mix, and thereby syncretize, beliefs and practices of the old faith with that of faith in Christ.

> It is as impossible to quote the legends of the gods so worshiped, as it is to quote the stories of the Incarnations of Krishna, whilst the accompanying circumstances of the worship were only less filthy than the lives of the divinities in whose honour they were performed. Suffice it to say that the temples of Ephesus and Corinth were no more the homes of virtue than the temples in Benares or Peking. The language of St. Paul in the Epistle to the Ephesians exactly describes the condition of the people from whom his converts came, and amongst whom they lived.[37]

This, then, epitomizes the divide between C1–C4 and C5–C6 theory and practice: how far is too far? Allen intimates above that Paul was careful not to confuse his new converts by syncretizing old practices with new belief. But then there are those instances where Paul apparently did not discourage utilizing old knowledge in order to introduce the new faith (e.g., the sermon on Mars Hill in Acts 17).

---

37   Ibid., 30. Allen then footnotes the verses to which he refers—Ephesians 4:17–19—which are rendered here in their entirety: "So I tell you this, and insist on it in the Lord, that you must no longer live as the Gentiles do, in the futility of their thinking. They are darkened in their understanding and separated from the life of God because of the ignorance that is in them due to the hardening of their hearts. Having lost all sensitivity, they have given themselves over to sensuality so as to indulge in every kind of impurity, with a continual lust for more" (NIV).

Allen is arguing that the antecedent conditions of his pointed question have not changed, just as the depravity of human sin has not changed. He therefore would caution against any of these "conditions" that would prompt a "charge of deception," regardless of the degree to which one accommodates the old life to the new. This is the tension to which the C Spectrum speaks in presenting Christianity to those who have not yet heard, whether to Muslims of the Philippines or elsewhere in the world. And this is the standard to which Allen held himself, and his readers, in presenting his material. Would we adhere to Paul's methods or ours (theirs)? For those in the challenge of ministry to Muslims, Allen's counsel should not be readily ignored.

Works Cited

Allen, Roland. *Missionary Methods: St Paul's or Ours?*, American ed. Grand Rapids: Eerdmans, 1962. First published 1912.

Corwin, Gary. "A Humble Appeal to C5 / Insider Movement Muslim Ministry Advocates to Consider Ten Questions." *International Journal of Frontier Missions* 24, no. 1 (Spring 2007): 5–21.

———, and Ralph Winter. "Reviewing the September–October *Mission Frontiers*." *Mission Frontiers* (January–February 2006): 17–20.

Cushner, Nicholas P. "The Abandonment of Tamontaka Reduction (1898–1899)." *Philippine Studies* 12, no. 2 (Manila: Ateneo de Manila University, 1964): 288–95.

Fuller, Jonathan. *Cross Currents: The Story of the Muslim and Christian Encounter in the Philippines.* Manila: OMF Literature, 2005.

Gordon, Richard J. "An Act to Declare April 27 of Every Year as a Special Non-working Holiday throughout the Country to Commemorate the Victory of Lapu-Lapu and His Men over the Spaniards Led by Fernando Magallanes in the Historic Battle of Mactan on April 27, 1521, to Be Known as Lapu-Lapu Day or *Adlaw ni Lapu-Lapu*." Fourteenth Congress of the Republic of the Philippines—First Regular Session, Senate S. No. 2162, Senate of the Philippines. Manila: Government of the Republic of the Philippines, 2008. Accessed December 3, 2011. http://www.senate.gov.ph/lis/bill_res.aspx?congress=14&q=SBN-2162.

Gowing, Peter G. "Muslim-American Relations in the Philippines, 1899–1920." In *The Muslim Filipinos: Their History, Society and Contemporary Problems,* edited by Peter G. Gowing and Robert D. McAmis, 33–41. Manila: Solidaridad, 1974.

Higgins, Kevin. "Acts 15 and Insider Movements among Muslims: Questions, Process, and Conclusions." *International Journal of Frontier Missions* 24, no. 1 (Spring 2007): 29–40.

Lewis, Rebecca. "A Note about the C-scale." *International Journal of Frontier Missions* 24, no. 2 (Summer 2007): 76.

Massey, Joshua. "God's Amazing Diversity in Drawing Muslims to Christ." *International Journal of Frontier Missions* 17, no. 5 (Spring 2000): 5–14.

———. "His Ways Are Not Our Ways." *Evangelical Missions Quarterly* 35, no. 2 (April 1999): 188–97.

Mayers, Marvin K. *Christianity Confronts Culture: A Strategy for Crosscultural Evangelism.* Revised and enlarged ed. Grand Rapids: Zondervan, 1987.

McKenna, Thomas M. *Muslim Rulers and Rebels: Everyday Politics and Armed Separatism in the Southern Philippines.* Berkeley: University of California Press, 1998.

Mesa, Jose M. de. "Doing Theology as Inculturation in the Asian Context." In *New Directions in Mission and Evangelization 3,* edited by James A. Scherer and Stephen B. Bevans. Maryknoll, NY: Orbis Books, 1999.

Pardue, Frank M. C. "The Philippines' Last Frontier." DMin diss., Columbia International University, 2001.

Parshall, Phil. "Danger! New Directions in Contextualization." *Evangelical Missions Quarterly* 34, no. 4 (October 1998): 404–6, 409–10.

PeacebuildersCommunity.org, "Update: April–June 2006; A Christian-Muslim Peacebuilding Partnership Begins! A Joint PBC and CIAPDI News Release." Accessed August 26, 2007. http://peacebuilderscommunity.org/archives/updates/2006.2q.htm.

Philippine Jesuits. "Jesuits in the Philippines." Accessed December 25, 2011. http://www.phjesuits.org/who-we-are/jesuits-in-the-philippines.

Scheurers, Peter. *The Rio Grande Mission: Jesuit Missionary Letters from Mindanao.* Manila: University of the Philippines Center for Integrative and Development Studies, 1990.

Stewart, James C. "Maguindanao." In *Muslim Peoples: A World Ethnographic Survey,* 2nd ed., edited by Richard V. Weekes, 462–67. Westport, CT: Greenwood, 1984.

Tennent, Timothy C. "The Challenge of Churchless Christianity: An Evangelical Assessment." *International Bulletin of Missionary Research* 29, no. 4 (October 2005): 171–77.

————. "Followers of Jesus (Isa) in Islamic Mosques: A Closer Examination of C-5 'High-spectrum' Contextualization." *International Journal of Frontier Missions* 23, no. 3 (Fall 2006): 101–15.

Travis, John. "The C1 to C6 Spectrum: A Practical Tool for Defining Six Types of 'Christ-centered Communities' ('C') Found in the Muslim Context." *Evangelical Missions Quarterly* 34, no. 4 (October 1998): 407–8.

Tuminez, Astrid S. "This Land Is Our Land: Moro Ancestral Domain and Its Implications for Peace and Development in the Southern Philippines." *SAIS Review* 27, no. 2 (Summer–Fall 2007): 77–91. Accessed December 18, 2008. http://muse.jhu.edu/journals/sais/summary/v027/27.2tuminez.html.

Williams, Mark S. "Revisiting the C1–C6 Spectrum in Muslim Contextualization." *Missiology* 39, no. 3 (July 2011): 335–51.

Woodberry, J. Dudley. "To the Muslim I Became a Muslim?" *International Journal of Frontier Missions* 24, no. 1 (Winter 2007): 23–28.

Woods, Scott. "A Biblical Look at C5 Muslim Evangelism." *Evangelical Missions Quarterly* 39, no. 2 (April 2003): 188–95.

Yango, Emo. "Towards a Hermeneutic of Affirmation for Local Theologizing in Closed Access Communities." DMiss diss., Asian Graduate School of Theology, 2009.

CONCLUSION

Missionary Methods:
The Questions that Still Dog Us

CRAIG OTT

David Hesselgrave wrote some years ago:

> The missiological enterprise is rooted in three kinds of source materials—God's revelation in Holy Scriptures and the church creeds and theological systems based on that revelation; the social and behavioral sciences that help us understand the world's peoples and their cultures, belief systems and customs; and past and present missionary experiences with its successes and failures. To explore any missiological issue without seeking out and examining relevant data from all three of these repositories of information is to truncate missiological inquiry and place both missionary theory and practice in jeopardy.[1]

As we seek to discern the most appropriate missionary methods for our day in various contexts and in the face of great complexity, Hesselgrave's warning rings true. This volume has brought together a collection of essays that explore the topic of missionary methods from these three perspectives: theology, history, and social science. The value of such a multidisciplinary approach is hopefully self-evident.

---

1   David J. Hesselgrave, Preface to *Missiology and the Social Sciences: Contributions, Cautions and Conclusions*, Evangelical Missiological Series 4, ed. Edward Rommen and Gary Corwin (Pasadena: William Carey Library, 1996), 1.

But then certain questions still linger; questions that—in different shapes and forms—missionary practitioners have encountered and with which missiologists have wrestled for centuries. This conclusion briefly discusses four of those questions that never seem quite resolved: the problem of pragmatism, the role of the social sciences, the interpretation and application of missionary methods found in the New Testament, and the challenge of contextualization. Each of these questions bears heavily on discerning appropriate missionary methods, and each generation of missionaries will need to answer them afresh for their time and place.

The search for effective missionary methods is as old as Christian mission itself. In the New Testament the missionary movement began with fits and starts (recall the controversy over the preaching of the gospel to the Gentiles in Acts 10–11), yet it is quite clear that the Apostle Paul was very intentional about his method of fulfilling the Great Commission (e.g., Rom 15:17–29). The history of the expansion of Christianity is a story of experimentation, reflection, and debate over missionary methods. In the thirteenth century Raymond Lull reflected deeply on the effective evangelization of Muslims. In the sixteenth and seventeenth century the Jesuits experimented with contextualization in Asia that sparked the "rites controversy." The nineteenth-century Protestant missionary movement gave rise to Venn and Anderson's famous three-self formula for planting indigenous churches. John L. Nevius' classic *The Planting and Development of Missionary Churches* (1899) bucked conventional missionary wisdom and spelled out a methodology that has been credited with contributing to the remarkable growth of the church in Korea. The twentieth century saw unprecedented specialization and the use of technology in missionary methods for everything from missionary aviation, to radio, to Bible translation and, yes, to the Internet.

Sometimes these methods were theologically reasoned. At other times they grew out of practical necessity. And at still other times they were the fruit of an entrepreneurial spirit and the search for more creative approaches to greater effectiveness and efficiency. Towards the end of the nineteenth and early twentieth centuries there was a veritable explosion of research and writing on missionary methods.[2] Roland Allen's landmark *Missionary Methods: St. Paul's or Ours?* (1912)

---

2   Titles from this period not discussed in this chapter include John Smith, *The Magnetism of Christ: A Study of Our Lord's Missionary Methods* (New York: Armstrong, 1904); Belle M. Brain and Delavan Leonard Pierson, *Holding the Ropes: Missionary Methods for Workers at Home* (New York: Funk & Wagnalls, 1904); Edwin Munsell Bliss, *The Missionary Enterprise: A Concise History of Its Objects, Methods And Extension* (New York: Revell, 1908); and Hugh Watt White, *Jesus the Missionary: Studies in the Life of Jesus as the Master, the Model, the Proto-type for All Missionaries* (Shanghai: Presbyterian

is perhaps the best-known attempt to critically assess missionary methods on the basis of the Pauline example. Birthed in the frustration of disappointing progress in the spread of the gospel and the establishment of healthy indigenous churches, Allen went back to the Bible. As evidenced by the essays in this volume and numerous other publications celebrating *Missionary Methods'* one hundredth anniversary, the issues he raised and questions about missionary methods remain relevant and no less controversial.[3] Gary Corwin's chapter provided us with a thumbnail overview of missionary methods. But this concluding essay briefly addresses those four aforementioned questions that have historically and to this day continue to dog the missionary enterprise when it comes down to discerning missionary methods.

The Question of Pragmatism

Missionaries tend to be characterized by two qualities: theological conservatism and methodological pragmatism. Most would not be missionaries if they were not convinced of the uniqueness of Christ, the necessity of conversion, and that the Bible is our authoritative and trustworthy guide. At the same time, because of the many challenges they face in cross-cultural ministry and the high personal and financial cost of mission work, they are keenly interested in discovering the most fruitful missionary methods. Simply put, they want to see results. After all, eternity is at stake. These two characteristics unfortunately (and unnecessarily) can create an unhealthy tension.

North American missionaries, though not alone, have been on the forefront of a pragmatic approach to missionary methods in a sometimes reckless quest for creative ways to "get the job done" whatever it takes. The desire for results (what I am loosely calling "pragmatism"[4]) can lead to several problems. First, it can lead to the ends justifying means that are inconsistent with biblical goals or values. One

---

Mission Press, 1916). For more general research and literature, including dissertations from this period, see George Gurganus, "A Study of Missionary Methods in Historical Perspective," *Restoration Quarterly* 9, no. 2 (January 1966): 79–90.

    3   See, for example, the July 2012 issue of *Transformation*, entirely dedicated to Roland Allen; Robert L. Plummer and John Mark Terry, *Paul's Missionary Methods: In His Time and Ours* (Downers Grove, IL: InterVarsity Press, 2012); J. D. Payne, *Roland Allen: Pioneer of Spontaneous Expansion* (North Charleston, SC: CreateSpace, 2012); and Robin Daniel, *Mission Strategies: Then and Now* (Chester, UK: Tamarisk, 2012).

    4   The philosophical school of pragmatism as advocated by Charles Sanders Peirce and others has been called the first truly American philosophy. I am, however, using the term here in a more popular sense.

can be tempted to neglect sound theological foundations in favor of shortsighted quick fixes and the endless search for the elusive "silver bullet." David Hesselgrave's chapter in this book highlights the temptation to avoid teaching the "stern doctrines" of the Bible for fear that they will offend. Second, not only may the end be justifying inappropriate means, but the end itself may be inappropriate. Often "results" are defined in terms of numbers alone (e.g., more conversions, more churches planted, more children fed, etc.). Quality may be sacrificed for quantity; for example, higher attendance but lower commitment.

The Church Growth Movement (CGM) from the late 1960s though the early 1990s represents an unprecedented pragmatic approach that produced vast amounts of research and literature in search of the most effective missionary methods.[5] It boldly employed empirical research and historical analysis to uncover principles for how and why people become Christians and how "people movements" develop. Though much of the harsh critique of the CGM was overstated or misunderstood the movement, there was truth enough in the critique that the movement lacked serious theological reflection leading to dubious practices.[6] The CGM was followed by other approaches with a pragmatic bent: church health, Natural Church Development, cell-church ministry, church planting movements, etc., though these have generally been more modest in their claims.

One attempted corrective to such human-oriented approaches to missionary methods arose from within the CGM itself with C. Peter Wagner's (and others') teachings on spiritual warfare and territorial spirits. Yet even this emphasis on prayer, power evangelism, and spiritual warfare took on a curious, pragmatic twist, becoming the new key for effective world evangelization, complete with how-to guidelines. This too raised a lively and at times divisive discussion among missiologists and theologians.[7] Robert H. Bennett's chapter in this collection, reflecting

---

5   The seminal works of Donald A. McGavran, father of the CGM, include *The Bridges of God* (New York: Friendship Press, 1955); and *Understanding Church Growth* (Grand Rapids: Eerdmans, 1970).

6   That weakness no doubt contributed to its decline as a movement. Another factor was the simple fact that the application of the principles generally did not deliver what they promised: more and larger churches. For a more current critical discussion of the CGM, see Elmer L. Towns and Gary McIntosh, eds., *Evaluating the Church Growth Movement: 5 Views* (Grand Rapids: Zondervan, 2004).

7   See, for example, two EMS series, volumes 3 and 5; C. Douglas McConnell, ed., *The Holy Spirit and Mission Dynamics* (Pasadena: William Carey Library, 1997); and Edward Rommen, ed., *Spiritual Power and Missions* (Pasadena: William Carey Library, 1999). See also the papers from the Lausanne consultation Deliver Us from Evil (DUFE), convened in Nairobi, Kenya, in A. Scott Moreau, Tokunboh Adeyemo, David G. Burnett, Bryant L. Myers, and Hwa Yung, eds., *Deliver Us from Evil* (Monrovia, CA: World Vision International, 2002).

upon Allen's discussion of the supernatural and missionary methods, offers a more balanced approach, specifically when engaging adherents of animistic religions.

The very word "pragmatic" evokes disdain in many, based upon the assumption that the quest for results inherently compromises biblical values and goals, as it too often has. The dismissive label "managerial mission" has been applied by some to anything in missions that smacks of measurability and efficiency.[8] Indeed, strictly speaking, we cannot manage or manipulate true effectiveness in ministry. These concerns have their justification. The value of works such as Allen's *Missionary Methods* is that they challenge us to recalibrate our ends and means in light of the word of God.

However, the alternative to an overemphasis on results cannot be to neglect them altogether with a simplistic "just be faithful and leave the results to God." While there is indeed no substitute for dependency upon God, such an attitude can end up as an excuse for ineffectiveness, wastefulness, repeating mistakes of the past, and promoting a view that human means are irrelevant to the sovereign working of God. Rightly understood, do we really want to be totally *un*pragmatic? Do we not care *at all* about efficiency and effective methods? Without a wink of compromise, the Apostle Paul sought to "win as many as possible" and became in his words, "all things to all people so that *by all possible means* I might save some" (1 Cor 9:19,22; italics mine). He then exhorts, "Run in such a way as to get the prize" (1 Cor 9:24). Surely good stewardship and accountability call us to give attention to the fruit (or lack thereof) of our ministry efforts. The Scriptures praise wisdom and understanding: "Desire without knowledge is not good—how much more will hasty feet miss the way" (Prov 19:2). Employing methods with greater likelihood of success is a sign of good stewardship and diligence, not necessarily lack of faith.

Scripture is clear that God alone gives spiritual growth. At the same time, we have the privilege of being God's fellow workers, and we are exhorted to build with care upon the foundation once laid, for the quality of our labors will be judged by God (1 Cor 3:9,10). Rather than speaking of being *either* pragmatic *or* biblical, perhaps we should speak of being *both* pragmatic *and* biblical. We need more theological clarity, more faith in God, more spiritual power, more divine guidance,

---

8   The term probably originated with Samuel Escobar, "Evangelical Missiology: Peering into the Future at the Turn of the Century," in *Global Missiology for the 21st Century*, ed. William D. Taylor (Grand Rapids: Baker Academic, 2000), 101–22. For a response, see Levi T. DeCarvalho, "What's Wrong with the Label 'Managerial Mission'?" *International Journal of Frontier Missions* 18, no. 3 (Fall 2001): 141–46, and Corwin's discussion of "managerial mission" in chapter 4 of this volume.

and more effective methods. God has provided us with the Bible, the Holy Spirit, and our intellects to this end. Let us not create a false dichotomy, but be committed to biblical priorities and in dependency upon God give our best to achieve them.

The Question of Social Science

Related to the previous question is the more specific matter of the role of the social sciences in the theory and practice of missions. Though the social sciences have a relatively short academic history, as Eugene Nida once aptly said, "Good missionaries have always been good 'anthropologists.'"[9] Whether that involved an intuitive appreciation of culture or more intentional and systematic approach, missionaries have been students of culture. Over the last half century the social sciences have come to have far-reaching influence on virtually every dimension of missionary practice: communication theory, linguistics, social change, moral theory, counseling, education, leadership development, church planting, community development, and more.

In the early twentieth century there were only a few missionaries who did research and writing using the social sciences—for example, the German Bruno Gutman,[10] who studied under the father of experimental psychology Wilhelm Wundt; and British Edwin W. Smith,[11] who became the only missionary elected to be president of the Royal Anthropological Institute. But it was the more pragmatically minded North Americans who would in the second half of the twentieth century make the social sciences a central, if not indispensable, feature of missiology and missionary training.[12] Books such as Eugene Nida's *Customs and Cultures* and Paul Hiebert's *Anthropological Insights for Missionaries* became required reading for thousands of missionaries. As doctoral programs were developed in missiology and intercultural studies, the vast majority of dissertations employed social science methodology and field-based research. John Mehn's doctoral research on church leadership and church planting in Japan, as summarized in his chapter in this volume, is a good example of this.

---

9   Eugene Nida, *Customs and Cultures* (New York: Harper, 1954), xi.

10   See Ernst Jśchke, "Bruno Gutman's Legacy," *Occasional Bulletin of Missionary Research* 4, no. 4 (October 1980): 165–69.

11   See W. John Young, "The Legacy of Edwin W. Smith," *International Bulletin of Missionary Research* 25, no. 3 (July 2001): 126–30.

12   For an overview of the use of anthropology in missiology, see Robert J. Priest, "Anthropology and Missiology: Reflections on the Relationship," in *Paradigm Shifts in Christian Witness*, ed. Charles E. Van Engen, Darrell Whiteman, and J. Dudley Woodberry (Maryknoll, NY: Orbis Books, 2008), 23–32.

Yet the growing influence of the social sciences in missiology has also raised many questions and suspicions. First, some missiologists began to fear they would overshadow theology altogether.[13] Is theology being left at the doorstep of the missiological house? Should missionary training be a matter of teaching social sciences, communication theory, and community development, or would not a solid foundation in biblical studies alone be adequate? Second, most social theories have their origins in secular ideologies that have little, if any, place for God and the supernatural, and they generally assume humanism. Finally, will dependence upon empirical research and emphasis upon natural causes and human agency lead to a lack of dependency upon God, or worse, to socially or psychologically manipulative missionary methods? This debate has a lively history[14] and has been the topic of numerous publications and conferences.[15]

Indeed social theories are not ideologically neutral. The missionary use of the social sciences must thus be cognizant of how such ideologies can potentially become a Trojan horse for unbiblical values and methods. But the option is not to ignore the social sciences, for to do so would be to adopt by default an implicit and unreflected social theory that could be no less damaging.[16] Rather, we must examine, discern, and chasten social theories in light of biblical teaching. We move as a hermeneutical community in an epistemological spiral from the Bible to social theory, to praxis, and back to the Bible. We thereby prayerfully reflect, correct, and expand our understandings of God's purposes and God's people, and thus discern appropriate practices to engage cultures with the transforming power of the gospel.

History is replete with examples of disastrous mistakes missionaries have made due to a failure to understand culture. Such mistakes unnecessarily hinder the spread of the gospel, the building of the church, and the betterment of the people. The challenges that missionaries face cannot be answered by a simplistic appeal to the

---

13   For example, Edward Rommen, "The De-theologizing of Missiology," *Trinity World Forum* 19 (1993): 1–4.

14   See, for example, Priest, "Anthropology and Missiology"; Darrell Whiteman, "Anthropology and Mission," in *Paradigm Shifts in Christian Witness*, ed. Charles E. Van Engen, Darrell Whiteman, and J. Dudley Woodberry (Maryknoll, NY: Orbis Books, 2008), 3–12; Paul G. Hiebert, "Critical Issues in the Social Sciences and Their Implications for Mission Studies," *Missiology* 24, no. 1 (January 1996): 65–82; and Charles R. Taber, *To Understand the World, to Save the World: The Interface between Missiology and the Social Sciences* (Harrisburg, PA: Trinity Press International, 2000).

15   For example, Edward Rommen and Gary Corwin, eds., *Missiology and The Social Sciences: Contributions, Cautions and Conclusions*, Evangelical Missiological Series 4 (Pasadena: William Carey Library, 1996).

16   It is naive to assume that biblical exegesis and theology are somehow uninfluenced by the theologian's social understandings.

Bible. Sound theology must be accompanied by insights into culture, linguistics, and religion in order to arrive at biblically faithful practices in contexts so different from those that we find in the Bible.

God chooses to most often work through human agents, and when employed with discernment the social sciences are an important tool in the missionary toolbox. The New Testament clearly demonstrates that the Apostle Paul adapted his preaching and ministry to his audiences. Thus, the question naturally follows: what influenced the adaptation? Paul was not a social scientist, but he did understand his audiences. The value of the social sciences is in helping us understand people and societies. Yet in and of themselves they do not prescribe methods. Determining the practical implications of what social sciences tell us about people remains a decision to be determined on other grounds; most importantly on the basis of biblical goals and values, and a biblical worldview. Joel Thiessen's chapter not only reminds us that the social sciences can prove "common sense" assumptions to be false and misleading, but also demonstrates how careful research can reveal overlooked spiritual needs and opportunities. Anthony Casey's chapter illustrates the value of understanding a people's communication and learning styles (e.g., orality) for effective disciple making. To the extent that the social sciences help missionaries understand a people's beliefs, worldview, values, communication processes, needs, etc., they will help missionaries adapt their methods in ways appropriate to that audience in the achievement of biblical ends.

A missionary's failure to have a clear understanding of a people, such as their understanding of sin and morality, can actually lead to a *less* biblically accurate communication of the gospel and cast unnecessary stumbling blocks before the feet of the audience.[17] Robert Priest argues that whereas Western theology has tended to make philosophy its discussion partner, the social sciences offer a potential partner for theologizing.[18]

To summarize: the answer is not to somehow pit theology against social science, but rather understand how each is important and how to exercise discernment in both the manner in which we do theology and the manner in which we utilize social science. Such an approach will help us arrive at missionary methods that are

---

17   A practical and enlightening example of this is provided by Robert Priest, "'Experience-near Theologizing' in Diverse Human Contexts," in *Globalizing Theology*, ed. Craig Ott and Harold A. Netland (Grand Rapids: Baker Academic, 2006), 180–95.

18   Ibid.

in alignment with God's purposes, dependent upon his working, and appropriate to the cultural realities of the people we serve.

The Question of New Testament Precedence

Here a double question arises: what are the missionary methods described in the New Testament, and to what extent are we to follow their example? This is on the one hand a historical and exegetical question, and on the other a hermeneutical question. The following discussion will focus primarily upon Pauline mission, which has been the focus of most scholarship on New Testament mission. More recently a question has emerged regarding the interpretation of John 20:21, the role of Jesus (versus Paul) as the model for mission, incarnational mission, and its implications for missionary methods.[19] Space does not allow that debate to be taken up here. However, John Cheong's chapter in this volume provides an excellent continuation of that discussion.

Defining New Testament Missionary Methods

Scholarly literature on New Testament missionary methods began to appear in earnest in the early twentieth century.[20] We have already noted Roland Allen's *Missionary Methods* appearing in 1912 which has a decidedly practical orientation, looking for answers to the challenges that the missionary endeavor faced. Allen followed up that work with *The Spontaneous Expansion of the Church and the Causes which Hinder It* in 1927. With his chapter in this volume Robert Gallagher joins numerous others in identifying the limitations of Allen's analysis, even in terms of description. Allen's Anglican background, his theological assumptions, and contemporary issues influenced his discussion of Paul's methods. This highlights the difficulty of arriving at even a description of Pauline missionary methods.

---

19   See, for example, Ross Langmead, *The Word Made Flesh: Towards an Incarnational Missiology* (Dallas: University Press of America, 2004); David J. Hesselgrave, "Incarnationalism and Representationalism," in *Paradigms in Conflict: 10 Key Questions in Christian Missions Today* (Grand Rapids: Kregel, 2005), 141–65; Christopher R. Little, *Mission in the Way of Paul* (New York: Lang, 2005), 78–86; and Craig Ott and Stephen J. Strauss, *Encountering Theology of Mission: Biblical Foundations, Historical Developments, and Contemporary Issues*, with Timothy C. Tennent (Grand Rapids: Baker Academic, 2010), 97–104.

20   See footnote 2 in this chapter.

The venerable mission historian Kenneth Scott Latourette, though praising Allen's work, notes several important facts to be remembered in light of mission history, two of which are relevant to this discussion.

> In the first place, we should recall that we really have little information of the methods by which the Gospel spread so rapidly ... In the second place, the spread of the Faith, while phenomenal, took place in only a small segment of the globe and, in the main, in one culture: it was limited chiefly to the Roman Empire and a few fringing areas.[21]

In other words, while we know some things about Paul's mission, there is much that we do not know. Details are lacking. Also, we can only speculate how Paul might have changed his methods had he ministered in a radically different context with which he was unfamiliar, such as East Asia or sub-Saharan Africa. Thus, dogmatic statements about missionary methods are difficult to make, either descriptive or prescriptive, based upon the biblical record alone.

The other most notable work of the time was Adolph Harnack's *The Mission and Expansion of Christianity in the First Three Centuries*[22] that appeared 1902 in German, ten years prior to Allen's landmark text and referenced by him. Compared to Allen's mere 173 pages, the English edition of Harnack's more scholarly work encompassed two volumes totaling 871 pages. Harnack was influenced by liberal theology and critical understandings of Scripture, making evangelicals uncomfortable with his work and conclusions. Evangelicals would have to wait exactly one hundred years for a scholarly and updated answer to Harnack with the appearance of Eckhard Schnabel's massive *Early Christian Mission*.[23]

Scholarly interest in New Testament mission following Harnack did not arise again until the 1960s with the appearance of Ferdinand Hahn's *Mission in the New Testament*,[24] and more specifically on missionary methods with Joseph A. Grassi's *A World to Win: The Missionary Methods of Paul the Apostle*.[25] No shortage of scholarly works on Pauline mission and strategy has followed. Two works are particularly

---

21   Kenneth Scott Latourette, "The Light of History on Current Missionary Methods," *International Review of Missions* 42, no. 2 (April 1953): 138.
22   2 vols., trans. James Moffatt (NewYork: Williams & Norgate, 1904/1905).
23   2 vols. (Downers Grove, IL: InterVarsity Press, 2004), German original 2002.
24   Trans. Frank Clarke (Naperville, IL: Allenson, 1965), German original 1963.
25   Maryknoll: Maryknoll, 1965.

noteworthy that reflect high scholarship and evangelical sentiments: Michael Green's now-classic *Evangelism in the Early Church*[26] and Rainer Riesner's masterful *Paul's Early Years: Chronology, Mission Strategy, Theology.*[27]

However, a new standard for New Testament mission history was set with the appearance of Schnabel's encyclopedic *Early Christian Mission*. With two volumes totaling 1928 pages, it stands unsurpassed as an authoritative study of early Christian mission based upon the biblical record and background information. The work concludes with a relatively brief chapter on implications for contemporary mission practice. In 2008 Schnabel released *Paul the Missionary: Realities, Strategies and Methods*[28] that summarizes large portions of *Early Christian Mission* in a more readable 518 pages focusing only on Pauline mission. Schnabel's discussion of Pauline method brings us much closer to answering questions (in part raised by Allen) such as: whether Paul intentionally departed from his church plants after a short time, and if Paul had a specific geographic strategy. However, Schnabel's discussion of implications for contemporary missionary practice is limited, and he is critical of most missiologists' attempts to draw principles for missionary methods from the book of Acts.

Learning from the Methods Described in the New Testament

This brings us to the next question of description versus prescription. Once we have understood the missionary methods of the New Testament (as far as that is possible), to what extent are they normative for missionary practice today? Should we imitate them? If not, what can we learn from them? Is it necessary to ask about every missionary method, "Did Paul do it this way?" Is that the right question to be asking? Evangelicals believe that all Scripture, including Acts, is profitable for instruction (1 Tim 3:6–17). Yet our world is so different from that of the New Testament that the practical lessons for today's practice of mission are not so self-evident.

This is a larger hermeneutical question than can be adequately addressed in this brief conclusion. On the one hand, restraint is warranted in attempts to imitate Pauline methods in detail. Turning Acts into a "handbook for missionaries" is a dubious undertaking. Efforts to draw a direct line of application from the Acts

---

26   Grand Rapids: Eerdmans, 1970.
27   Trans. Doug Scott (Grand Rapids: Eerdmans, 1998), German original 1994.
28   Downers Grove, IL: InterVarsity Press, 2008.

narrative to specific contemporary challenges is a complex task.[29] Luke's purpose is more to demonstrate the Spirit-empowered advance of the gospel into the Gentile world and its universal efficacy than to provide a practical manual on missionary methods.[30] The implications of Acts for missionary methods today will be less in discerning rigid guidelines, imitating specific methods, or sorting out what applies and what does not.[31]

If restraint in naive imitation is warranted on the one hand, we must on the other hand with confidence follow the broad trajectory of the Acts narrative and hold all the more firmly to its theological foundations and rationale. Many of Allen's observations are in keeping with such an approach, such as his emphasis upon the Holy Spirit, as argued by Rob S. Hughes in his chapter of this book. Acts portrays the advance of the gospel in the power of the Spirit, with many surprises along the way and in the face of internal and external opposition. We observe bold preaching that challenges idolatry and calls for repentance. An unwavering commitment to the truth of the gospel is accompanied by a nuanced approach to culture and a call to love and holiness. A concern to preach the gospel where Christ is not yet known is balanced with a concern for the spiritual maturity of believers.[32] The spiritual dynamics, the interpersonal dynamics, the ecclesial dynamics, and the cultural dynamics we observe in Acts and the Pauline corpus all evidence a fluid movement greater than ourselves, yet strangely linked to human means. We can expect the Holy Spirit to continue to surprise us, raising up new and creative methods as we face new and daunting challenges, while at the same time remaining rooted in the unchanging gospel of the kingdom. We can trust the Spirit to empower the progress of the gospel, transform lives, create believing communities, equip and gift new leaders, and advance to the ends of the earth by reproducing disciples, missionaries, and churches. Our methods and strategies must in this sense be continually "resubmitted" to the Word and the Spirit of God.[33]

---

29   Little, *Mission*, is one of the better attempts to apply a careful examination of Pauline practice to contemporary methods of international partnership and resource sharing.

30   For an overview of interpretations and understandings of Acts, see Mark Allan Powell, *What Are They Saying about Acts?* (Mahwah, NJ: Paulist, 1991).

31   Some popular hermeneutic texts, such as Gordon D. Fee and Douglas K. Stuart, *How to Read the Bible for All Its Worth: A Guide to Understanding the Bible* (Grand Rapids: Zondervan, 1993), list guidelines for sorting out normative versus descriptive teaching in narrative texts such as Acts. But such a method can lead to a hermeneutical separating of the wheat from the chaff: "This applies to us, and that does not."

32   This is explicit in Paul's letters (e.g., Rom 15:20; Col 1:28).

33   See David J. Hesselgrave, "Paul's Missions Strategy," in *Paul's Missionary Methods: In His Time and Ours*, ed. Robert L. Plummer and John Mark Terry, 127–45 (Downers Grove, IL: InterVarsity Press,

Hermeneutical approaches such as Kevin Vanhoozer's *theodrama*[34] point to fresh avenues of understanding and application, whereby we become the actors on God's stage, playing our role, acting in wisdom, and consistent with the unfolding story line of salvation history. A similar alternative approach employs game logic—much the way the rules and goals of a game remain the same but strategies change with changing circumstances. So too, specific strategies for participation in God's mission will change with changing contexts, while the rules and goals remain the same. In the New Testament, particularly in Acts, we see the goals, rules, and strategies of mission being played out under divine direction.[35]

The Question of Contextualization

Though the term "contextualization" is of relatively recent coinage, the practice is certainly not. Dean Flemming's *Contextualization in the New Testament* demonstrates that the entire New Testament itself is an example of contextualization. The Apologists of the first centuries of church history attempted to appropriate Greek philosophy in evangelism and theology. The Jesuits in Asia boldly experimented with what was considered radical accommodation of local culture, which led to a century-long debate in the Roman Catholic Church. Though there were some remarkable exceptions,[36] much of nineteenth-century missions so associated with colonialism represent what Paul Hiebert called the era of noncontextualization.[37] Early liberation theologians created controversy with a praxis-oriented approach to contextualization utilizing Marxist social theory. In short, missionaries have always wrestled with how their methods will challenge, accommodate, transform, and/or adopt local culture. Though the discussions may seem at times rather theoretical, questions of contextualization present some of the thorniest practical challenges that missionaries face: how to translate the Bible, how to deal with traditional practices,

---

2012); and Michael Pocock, "Paul's Strategy: Determinative for Today?" in Plummer and Terry, *Paul's Missionary Methods*, 146–59.

34   Kevin J. Vanhoozer, *The Drama of Doctrine* (Louisville: Westminster John Knox, 2005).

35   See Crait Ott, "Contextualization, the Bible, and Games: What I Learned about Theology from The Settlers of Catan" *Evangelical Review of Theology* 37:3 (July 2013):210–226.

36   See, for example, Steven Kaplan, "The Africanization of Missionary Christianity: History and Typology," in *Indigenous Responses to Western Christianity*, ed. Steven Kaplan (New York: New York University Press, 1995), 9–28.

37   Paul G. Hiebert, "Critical Contextualization," in *Anthropological Reflections on Missiological Issues* (Grand Rapids: Baker, 1994), 75–92.

how to engage non-Christian religions, how to affect social change, how to answer ethical dilemmas, how to address syncretism.

The controversial nature of this challenge and its implications for missionary methods have become painfully evident in the current debate over so-called Insider Movements (IM). During the last fifteen years a mountain of literature has been published (mostly in missiological journals) pro and con over the question of how to best evangelize and disciple Muslims. Mark S. Williams' chapter in this volume illustrates how this has played out historically in the Philippines. The issues are deeper than mere adaptation of outward cultural forms, but strike at the very heart of Christian conversion, identity, and ecclesiology. Consensus does not yet appear in sight. The IM debate exemplifies how missionary methods relating to contextualization are not only complex but also emotional. The stakes are high in terms of their practical, ecclesial, and theological implications.

Among the most important tasks that missionary methods must address is the building of the bridge between the teachings of the Bible in its original context, and the realities of culture in the missionary context. This task demands the best of both theological acumen and cultural insight. Some missionaries know their Bible well but cannot connect it to their world of ministry. Others know their culture well, but cannot connect it to the teaching of the Bible. Missionaries must be taught skills in both directions if they are to teach and apply the Bible in a way that is both relevant and prophetic. Both the tools of understanding Scripture and the tools of understanding culture are indispensable. Contextualization is then the metaskill that brings these two tools together in the task of theological reflection and cultural engagement. This is the art of contextualization, and it is essential to carrying out the Great Commission and the Great Commandment in ways faithful to Scripture in any given local setting.

Closing

Solomon once wrote, "Of making many books there is no end, and much study wearies the body" (Eccl 12:12). It might also be said, "Of inventing missionary methods there is no end, and much debate about them wearies the missionary!" Shouldn't we just get on with the job and not make this too complicated? But then what methods *will* we use?

Fortunately the Holy Spirit can use a crooked stick to draw a straight line, and he has been doing that since Pentecost. God works not only because of our missionary methods, but perhaps more often in spite of them. This is our great comfort and hope. But this confidence does not excuse us from the hard work of seeking God's guidance in the Scriptures and employing our God-given intellect to better understand the people we seek to serve. We must discern the most appropriate ways to achieve God's purposes. Our rapidly changing world will not allow us to depend solely upon the methods of yesterday. Thus, the search will rightly continue to discover best practices that are both biblical and effective. And yet the temptation is ever crouching at the door to allow our hunger for success to compromise biblical wisdom and integrity. Therefore we must remember that the message of Christ crucified will ever remain an offense and stumbling block, while at the same time being God's power and wisdom (1 Cor 1:23,24). There are no shortcuts on the path of discipleship. It is Jesus who will build his church (Matt16:18), and only by abiding in him will our lives and ministries bear much fruit (John 15:1–8).

Works Cited

Bliss, Edwin Munsell. *The Missionary Enterprise: A Concise History of Its Objects, Methods and Extension.* New York: Revell, 1908.

Brain, Belle M., and Delavan Leonard Pierson. *Holding the Ropes: Missionary Methods for Workers at Home.* New York: Funk & Wagnalls, 1904.

Daniel, Robin. *Mission Strategies: Then and Now.* Chester, UK: Tamarisk, 2012.

DeCarvalho, Levi T. "What's Wrong with the Label 'Managerial Mission'?" *International Journal of Frontier Missions* 18, no. 3 (Fall 2001): 141–46.

Escobar, Samuel. "Evangelical Missiology: Peering into the Future at the Turn of the Century." In *Global Missiology for the 21st Century,* edited by William D. Taylor, 101–22. Grand Rapids: Baker Academic, 2000.

Fee, Gordon D., and Douglas K. Stuart. *How to Read the Bible for All Its Worth: A Guide to Understanding the Bible.* Grand Rapids: Zondervan, 1993.

Grassi, Joseph A. *A World to Win: The Missionary Methods of Paul the Apostle.* Maryknoll, NY: Maryknoll, 1965.

Green, Michael. *Evangelism in the Early Church.* Grand Rapids: Eerdmans, 1970.

Gurganus, George. "A Study of Missionary Methods in Historical Perspective." *Restoration Quarterly* 9, no. 2 (January 1966): 79–90.

Hahn, Ferdinand. *Mission in the New Testament.* Translated by Frank Clarke. Naperville, IL: Allenson, 1965. German original 1963.

Harnack, Adolph. *The Mission and Expansion of Christianity in the First Three Centuries.* 2 vols. Translated by James Moffatt. New York: Williams & Norgate, 1904/1905.

Hesselgrave, David J. "Incarnationalism and Representationalism." In *Paradigms in Conflict: 10 Key Questions in Christian Missions Today*, 141–65. Grand Rapids: Kregel, 2005.

———. "Paul's Missions Strategy." In *Paul's Missionary Methods: In His Time and Ours,* edited by Robert L. Plummer and John Mark Terry, 127–45. Downers Grove, IL: InterVarsity Press, 2012.

———. Preface to *Missiology and the Social Sciences: Contributions, Cautions and Conclusions,* edited by Edward Rommen and Gary Corwin, 1–3. Evangelical Missiological Series 4. Pasadena: William Carey Library, 1996.

Hiebert, Paul G. "Critical Contextualization." In *Anthropological Reflections on Missiological Issues,* 75–92. Grand Rapids: Baker, 1994.

———. "Critical Issues in the Social Sciences and Their Implications for Mission Studies." *Missiology* 24, no. 1 (January 1996): 65–82.

Jśchke, Ernst. "Bruno Gutman's Legacy." *Occasional Bulletin of Missionary Research* 4, no. 4 (October 1980): 165–69.

Kaplan, Steven. "The Africanization of Missionary Christianity: History and Typology." In *Indigenous Responses to Western Christianity,* edited by Steven Kaplan, 9–28. New York: New York University Press, 1995.

Langmead, Ross. *The Word Made Flesh: Towards an Incarnational Missiology.* Dallas: University Press of America, 2004.

Latourette, Kenneth Scott. "The Light of History on Current Missionary Methods." *International Review of Missions* 42, no. 2 (April 1953): 137–43.

Little, Christopher R. *Mission in the Way of Paul.* New York: Lang, 2005.

McConnell, C. Douglas, ed. *The Holy Spirit and Mission Dynamics.* Pasadena: William Carey Library, 1997.

McGavran, Donald A. *The Bridges of God.* New York: Friendship Press, 1955.

———. *Understanding Church Growth.* Grand Rapids: Eerdmans, 1970.

Moreau, A. Scott, Tokunboh Adeyemo, David G. Burnett, Bryant L. Myers, and Hwa Yung, eds. *Deliver Us from Evil: An Uneasy Frontier in Christian Mission.* Monrovia, CA: World Vision International, 2002.

Nida, Eugene. *Customs and Cultures*. New York: Harper, 1954.

Ott,Craig, "Contextualization, the Bible, and Games: What I Learned about Theology from The Settlers of Catan" *Evangelical Review of Theology* 37:3 (July 2013): 210–26.

———, and Stephen J. Strauss. *Encountering Theology of Mission: Biblical Foundations, Historical Developments, and Contemporary Issues*. With Timothy C. Tennent. Grand Rapids: Baker Academic, 2010.

Payne, J. D. *Roland Allen: Pioneer of Spontaneous Expansion*. North Charleston, SC: CreateSpace, 2012.

Plummer, Robert L., and John Mark Terry, eds. *Paul's Missionary Methods: In His Time and Ours*. Downers Grove, IL: InterVarsity Press, 2012.

Pocock, Michael. "Paul's Strategy: Determinative for Today?" In *Paul's Missionary Methods: In His Time and Ours*, edited by Robert L. Plummer and John Mark Terry, 146–59. Downers Grove, IL: InterVarsity Press, 2012.

Powell, Mark Allan. *What Are They Saying about Acts?* Mahwah, NJ: Paulist, 1991.

Priest, Robert J. "Anthropology and Missiology: Reflections on the Relationship." In *Paradigm Shifts in Christian Witness*, edited by Charles E. Van Engen, Darrell Whiteman, and J. Dudley Woodberry, 23–32. Maryknoll, NY: Orbis Books, 2008.

———. "'Experience-near Theologizing' in Diverse Human Contexts." In *Globalizing Theology*, edited by Craig Ott and Harold A. Netland, 180–95. Grand Rapids: Baker Academic, 2006.

Riesner, Rainer. *Paul's Early Years: Chronology, Mission Strategy, Theology*. Translated by Doug Scott. Grand Rapids: Eerdmans, 1998. German original 1994.

Rommen, Edward. "The De-theologizing of Missiology." *Trinity World Forum* 19 (1993): 1–4.

———, ed. *Spiritual Power and Missions*. Pasadena: William Carey Library, 1999.

———, and Gary Corwin, eds. *Missiology and the Social Sciences: Contributions, Cautions and Conclusions*. Evangelical Missiological Series 4. *Pasadena: William Carey Library, 1996*.

Schnabel, Eckhart. *Early Christian Mission*. 2 vols. Downers Grove, IL: InterVarsity Press, 2004. German original 2002.

———. *Paul the Missionary: Realities, Strategies and Methods*. Downers Grove, IL: InterVarsity Press, 2008.

Smith, John. *The Magnetism of Christ: A Study of Our Lord's Missionary Methods.* New York: Armstrong, 1904.

Taber, Charles R. *To Understand the World, to Save the World: The Interface between Missiology and the Social Sciences.* Harrisburg, PA: Trinity Press International, 2000.

Towns, Elmer L., and Gary McIntosh, eds. *Evaluating the Church Growth Movement: 5 Views.* Grand Rapids: Zondervan, 2004.

Vanhoozer, Kevin J. *The Drama of Doctrine.* Louisville: Westminster John Knox, 2005.

White, Hugh Watt. *Jesus the Missionary: Studies in the Life of Jesus as the Master, the Model, the Proto-type for All Missionaries.* Shanghai: Presbyterian Mission Press, 1916.

Whiteman, Darrell. "Anthropology and Mission." In *Paradigm Shifts in Christian Witness,* edited by Charles E. Van Engen, Darrell Whiteman, and J. Dudley Woodberry, 3–12. Maryknoll, NY: Orbis Books, 2008.

Young, W. John. "The Legacy of Edwin W. Smith." *International Bulletin of Missionary Research* 25, no. 3 (July 2001): 126–30.

General Index

Scripture Index